THE
UNCOLLECTED VERSE OF
APHRA BEHN

EDITED, WITH AN
INTRODUCTION AND NOTES,
BY
Germaine Greer

STUMP CROSS BOOKS
1989

Stump Cross Books, Walden Road, Stump Cross, Essex CB10 1RW

© Stump Cross Books, 1989
First published 1989

ISBN 1 872029 00 0

Typeset and printed by BluePrint, Cambridge, England.

ACKNOWLEDGMENTS

Grateful acknowledgment is here made to the Bodleian Library of the University of Oxford for permission to quote from Bodleian MSS Firth c. 15, Firth c. 16, Don. b. 8 and Eng. Poet. c 18, and to the British Library for permission to quote from Harleian MS 7319.

And in a decent Garb the naked Piety;
Justice from Fraud and Perjury fore'd to fly;

TABLE OF CONTENTS

WORKS CITED BY SHORT TITLE

Alden   Alden, J. E., *The Muses Mourn: a Checklist of
         Verse occasioned by the death of Charles II*,
         Charlottesville, 1978.

ARP   D. M. Vieth, *Attribution in Restoration Poetry:
         A Study of Rochester's Poems of 1680*, Newhaven
         and London, 1963.

'Astrea's Booke'   'Astrea's Booke for Songs and Satyrs',
         Bodleian MS Firth c. 16.

Covent Garden Drolery
         *Covent Garden Drolery, or a Colection, Of all
         the Choice Songs, Poems, Prologues and Epi-
         logues... Written by the refinedst Witts of the
         Age.* And *Collected by A. B. London... 1672.*

CSPD   *Calendar of State Papers Domestic*, reign of
         Charles II, 6 vols., ed. F. H. B. Daniell and
         F. Bickley, London, H. M. S. O. 1921-1938.

Familiar Letters   *Familiar Letters of Love, Gallantry, And several
         Occasions, By the Wits of the last and present
         age...* London, 1718.

Harris   Harris, Brice, 'Aphra Behn's "Bajazet to
         Gloriana"', *Times Literary Supplement*, 9
         February, 1933.

Haswell Haswell, Jock, *James II, Soldier and Sailor*,
         London, 1972.

Hatton *Correspondence of the Family of Hatton...* 1601-
         1704, ed. E. M. Thompson, 2 vols., 1878.

Jerome   Jermome Joseph, *Montague Summers: A
         Memoir*, London, 1965.

Kitchin Kitchen, George, *Sir Roger L'Estrange*,
         London, Kegan Paul, 1915.

KTR   *Kissing the Rod: An Anthology of Seventeenth-
         Century Women's Verse*, ed. G. Greer, S.
         Hastings, J. Medoff, M. Sansone, London
         1988.

Luttrell	Luttrell, Narcissus, *A Brief Relation of State Affairs from September 1678 to April, 1714*, 6 vols., Oxford, 1939.
Miscellany, 1685	Behn, Aphra, ed., *Miscellany, Being a Collection of Poems by Several hands, Together with Reflections on Morality, or Seneca Unmasqued.* London, printed for J. Hindmarsh... 1685.
North, *Examen*	North, Roger, *Examen; or, An Enquiry into... a Pretended Complete History...*, London, 1740.
Observator	Sir Roger L'Estrange, *The Observator in Dialogue*, 3 vols. in 2, London, 1687.
O'Donnell	O'Donnell, Mary Ann, *Aphra Behn: An Annotated Bibliography of Primary and Secondary Sources*, New York and London, 1986.
OED	*Oxford English Dictionary*, ed. Sir J. A. H. Murray et al., 13 vols, Oxford, 1933.
Oman	Oman, Carola, *Mary of Modena*, London, 1962.
Ovid's Epistles	*Ovid's Epistles Translated by Several Hands...* London... 1680.
Phipps	Phipps, Christine, ed., *Buckingham: Public and Private Man: The Prose, Poems and Commonplace Book of George Villiers, Second Duke of Buckingham (1628 to 1687)*, New York and London, 1985.
Plomer	Plomer, Henry H., *A Dictionary of the Printers and Booksellers who were active... from 1668 to 1725*, Oxford, 1922.
POAS	*Poems on Affairs of State: Augustan Satirical Verse, 1660-1714*, 7 vols Newhaven and London, 1968-1971.
POAS 1697	*Poems on Affairs of State from the Time of Oliver Cromwell to the Abdication of K. James the Second...* Printed in the Year 1695.
POAS 1705	*A New Collection of Poems Relating to State Affairs...*London, 1705.

Price   Price, Cecil, *Cold Caleb: The Scandalous Life of Forde Grey, First Earl of Tankerville, 1655-1701*, London 1956.

Roxburghe Ballads   *The Roxburghe Ballads: Illustrating the Last Years of the Stuarts*, ed. J. Woodfall Ebsworth, 8 vols., Hertford, The Ballad Society, 1878-1896.

Summers   Summers, Montague, ed., *The Works of Aphra Behn*, 6 vols., Oxford, The Shakespeare Head Press, 1915, reprint Phaeton Press, New York, 1967.

Thorn-Drury   Thorn-Drury, George, *Covent Garden Drollery: A Miscellany of 1672*, London 1928.

Verney   *Memoirs of the Verney Family During the Seventeenth Century* ed. F. P. Verney and M. M. Verney, 2 vols. 1907.

Ward   Ward, E. F., *Christopher Monck, Duke of Albemarle*, London, 1915.

Wilson, 1976   Wilson, John Harold, *Court Satires of the Restoration*, Columbus, 1979.

MONTAGUE SUMMERS AND
The Works of Aphra Behn

In 1914 the fortunes of thirty-four-year-old Augustus Montague Summers were at a low ebb. He had gone down from Oxford six years before with a third-class honours degree in Theology, been ordained deacon and appointed to a curacy near Bath. Then he went to another at Bitton near Bristol, where his career in the Anglican clergy met a sudden check. He was removed from the curacy in mysterious circumstances not un-connected with a trial for pederasty in which nothing was proven. The next year he was baptised a Catholic, took the additional names of Alphonsus Joseph-Mary, and entered St John's Seminary to study for the priesthood, only to leave a few months later, probably at the request of his superiors. A persistent verbal tradition among the Catholic clergy holds that Summers' ordination as a Catholic priest was cancelled at the last minute. Though no record of an ordination has ever been found, from 1913 to the end of his life Summers claimed that he was a Catholic priest.

Since 1911 Summers had been supplementing the allowance he had from his father, a Bristol banker, with a schoolteacher's salary. In 1914 he was teaching English, French, History and Latin at the Central School of Arts and Crafts in Holborn where he made himself remarkable in that 'He wore clerical dress and said his Office from a Roman breviary after he had got [the students] going on [their] lessons' (Jerome, 25). In 1910 he met Arthur Henry Bullen, at whose house in Stratford-on-Avon he often stayed. In his MS autobiography, 'The Galanty Show', now lost, Summers told how Bullen had encouraged him to become an editor: 'Your demesne', he is supposed to have said, 'is the Restoration Drama. Let us draw up our private prospectus. First we'll have the play that satirises all the other plays, Buckingham's *Rehearsal*.' In 1914 the Shakespeare's Head Press produced a quarto of Buckingham's play edited by Montague Summers in 510 numbered copies.

'It was decided, for I pressed my point strongly, that the Works of Aphra Behn should follow. Plays, novels, and poems were to be included, and it soon became evident that this meant at least half-a-dozen volumes. Bonny Mrs Behn had never been edited, and hence (as may well be supposed) my hands were fairly full.' (Jerome, 30). In fact Summers himself paid for the printing of the 760 numbered sets of his six volume edition of *The Works of Aphra Behn*. If he had tried to publish everything that he knew Behn had written, he would have had to find the money to produce at least two more volumes. It would be churlish therefore in a modern scholar to sneer at him for the manifest shortcomings of his edition, nevertheless they are grave.

In his dedication to his friend Francis James, Father Summers, as he liked to be called, described *The Works of Aphra Behn* as 'the first collected edition of Aphra Behn', being of the opinion apparently that nearly two hundred and fifty years of obloquy had come to an end and Aphra Behn was about to be studied by more serious scholars than he. He was, of course, quite mistaken. No one would have been more surprised than Summers to find that his rather hasty compilation would remain the only collected edition of Behn's work until the tercentenary of her death, when his limited edition had swollen into a facsimile edition selling constantly and steadily to a new and huge readership created by the feminist movement of the nineteen-sixties, -seventies and -eighties, which is nowhere more energetic than in the literature departments of our universities. If he had guessed that Mrs Behn's reputation was to be in his hands for the rest of the century, Summers might have taken his self-imposed task a little more seriously, and curbed his natural proclivity for displaying his wit, charm and peculiar erudition at her expense.

Summers was not without assistance in his undertaking; as he said himself in the Preface, with typical pomp and archaising: 'Mr Edmund Gosse, C.B., has shown the liveliest interest in the book from its inception, and I owe him most grateful recognition for his kindly encouragement and aid. Nay, more, he did not spare to lend me treasured items from his library so rich in first, and boasting unique editions of Mrs Behn. Mr G. Thorn Drury, K.C., never wearied of answering my enquiries... To him I am obliged for the transcript of Mrs Behn's letter to Waller's daughter-in-law' (now in the Folger) 'and also the Satire on Dryden... The unsurpassed library of Mr T. J. Wise, the well-known bibliographer, was freely at my disposal.'.

Despite the assistance of such distinguished scholars, Summers fell into the most egregious errors. He noted with little compassion that most sources had Aphra Behn's family name wrong and confidently asserted that she was none other than the Aphra Amies who was christened with her twin brother at the parish church in Wye on 10 July 1640; if he had turned the page he would have noticed that this Aphra was buried a few weeks later. His certainy on this point is the more inexplicable, when on p. liv of the same Memoir he cites Colonel Culpepper's MS 'Adversaria' where he must also have found a completely different account of Behn's birth and breeding. He suggests on no evidence whatever that *The Young King* was written in Surinam in 1658 and that in about 1669 Behn 'accepted the protection of some admirer' (I, xviii).

Summers' attitude to Behn's works is if anything more cavalier than his concern for her biography; though he knew that 'A Letter to Mr Creech at Oxford, Written in the last Great Frost' (see below) was by Aphra Behn, he did not reprint it; though he says that *Love Letters between a Nobleman and his Sister* is 'certainly the work of Mrs Behn' he does not reprint that either, thus suppressing 450 pages of Behn's best work. Though he says that 'her Pindarics rank high amongst the semi-official, complimentary, threnodic or pastoral pseudo-Dithyrambs, of which the age was so bounteous', of them he chooses to reprint only one, that to Dr Burnet. He does not mention *To Poet Bavius* probably because he had never come across it. Behn's translation of La Rochefoucauld's Maxims, 'Reflections on Morality', described rather mysteriously by Summers as 'a number of clever apophthegms tersely turned,' is not reprinted either. The 'Reflections on Morality' are 394 in number, some of them far from terse. Though Summers reprinted Behn's version of De Bonnecorse's La *Montre* he chose not to print her translations from Fontenelle, *The History of Oracles and the Cheats of the Pagan Priests*, 'a book of great interest' by his own account, and *The Theory of the System of Several new Inhabited Worlds*. In the 'Memoir of Mrs Behn' in which all these works are mentioned, he describes too her contribution to Barlow's *Æsop's Fables*, and her translation of the sixth book of Cowley's *De Plantarum* but again does not reprint either. Nowhere in *The Works of Aphra Behn* are these omissions justified, nor is a bibliography or chronology of her work appended, in case a reader could see at a glance that Summers has left out almost half of her life's work.

Editors can do worse than leave out some of their authors' work; they can include work that is not by their authors at all. Summers includes among the works of Aphra Behn that he chose to reprint, a song from *Westminster Drollery* (1671) although his own note states that 'it cannot, originally be Mrs Behn's since it appears in a fuller form as *To his whore who askt money of him* (*Wit and Drolery 1656*)' (VI, 364, 430-431). From Gildon's *Chorus Poetarum* (1694) with his ascription 'By Madam Behn,' but without the title that Gildon gave it, he reprints 'Sappho addrest to his Grace the Duke of Buckingham'. In fact the poem is an imitation by William Bowles of Boileau's paraphrase of Sappho's Ode to Venus, published under Bowles's name in *Poems by Several hands and on Several Occasions* collected by Nahum Tate and printed for J. Hindmarsh in 1685. In the *Miscellany* which she edited the same year, Behn included another version of Boileau's paraphrase, by 'a Lady of Quality'. Bowles's poem was hijacked by Gildon to supply more fascinating detail about Aphra Behn whose posthumous literary reputation and remains he was living off. Behn, or 'Sappho', is depicted in the poem rapt in contemplation, not of Venus, but of George Villiers, Duke of Buckingham, whose sexual gormandising was notorious. The application of Bowles's poem to Mrs Behn is just another libel upon her, but Summers has no compunction in repeating such scurrilities although he presents himself as her champion. Summers' failure to question the identification of the putative speaker with the poet is evidence of thoughtlessness, the result of his deep indifference to literature, which is in direct proportion to his prurient interest in the green-room gossip of the Restoration.

Given Summers' lack of interest in authenticity it is not surprising that he prints 'On Mr Dryden, Renegate', in a text which he had from Thorn Drury who had copied it from an old MS then in the possession of Haslewood, now lost; the only seventeenth century MS version of this poem, in 'Astrea's Booke for Songs and Satyrs' (Bodleian MS Firth c.16) differs substantially from the version reproduced by Summers and does not show the attribution to Mrs Behn. Professor Mary Ann O'Donnell considers that 'Astrea's Booke' is partly in Behn's own hand, so the lack of ascription may indicate that is by her, but for the time being 'On Mr Dryden Renegate' must be thought an unlikely member of the Behn canon, for it attacks a friend and colleague who had rendered her several good offices, and converted to the religion which is most likely to have been Behn's own. That she might have made a copy of the poem for her own use is not evidence that she sympathised with the sentiments expressed in it; she may have intended at some juncture to write an answer to it. Though Summers notes the unlikeliness of the ascription, and had not the additional evidence of the Bodleian MS to justify it, he cannot resist including such a piquant morsel.

At the time that he compiling his edition of Behn, Summers either did not know of the existence of *Covent Garden Drolery* (1672) or, if he did, he did not trouble himself to examine the volume to see if Behn poems were to be found in it. This is all the more surprising because he had looked at *Westminster Drollery* and there is more reason to connect Behn with Covent Garden than Westminster. Stranger still, when he edited *Covent Garden Drolery* himself twelve years later Summers did not recognise poems that he had already edited and annotated as by Behn. He had reprinted the lyric beginning 'I led my Sylvia to a Grove,' twice, both as a song in Act II of *The Dutch Lover* and as one of the *Poems on Several Occasions*, and yet he did not recognise it, nor did he know 'Come my Phillis let us improve' when he saw it again as 'A Song to a Schotish tune' or 'Phillis you ask me' as 'Damon being asked a reason for loving'.

Behn had faded so far from his consciousness that he made the absurd mistake of supposing that the compiler of *Covent Garden Drolery*, given by initials as 'A. B.', was Alexander Brome. The very next year Summers' friend, George Thorn-Drury edited a reprint of the second edition, called the 'Second Impression with Additions', of *Covent Garden Drolery*; as there is very little difference between the two editions, Thorn-Drury's motive must have been correction of the earlier editor's mistakes. He does not mention Summers by name, but regarding Alexander Brome he says:

He it was, it was boldly alleged, who collected Covent Garden Drollery:

an unhappy choice, for Alexander Brome, as he signed himself, died June 30th, 1666. Identification by initials, even when one has taken the trouble to make sure that the person chosen to fit them was alive at the material date, is always a perilous business.

Thorn-Drury produces a much more likely candidate to fit the initials; not only was she alive at the time, there is a pre-dominance of female personages and female themes in the collection, the editor has some connection with the theatre, and Behn's poems are printed as a group. Evidence of a different kind is to be found in *Bristol Drollery*, in which, should the publication prove unsuccessful, the Bristol muse is advised 'humbly to cast herself on Madam Bhen'. At this date, January 1673/4, only three of Behn's plays had been published, so it is thought that the Bristol editor is referring to his London original (Thorn-Drury, xvi-xviii).

As an annotator Summers' shortcomings are even more obvious: while he can be relied upon to retail all that is to be known of the career of an actress like Sarah Cook, including the imputation to her of numerous abortions, he is quite uninterested in comparing texts, or close textual analysis. His annotations to 'On a Juniper-Tree, cut down to make Busks' are typical of his lack of serious concern for authenticity: in his edition of Behn he notes that the poem appeared in 1680 as one of the *Poems on Several Occasions by the Rt. Hon. the Earl of R—*, but stated firmly, 'It must not however be for a moment supposed that the Earl of Rochester has any claim to the authorship of this piece'. In his edition of Shadwell (1927) he hedges his bets, and declines to attribute the poem to Aphra Behn. (Modern scholarship gives it to Behn on internal evidence and on the evidence of a note 'By Mrs A. Behn' in the Harvard MS of Rochester's works.) Summers textual commentary on the poem is pseudo-scholarly prurience at its worst; he compares the opening lines with Horace, *Sermonum*, I, viii. solely for the sake of introducing a reference to phallic idols of the garden god, for the lines quoted have no demonstrable relevance to the style or content of Behn's poem. The obvious gloss is Behn's translation of the animadversions on the juniper in Cowley's *De Plantarum*, but Summers ignores it.

Though Summers noticed that 'Young Jemmy was a lad' appears in the second edition of *Female Poems on Several Occasions* (1682) he did not see that 'The Surprize' ('Phyllis, whose Heart was unconfin'd') appears there too. Though it is understandable that he could be unaware of the existence of an earlier version of the song, 'Ah! what can mean that eager joy' in *The Compleat Courtier* (1683) it is inexcusable that, though he knew that the book of Edward Howard's failed play, *The Six Days Adventure or the New Utopia* (1671) contained the commendatory poem Behn wrote, (one of her earliest appearances in print), he missed the opportunity of comparing the text as it appeared there with the version Behn prepared for publication thirteen years later. The version of Behn's commendatory poem published in the second edition of Creech's translation of Lucretius is significantly different from the version she chose to include in *Poems on Several Occasions*, but Summers does not bother to collate the two versions. If he had he would have seen that, at this period in her life at least, Behn was not afraid of expressing the most extreme form of the libertine philosophy, which carried scepticism so far as to doubt the existence of God.

It seems likely that most of the work of transcription for Summers' edition, transcription which is for the most part remarkably accurate it must be acknowledged, was done by amanuenses who simply wrote out everything contained in their copy text; otherwise it is hard to account for Summers' not remarking on duplications in his edition: for example, 'Song. On her loving two equally. Set by Captain Pack' as printed from *Poems on Several Occasions* in Vol. VI of Summers' edition is another version of the song in Act IV of *The False Count* that appears in Vol. I, but Summers' note does not mention the fact. He does not advise the reader either that 'The Counsel. A Song' is the same as 'A Pox upon this needless Scorn' from Part II of *The Rover*. He can be excused for not knowing that 'The Invitation' ('Come my Phyllis, let us improve') had appeared earlier in *Covent Garden Drolery*, but not that he had reprinted four lines of it himself in Vol. II, where they are quoted in Act V, Sc. ii of *The Town-Fopp* (1677); the reader who consults his first-line index will learn that Summers printed the Song from *The Town Fopp* twice, once in Vol. III as it appears in the published version of play, and once in Vol. VI as it appeared in *Poems on Several Occasions*. Although he has a lengthy note on the song 'Amyntas led me to a grove' in Vol.

VI, identifying it as the same poem that appeared in *The Muses'
Mercury* in 1717 with the first line 'I led my Sylvia to a grove', he omits
to mention that it is one of the songs from *The Dutch Lover* or that
it shows some minor but significant authorial emendations. How
these can be reconciled with the version also edited by Behn for
Covent Garden Drolery in 1672 with the first line 'I led my Sylvia to a
grove' he cannot of course suggest. Why Summers does not tell the
reader of Vol. VI that 'Love in fantastic triumph sat' can also be seen
in Vol. II as a song from the first act of *Abdelazar*, is inexplicable.
When Behn goes to the lengths of describing an occasion for 'In vain
I have labour'd the Victor to prove', calling it 'The Sence of a Letter
sent me, made into Verse; To a New Tune' it is useful to know the
poem is also a song from Act II of *The Amorous Prince*. If Behn is
actually quoting fragments from her own lyrics in her plays, it seems
likely that they were already familiar to some of her audience
through manuscript circulation. That the songs existed before the
plays is borne out by her use of two songs in *Covent Garden Drolery*
in 1672 that were not used in plays until 1673 and 1677. If Behn was
involved in the same kind of sophisticated interchange as the other
gallant versifiers of the 1660's, a radical re-thinking of her career as
professional writer would appear to be in order. While we cannot
blame Summers for failing to sift the manuscript miscellanies for
evidence of Behn's earlier activity as an amateur versifier among the
coteries, we may hold against him that he did not suggest that such
a search could well bear fruit.

Most astonishing perhaps is his failure to inform the reader that
the 'Paraphrase on *Ovid*'s Epistle of Oenone to Paris' was commissioned by Dryden for inclusion in *Ovid's Epistles translated by Several
Hands* (1680); strictly speaking the earlier publication is the *editio
princeps* and should have been Summers' copy text; if he had chosen
to print the later version because it was edited by the author herself
he should have said so. If indeed the substantive variants in the
earlier edition are the result of Dryden's editorial intervention, the
fact is not without interest. By the same token the *editio princeps* of
three other important poems, 'The Disappointment', 'On a Juniper
Tree', and 'On the death of Mr Greenhill' is *Poems on Several
Occasions by the Right Honourable, the E. of R—* (1680).

INTRODUCTION

The four stanzas of 'Young Jemmy' that are by Behn first appeared as 'A Most Excellent New Ballad' in broadside, 1681, and again in the same year expanded into a longer broadside ballad, and again in the second edition of *Female Poems on Several Occasions* by Ephelia (1682). Though Summers gives some account of these appearances he does not compare the texts with the version preferred by Behn in 1684. By failing to note these repeated appearances, Summers fails to project any impression of the nature and magnitude of Behn's contribution to Restoration literature. Behn's songs were so well-known that they were quoted in new contexts by way of comment, much as we might reapply the words of a pop song to a situation for which they were never intended. Behn's first songs of young Jemmy may have had no specific reference to James Scott, Duke of Monmouth, at all, but they were soon applied to him and they stuck, so that even Behn made satiric use of the same material.

Summers was rather more interested in the theatre than he was in literature but even here he is less than scrupulous. His notes on the plays are more likely to give details of the casting of revivals long after Behn's death, than they are to enlighten us about the text. While he may be excused for not knowing of the broadside of Behn's prologue and epilogue to *The Jealous Lovers* (see below, p.18) his reference to Langbaine is downright misleading, and the cast he suggests simply conjecture.

It is not the purpose of this small book to remedy all the defects of *The Works of Aphra Behn*. The only way this pressing necessity could be met is by the production of a new scholarly edition of all the works, including those plays anonymously published that we now know to be by Behn and the prose and poetry that Summers left out. Behn's work deserves to be properly annotated, dated, placed in its context and collated. There are limitations to the appropriateness of the study of seventeenth century poetry in what a more distinguished scholar than I has called 'author-shaped parcels', but Aphra Behn is too important a figure to be allowed to exist in the distorted guise of Summers' edition. In order to understand how her work overlaps with the work of others we have to pay more and more intelligent attention to her individual contribution, in particular to her awareness of continental literature, not only French but Italian

9

and Spanish as well, to the development of her idea of the lyric, and the equivocal role of her personae, especially when considered in relation to her actual invisibility.

The Aphra Behn of Summers' *Works of Aphra Behn* is his creature:

So she comes before us. A graceful comely woman, merry and buxom, with brown hair and bright eyes, candid, sincere, a brilliant conversationalist in days when conversation was no mere slipshod gabble of slang (etc., etc., I, liv)

Her contemporaries, though they libelled her out of hand, had more respect for 'Machiavellian Behn' than to depict her as a friendly barmaid peddling milk punch. The mainspring of her existence, especially in the last ten years of her life, was royalist politics; while Summers is sympathetic to her Jacobitism, he does not see that her concern goes beyond partisanship. Aphra Behn was a committed European, drawing her intellectual life-blood from Catholic Europe, at a time when England had cut herself adrift in order to exploit her imperialist, mercantilist, capitalist supremacy. If we are ever to understand Aphra Behn, we will have to study her work in its real context; in order to evaluate her relations with Buckingham and Rochester, Mulgrave and Etherege, D'Urfey and Tate, Creech and Otway, Ravenscroft and Dryden, we need to assess her reading of Bonnecorse, Fontenelle, Boileau, Tallemant, and La Rochefoucauld, to name only five of the dozens of continental authors who were her daily reading.

The most creditable of Summers' activities were those involved with the Phoenix Theatre from 1919 to 1926, when he played an important role in the revival of plays from the Jacobean period to the Restoration. During this period he was quite famous in England; a cartoon in one of the daily papers showed his by-then well-known figure, usually to be seen in shovel hat and cape, with his hair now combed flat over his brow and curled over his ears like a periwig. In portrait frontispieces to his works his flabby moon-face, with its strangely horned eye-brows and staring fish-eyes, droops over a clerical collar. In the seven years of Summers' guidance the Phoenix put on twenty-six plays, not one of them by Aphra Behn.

It is typical of Behn's chequered literary fortunes that she should have found an editor shadier than herself, who divided his intellectual attention unevenly between satanism, theatricals and literature, in descending order of importance, and that we should be indebted to his eccentricity for the only edition of her works that we have. We cannot continue to leave Behn's survival to the whims of gentlemen amateurs. While recognising the debt we owe to Montague Summers, we must resolve to cancel that debt as soon as possible. This small volume is a first contribution towards the compilation of a new edition. As matters stand *The Uncollected Verse of Aphra Behn* will have to function as a companion volume to Summers' *The Works of Aphra Behn*. We hope to issue the uncollected prose within a year, and the supposititious plays soon after.

THE PROLOGUE TO *Like Father, Like Son*

Spoken by Mrs. *Butler*

Lord what a House is here, how Thin 'tis grown!
As Church 'ere Conventicling was put down:
Since all the Brave are to *Newmarket* gone!
Declining States-men are abandon'd too,
Who scarce a heartless *Whigg* will visit now: 5
Who once had Crowds of Mutineers in Fashion,
Fine drawn in Cullys of th'*Association*,
Sparks, Justices, and Jurymen by Dozens,
Whom his perverted late betrays and Cozens.
But change of Scene, having unvail'd their Cheats,   10
Pensive State Puss alone, Majestick Sits;
Purr's on his pointless Mischiefs, tho' in vain;
Verses are all the Darlings of his Brain.
So we who having Plotted long to please,
With new Parts, new Cloathes, new Face, new Dress;   15
To draw in all the yielding Hearts o'th'Town.
His Highness comes, and all our Hopes are gone.
Ah Fickle Youth, what lasting Joys have we,
When Beauty thus is left for Loyalty;
I would to Heaven ye had been all *Whiggs* for me: 20
Whilst honest *Tory* Fools abroad do Roame,
Whigg Lovers Stay and Plot, and Love at Home.
Nay one Advantage greater far than this,
The Party helps to keep their Mistresses.
The Devils it't (*sic*)if I'm not Fine and Vain,   25
Whom publick Bank contribute to Maintain.

Epilogue. Spoken by Mr. *Gevan*.

And now *Messiers!* what do you say
Unto our Modern, Conscientious Play?
Nor *Whigg*, or *Tory* here can take Offence,
It Libels neither Patriot, Peer, or Prince,
Nor Sheriff, nor Burgess, nor the Reverend Gown;   5
Faith here's no Scandal worth Eight Hundred Pound.
Your Damage is at most but Half a crown.
Only this Difference you must allow,
That you receive th'Affront and pay us too,
Woud some Body had manag'd matters so.   10
Here's no Reflections on Damn'd Witnesses,
We scorn such out of fashion things as these;
They fail to be Beloved, and fail to Please.
No *Salamanchian* Doctorships abus'd,
a Malicious *State'man* here accus'd.   15
Tho' here are Fools of every Fashion
Except State Fools, the Fools of Reformation.
And these Originals decline so fast

Substantive Variants in *Miscellany* 1685
Title 1685 *Epilogue to the Jealous Lovers. By Mrs.* Behn, *in* 1682.
1   And now Messiers / And how, and how, Mesieurs 1685
2   Unto our Modern, / To our good Moderate 1685
3   Nor *Whigg* / Not Whig 1685
5   Nor Sheriff / Nor *Shrieve* 1685
9   That / 'Tis 1685
10   some Body / Rebell WARD 1685
12   out of fashion / out-of-Fashion'd 1685
13   Beloved / believ'd 1685
14   *Salamanchian* Doctorships / *Salamanca* Doctor-ship 1685
15   Nor a malicious *State'man* / Not a Malicious *States-man* 1685
16   1685 A new couplet inserted:
    No Smutty Scenes, no intrigues up Stairs,
    That make your *City* Wives in love with *Players*.
16-17 1685 But here are fools of every sort and Fashion,
    Except State-Fools, the Tools of *Reformation*,

We shall have none to copy by at last;
                  Pointing at Mr. *Williams* Mr. *Wiltshire*
Here's *Joe*, and *Jack*, *a pair of Whining Fools*,   20
And *Leigh* and *I*, Dull, Lavish, Creeping Tools
Bowmans for Mischief all, and carrys on
With Faune and Sneer as Gilting *Whigg* has done.
But like theirs too, his Projects are o'r thrown.
Sweet Mistris Corall here has lost her Lover,   25
Pshaw, *English* or *Irish* ground shall find another.
                     To Mrs. *Butler*
Poor Madam Butler too, are you defeated,
You never were before so basely Cheated.
Here Mistris *Betty*, Hah! she's grown a very Woman,
Thou'st got me Child, better than no man.   30
Here's blundering *Richards* is my Huffing Esquire,
Damn me, the best in E*ngland's* sort, d'e hear.
Is that your Cue come nearer Faith thy Face
Has features not unlike Joe *Haines's* Grace,
Impudence assist thee, and boldly try   35
To speak for us, and for the Comedy

Mr *Richards* speaks.

I'le do't Gallants, I'le Justify this Play;
Od Zoons 'tis Good, and if you lik'd you may.

---

18 1685 A new (and meaningless) line inserted:
    Or Cullys of the Court — *Association*
18 And these / and those 1685
20 *Joe* / *Jo* 1685
21 *Leigh* /*Ligh* 1685; Dull, lavish, Creeping Tools / brisk, lavish keeping Fools 1685
22 Bowmans / He's 1685; carry's on / carry's it on 1685
24 But / And 1685
25-38 not included in 1685

POEMS FROM *Miscellany*, 1685

A Letter to Mr. *Creech* at *Oxford*, Written in the last great Frost.

Daphnis, because I am your debtor,
(And other causes which are better)
I send you here my debt of Letter.
You shou'd have had a scrap of Nonsense,
You may remember left at *Tonsons.*   5
(Tho by the way that's scurvy Rhime Sir,
But yet 'twill serve to Tagg a Line Sir.)
A *Billet Deux* I had design'd then
But you will say I was in Wine then,
Because it being cold, you know   10
We warm'd it with a Glass — or so,
I grant you that Shie Wine's the Devil,
To make ones memory uncivil;
But when 'twixt every sparkling Cup,
I so much brisker Wit took up;   15
Wit, able to inspire a thinking;
And make one solemn even in Drinking;
Wit that would charm and stock a Poet,
Even instruct —— who has no Wit;
Wit that was hearty, true and loyal,   20
Of Wit, like Bays Sir, that's my Tryal;
I say 'twas most impossible,
That after that one should be dull.
Therefore because you may not blame me,
Take the whole Truth as—— shall sa'me.   25
 From*White-Hall* Sir, as I was coming,
His Sacred Majesty from Dunning;
Who oft in Debt is, truth to tell,
For Tory Farce, or Doggerell,
When every Street as dangerous was,   30

As ever the *Alpian* Hills to pass.
When melted Snow and Ice confound one,
Whether to break one's neck or drown one,
And *Billet Deux* in Pocket lay,
To drop as Coach shou'd Jolt that way,   35
Near to that place of Fame call'd Temple,
(Which I shall note by sad Example)
Where Colledg Dunce is cur'd of Simple,
Against that Sign of Whore call'd Scarlet,
My Coachman fairly laid Pilgarlick.   40
    Tho Scribling Fist was out of joynt,
And ev'ry Limb made great complaint;
Yet missing the dear Assignation,
Gave me most cause of Tribulation.
To Honest H—le I shou'd have shown ye,   45
A Wit that wou'd be proud t'have known ye;
A Wit uncommon, and Facetious,
A great admirer of *Lucretius*;
But transitory hopes do vary,
And high Designments oft miscarry,   50
Ambition never climb'd so lofty,
But may descend too fair and softly,
But would you'd seen how sneakingly
I look'd with this Catastrophe.
So sawcy Whigg, when Plot broke out,   50
Dejected hung his sniv'ling snout;
So *Oxford* member look'd, when *Rowley*
Kickt out the rebel Crew so foully;
So *Perkin* once that God of Wapping,
Whom slippery turn of State took napping,   55
From hopes of *James* the second fell
Into the native Scounderell.
So Lover look'd of Joy defeated,
When too much Fire his Vigour cheated,
Even so look'd I, when Bliss depriving,   60
Was caus'd by over-hasty driving,
Who saw me cou'd not chuse but think,

I look'd like Brawn in sowsing drink.
Or Lazarello who was show'd
For a strange Fish, to'th'gaping Crowd.   65
Thus you by fate (to me, Sinister,
At Shop of Book my Billet mist Sir.
And home I went as discontent,
As a new routed Parliament,
Not seeing *Daphnis* ere he went.   70
And sure his grief beyond expressing,
Of Joy propos'd to want the Blessing;
Therefore to Pardon pray incline,
Since disappointment all was mine;
Of Hell we have no other notion,   75
Than all the Joys of Heav'ns privation;
So Sir with Recommendments fervent,
I rest your very humble Servant.

POSTCRIPT

On Twelfth night Sir, by that good token,
When lamentable Cake was broken,   80
You had a Friend, a Man of Wit,
A Man whom I shall ne're forget;
For every word he did impart,
'Twas worth the keeping in a heart:
True Tory all! and when he spoke,   85
A God in Wit, tho Man in look.
—This to your Friend— *Daphnis* address
The humblest of my Services;
Tell him how much— yet do not too,
My vast esteem no words can shew;   90
Tell him— that he is worthy— you.

OVID to *JULIA.*

A

LETTER,

By an Unknown Hand.

Fair Royal Maid, permit a Youth undone
To tell you how he drew his Ruin on;
By what degrees he took that Poison in,
That made him guilty of *Promethius* sin;
Who from the Gods durst steal Cœlestial fire,   5
And tho with less success, I did as high aspire.
Oh why ye Gods! was she of Mortal Race?
And why twixt her and me, was there so vast a space?
Why was she not above my Passion made
Some Star in Heaven, or Goddess of the Shade?   10
And yet my haughty Soul cou'd ne'er have bow'd
To any Beauty, of the common Crowd.
None but the Brow, that did expect a crown
Cou'd Charm or Awe me with a Smile, or Frown;
I had the Envy of th'*Arcadian* Plains,   15
Sought by the Nymphs, and bow'd to by the Swains;
Where I pass'd, I swept the Fields along,
And gather'd round me all the gazing throng:
In numerous Flocks and Herds I did abound, ⎫
And when I spread my wanton wishes round, ⎬   20
They wanted nothing but my being Crown'd. ⎭
Yet witness all ye spightful Powers above,
If my Ambition did not spring from Love!

Substantive variants from 'Bajazet to Gloriana' *Poems on Affairs of State* 1697
4   Promethius / Promethean 1697
7   Oh why ye Gods! / Ah, why (you Gods) 1697
17 Fields / Street 1697
20 spread my wanton / vainly spread my 1697

Had you my Charming *Julia* been less fair,
Less Excellent, less Conqu'ring than you are,   25
I had my Glorious Loyalty retain'd,
My Noble Blood untainted had remain'd,
Witness ye Groves, witness ye Sacred Powers!   ⎫
Ye shaded Rivers Banks, and beds of Flowers,   ⎬
Where the expecting Nymphs have past their Hours. ⎭   30
Witness how oft, all careless of their Fame,
They languish'd for the Author of their flame,
And when I came reproach'd my cold reserve;
Ask'd for what Nymph did I my Joys preserve?
What sighing Maid was next to be undone?   35
For whom I drest and put my Graces on?
And never thought, (tho I feign'd every proof
Of tender Passion) that I lov'd enough.
While I with Love's variety was cloy'd;
Or the faint pleasure like a Dream injoy'd.   40
'Twas *Julia's* brighter Eyes my soul alone
With everlasting gust, could feed upon.
From her first bloom my Fate I did pursue,   ⎫
And from the tender fragrant Bud, I knew   ⎬
The Charming Sweets it promis'd, when it Blew.   ⎭   45
This gave me Love, and 'twas in vain I try'd
The Beauty from the Princess to divide;
For he at once must feel, whom you inspire,
A soft Ambition, and a haughty fire,
And Hopes the Natural aid of young desire.   50

---

24 you my Charming *Julia* / you, my bright *Gloriana* 1697
25 Conquering / Charming 1697
26 Glorious / honost(*sic*) 1697
28 1697 Witness ye Graces, witness you Sacred Bowers!
29 Rivers / River 1697
31 oft, all careless of their Fame / oft (all careless of their Fame) 1697
34 did I / I did 1697
41 *Julia's* / *Gloriana's* 1697
46 This gave me Love / They gave me hope 1697

My unconsidering Passion had not yet
Thought your Illustrious Birth for mine too great,
'Twas Love that I pursu'd, vast Love that leads
Sometimes the equall'd slave, to Princes Beds.
But I forgot that Sacred Flame must rest   55
In your bright Soul, that makes th'Adorer blest;
Your generous fire alone must you subdue,
And raise the Humbler Lover up to you;
Yet if by Chance m'Ambition met a stop,
By any thought that check'd m'advancing hope,   60
This new one straight would all the rest confound,
H‍   ‍ev'ry Coxcomb aim'd at being Crown'd;
The vain young Fool with all his Mothers parts,
(Who wanted wit enough for little Arts,)
With Crowds and unmatch'd nonsense, lays a claim   65
To the Glorious title of a Sovereign;
And when for Gods such wretched things set up,
Was it so great a crime in me to hope?
No Laws of Heaven, or Man my Vows reprove;
There is no Treason in Ambitious Love.   70
That Sacred Antidote, i'th'poison'd Cup,
Quells the Contagion of each little drop,
I bring no Forces, but my sighs and tears,

---

53 vast Love / that God 1697
55 But I forgot / But oh, I had forgot 1697
57 generous / sacred 1697
58 'Tis that, not mine, can raise me up to you;
59 If / Yet... met / meet 1697
60 By / With 1697
64 wit / sense 1697
1697   Four lines, probably not by Behn, inserted between 64 and 65:
        Whose composition was like *Cheder* Cheese,
        (In whose Production all the Town agrees.)
        To whom, from Prince to Priest was added Suff,
        From great King Charles e'en down to Father *Goff*;
65 Yet he with vain Pretension lays a claim 1697
68 in / for 1697

My Languishment, my soft complaints and Pray'rs,
Artillery which I ne'r sent in vain,   75
Nor Sail'd (*sic*) where e'er address'st, to wound with pain:
Here, only here! rebated they return,
Meeting the sollid Armour of your Scorn;
Scorn! By the Gods! I anything could bear,
The Rough Fatigues and Storms of dangerous War;   80
Long Winters Marches, or the Summer heat,
May even in Battel, from the Foe defeat;
Scars on my face, Scars, whose dull recompence,
Would ne'er attone, for what they rob from thence.
Scandal of Coward, nay half witted too,   85
Or siding with the Pardon'd Rebell Crew;
Or any thing but scorn, — and yet frown on,
Your Slave was destin'd thus to be undone.
You the Avenging Deity appear,
And I a Victim fall to all the injur'd Fair.   90

---

75   I / was 1697
76   1697 Nor fails, where'e'er it lights, to wound or pain.
83   my / this 1697
87   1697 Or ought but scorn, and yet you must frown on,

A
PINDARICK
ON THE
DEATH
Of Our Late
SOVEREIGN
With An Ancient Prophecy on His
Present MAJESTY

STANZA I.

Sad was the *Morn'*, the sadder *Week* began,
And heavily the God of Day came on:
From Ominous *Dreams* my wondering Soul lookt out,
And saw a Dire *Confusion* round about.
My Bed like some sad Monument appear'd,   5
Round which the Mournful Statues wring their hands and weep;
Distracted Objects all! with mighty Grief, prepar'd
    To rouse me from my painful Sleep.
Not the sad Bards that wail'd *Jerusalems* woes,
(With wild neglect throu'out the peopl'd street,   10
With a Prophetick rage affrighting all they meet)
Had mightier Pangs of sorrow, mightier throes;
Ah! wretch, undone they Cry! awake forlorn,
The King! the King is Dead rise, rise and Mourn.

II.

Again I bid 'em tell their sorrows Theam,   15
    Again they Cry *The King! the King is Dead!*
Extended, Cold and Pale upon the Royal Bed;
    Again I heard, and yet I thought it *Dream.*
        Impossible (I raving Cry)
    That such a *Monarch*! such a *God* should dye!   20

22

And no *Dire Warning* to the World be given:
No *Hurricanes* on Earth! no *Blazing Fires* in Heaven!
The Sun and Tyde their *constant Courses* keep:
That Cheers the *World* with its Life-giving Reign,
This hasts with equal Motion to the *Deep*;   25
And in its usual turns revives the Banks again,
    And in its soft and easie way,
Brings up no *Storms* or *Monsters* from the Sea,
No *Show'rs* of Blood, no Temples *Vale* is rent,
But all is *Calm*, and all is *Innocent*.   30
When *Nature* in Convulsions should be hurl'd,
And *Fate* should shake the Fabrick of the World;
Impossible! Impossible I Cry!
So Great a King! So much a God! so silently should dye!

III.

True I Divin'd! when loe a *Voice* arriv'd,   35
Welcom as *that* which did the Crowd Surprise,
When the Dead *Lazarus* from the Tomb reviv'd,
And saw a *Pitying God* attend his rise!
Our Sovereign lives! it cry'd! *rise and Adore!*
Our Sovereign lives! Heaven adds one *Wonder more;*   40
To the *Miraculous History of his Num'rous store:*
  Suddain as *thought,* or *winged Light'ning* flys,
This chas'd the Gloomy *Terrors* from our Eyes,
And all from *Sorrows,* fall to *Sacrifice.*
Whole Hecatoms of *Vows* the Altars Crown,   45
To clear our *Sins* that brought this Vengeance down;
So the *Great Saviour* of the World did fall,
A Bleeding Victim to *attone* for all!
Nor were the Blest *Apostles* more reviv'd,
When in the *Resurrection* they beheld   50
Their *Faith* Establisht, and their *Lord* surviv'd,
And all the *Holy Prophesies* fulfill'd.
Their Mighty *Love,* by Mighty *Joy* they show'd!
  And if from *feabler Faith* before,

They did the Deity, and Man Adore: 55
What must they pay, when He *confirm'd* the God?
Who having *finisht* all His wonders here,
    And *full Instructions* given,
To make his bright *Divinity* more *Cleer*;
Transfigur'd all to Glory, Mounts to Heaven!   60

IV.

So fell our *Earthly God*! so Lov'd, so Mourn'd,
    So like a God again return'd.
For of His *Message*, yet a *part* was unperform'd,
    But oh! our *Pray'rs* and *Vows* were made *too late*,
    The Sacred *Dictates* were already past;   65
And open laid the *Mighty Book* of *Fate*,
    Where the *Great MONARCH* read his lifes *short date*,
    And for *Eternity* prepar'd in hast.
      He saw in th' ever lasting Chains
Of long past Time and Numerous Things,   70
      The Fates, Vicissitudes, and pains,
Of Mighty *Monarchies*, and Mighty *Kings*,
And blest his Stars that in an Age so Vain,
    Where Zealous *Mischiefs*, *Frauds*, *Rebellions*, Reign:
    Like *Moses*, he had led the Murm'ring Crowd,   75
Beneath the *Peaceful Rule* of his Almighty Wand;
    Pull'd down the *Golden Calf* to which they bow'd,
    And left 'em *safe*, entring the promis'd Land;
    And to *good JOSHUA*, now resigns his sway,
JOSHUA, by *Heaven* and *Nature* pointed out to lead the way.   80

V.

Full of the *Wisdom* and the *Pow'r* of God,
The *Royal PROPHET* now before him stood:
On whom His Hands the Dying *MONARCH* laid,
And wept with tender Joy, and Blest and said:
To Thee, kind Aid in all my Fates and Pow'rs,   85

Dear Partner of my Sad and Softest Hours,
Thy Parting King and Brother recommends
His frighted Nations, and his Mourning Friends,
Take to Thy Pious Care, my Faithful Flock.
    And tho' the Shelt'ring Cedar Fade,   90
Regard said he, regard my tender Stock;
    The Noble Stems may shoot and grow
    To Grace the Spacious Plains, and bow
Their Spreading Branches round Thee a defensive shade.
The *Royal SUCCESSOR* to all he hears   95
With *sighs* assented, and confirming *Tears.*
Much more he spoke! much more he had Exprest,
But that the *Charming* Accents of his *Tongue*
Flew upwards to Compose a Heav'nly Song,
And left his speaking Eyes to *Bless* and *tell* the rest,   100
His Eyes so much Ador'd! whose less'ning light
Like setting Suns that hasten on the Night;
(Lending their Glories to another Sphere)
    Those Sacred Lights are fading here,
Whilst every Beam above informs a Star,   } 105

VI.

    Which shall a Nobler Business know,
And Influence his best lov'd Friends below.
But oh!
No *Humane* thought can paint the *Grief* and *Love*,
    With which the *Parting Hero's* strove.   110
Sad was the Scene, *soft looks* the *Voice* supplies,
Anguish their *Hearts,* and *Languishment* their *Eyes*;
Not God-like *Jonathan* with greater pain,
Sigh't his last Farewell to the *Royal Swain;*
While *Awful silence* fill'd the Gloomy place,   115
And *Death* and *Midnight* hung on ev'ry Face.
And now the *fatal Hour* came on,
And all the Blessed Pow'rs above,
In hast to make him ALL their own,

Around the *Royal Bed* in shining order move. 120
Once more he longs to see the *Breaking Day*,
The *last* his Mortal Eyes shall e're behold,
   And oft he ask'd if no *Kind Ray*,
     Its *near Approach* foretold,
   And when he found 'twas *Dawning* in, 125
(With the Cold *Tide* of Death that flow'd all o're)
Draw, draw, said he, *this Clowd that hangs between,*
   And let me take my last adieu;
   Oh let me take my last soft view,
For I shall never, never see it more. 130
And Now ———
Officious Angels catch his dying *Sighs,*
And bear 'em up in Triumph to the Skys,
Each forms a Soul of the *Divinest* dress!
For *New-born Kings* and *Heroes* to possess. 135
The *last,* that from the Sacred *Fabrick flew,*
Made C*HARLES* a *God* and *JAMES* a *Monarch* too!

To His Sacred MAJESTY,
KING JAMES II.

A*LL* Hail *Great Prince!* whom ev'ry *Miracle*
   Preserv'd for *Universal Rule;*
  When Time Your *wond'rous Story* shall unfold,
Your *Glorious Deeds* in *Arms,* when yet but Young;
Your strange *Escapes,* and *Danger* shall be told, 5
Your Battails *Fought,* Your Gilded Lawrels *won,*
When yet the *Elder* Generals (not in *Fame*)
   Your *Perils* dar'st not share,
Alone the raging Torrent You wou'd stem,
And bear before You the fierce Tide of War. 10
   How *Spain* Records Your Glorious Name,
And how when *Danger* call'd, for *Britains* good,
You paid the *lavish Ransom* of Your Blood.
   When the Ingrates shall Blushing read,

How far *great* Souls the *Vulgar* can exceed   15
In *Patience*, *Suffering*, and *Humility*,
    Your *Condiscention*, and Your *Banishment*,
    Then let the *Obstinate* (convinc'd) agree;
You only were preserv'd, and fit, for S*acred Government*.

Come listen all, whom *needless fears* possess,   20
    And hear how Heav'n *confirms* Your Happiness:
        Behold the Sacred Promis'd Prince,
        Whom wond'rous Prophets Ages since
Told, When the Mistick Figures of the Year,
        To such a Number should Amount,   25
        (As fill this Lucky Years Account)
O're England there should Reign a Star
    Of that Divine and Gracious Influence,
    Should make proud Neighbouring Nations fear:
And Mightier Britains happy Genius prove,   30
And bless the Land with Plenty, Peace, and Love.
'Tis YOU, oh Sacred Sir, for *Empire* Born,
        Shall make the great *Prediction* true,
        And this last *Miracle* perform,
To make us *Blest*, and make us *own* it too.   35
Oh may Your *Luster* with Your *Life* renew!
Long may You Shine, and spread Your Beams as far,
    As from the Morning to the Ev'ning Star;
    'Till Your *Convincing Rays*, Your Foes o're come,
And for Your *Glorious Magnitude* the scanted Globe want room.

FINIS.

A
POEM
ON HER
Sacred Majesty
Catherine Queen Dowager.

Pardon! Oh *Sacred Mourner*! that we paid
Our first sad Tributes to the *Royal Dead*;
Which did our Souls to rending sighs convert,
Drain'd our fixt eyes, and pierc'd the bleeding heart;
And for a *Loss* that Heav'n can ne're redress,   5
Our *Raging Griefs* were rude in their excess:
Which, while with *wild Devotion* we pursue,
Ev'n *Heav'n* neglected lay, ev'n Sacred *YOU* ;
Our *own* dire *Fates* did *all* our Tears employ,
Griefs have self-interest too as well as *Joy*.   10
But when *such Sacrifice* from *us* is due,
What must the *Mighty Loss* exact from *You*,
Who Mourn a *King*, and dear lov'd Husband too!
How shall we measure that vast tide of 𝔚𝔬𝔢,
That did Your Royal *breaking Heart* o'reflow?   15
And almost, with a high imperious force,
Bore down the Banks of *Life* in its too rapid course.
Your *Languishments* and *Sorrows*, who repeats,
Or by his *own*, on *Yours* a *Value* sets,
Compares *deep Seas* to *wandr'ing Rivolets*;   20
Who though a while in their own Meads they stray,
Lose their young streams at last in the unbounded Sea.
Shou'd all the Nations tenderest griefs combine;
And all our *Pangs* in one vast body joyn,
They cou'd not sigh with *Agonies* like *Thine*.   25
That You survive, is Heav'ns peculiar care;
To *charm* our *Grief*, and *heal* our wild *Despair*;
While we to *Charles's* Sacred Relick bow,

28

Half the *great Monarch* we Adore in You:
The *rest*, our Natural Devotions grant;   30
We *bless* the *Queen*, and we *Invoke* the *Saint*:
Nor fades your *Light* with *England's* Worship'd Sun,
Your *Joys* were set, but still Your *Glory* shon:
And with a Luster that shall still increase,
When worlds shall be no more, and Natures self shall cease;   35
For never in *one mortal Frame* did joyn
A *Fortitude* and *Vertue* more Divine:
Witness the *Steady Graces* of your Soul   ⎫
When charg'd by *Perjuries* so black and foul,   ⎬
As did *all Laws*, both *Humane* and *Divine* controul. ⎭   40
When Heaven (to make the *Heroin* understood;   ⎫
And Hell it self permitted loose abroad)   ⎬
Gave you the *Patience* of a *Suffering God*.   ⎭
So our blest *Saviour* his *Reproaches* bore   ⎫
When Piercing Thorns His *Sacred Temples* wore;   ⎬   45
And stripes compell'd the Rich *redeeming Gore*. ⎭
Your pretious *Life* alone, the Fiends disdain'd
To Murder home; your *Vertue* they prophan'd;
By Plots so rude, so Hellish a Pretence
As ev'n wou'd call in question *Providence*:   50
Or why Avenging *Thunder* did not strike
Those *Cursed Hands* durst touch the Sacred *Ark*;
But as where *long* the Sun is *set* in *Night*,
They with *more joy* Salute the breaking *light*;
Heav'n cast this *Cloud* before your radient *Beams*   55
To prove their *Force* by contrary *Extreams;*
The Nations all with new Devotion bow,
To *Glories* never understood till now:
'Twas *Majesty* and *Beauty* Aw'd before;
But now the *Brighter Vertue* they adore   60

    This the *Great Lord* of all Your Vows beheld;
And with disdain Hells baffl'd rage repell'd;
He knew your *Soul* and the soft *Angel* there;

And long (kind Rivals) did that Empire share;
And all your Tears, your pleading Eloquence   65
Were needless Treasures; lavish'd to convince
Th'Adorer of your known and Sacred *Innocence*
When not for *Life* the Royal *Suppliant* mov'd;
But *His belief*; whom more than Life she lov'd;
From whom, if e're a frown she cou'd receive   70
'Twas when She *doubted* that He cou'd believe;
While he repeats the dear confirming Vows;
And the *first* soft addressing *Lover* shows.

   By your *reflecting Smiles* the World was gay;
Faction was fled; and *Universal Joy*   75
Made the glad business of the welcome day.
Ah! too secure we baskt beneath the *Sun*;
And little thought his *Race* so near was run;
But as if *Phaeton* had usurp'd its Rule;
In the full Brightness of its course it fell;   80
Whilst all the *frighted World* with wonder gaz'd;
And *Nature* at her own disorder stood amaz'd:
While you, ah *Pious Mourner* did prepare
To offer up to *Heav'n* your early Prayer;
You little thought 'twou'd meet your dear-lov'd Monarch there:
But on the Wings of Death the News approach't;
And e'ne destroy'd the wondring sense it toucht;
O Mighty *Heav'n-Born* Soul! that cou'd support
So like a God! this cruel *first effort!*
Without the *Feebler Sexes* mean replies,   90
The *April Tributes* of their *Tears* and *Cries*,
Your *Valu'd* Loss a *Noysey Grief* disdain'd,
Fixt in the *heart*, no outward sign remain'd;
Though the *soft Woman* bow'd and dy'd within;
Without, Majestick Grace maintain'd the *Queen*!   95
Yet swiftly to the *Royal Bed* You fly,
Like short-liv'd Lightning from the parted sky
Whose new-born Motions do but flash and dy.
Such *Vig'rous Life* ne're mov'd your steps before,

But here——they *sunk* beneath the *Weight* they bore.   100
Princes we *more* than *Humane* do allow,
You must have been *above* an *Angel* too;
Had You *resisted* this sad *Scene* of War;
So the *Blest Virgin* at the Worlds great loss,
Came, and beheld, then *Fainted* at the Cross.   105

    Methinks I see, You like the Queen of *Heav'n*,
To whom all *Patience* and all *Grace* was giv'n;
When the Great *Lord* of *Life* Himself was laid
Upon her Lap, all wounded, Pale and Dead;
Transpierc'd with Anguish, ev'n to Death *Transform'd*,   110
So She *bewail'd* Her God! so *sigh'd*, so *Mourn'd*;
So His blest *Image* in Her Heart remain'd,
So His blest *Memory* o're Her Soul still *Reign'd*!
She Liv'd the *Sacred Victim* to deplore,
And never *knew*, or *wisht* a Pleasure more.   115

    But when to Your Apartment You were brought,
And *Grief* was Fortify'd with *Second Thought*;
O how it burst what e're its Force withstood,
Sight to a *Storm*, and swell'd into a *Flood*;
Courage, which is but a peculiar Art   120
By *Honour* taught; where *Nature* has no Part:
When e're the *Soul* to fiercer Passions yield,
It ceases to be brave, and quits the field;
Do's the abandon'd sinking *heart* expose
Amid'st Ten Thousand Griefs, its worst of Foes.   125

    Your *Court*, what Dismal *Majesty* it wears,
Infecting all around with *Sighs* and *Tears*;
No Soul so *dull*, so *insensible* is found,
Without concern to tread the hallowed Ground;
Awful, and *silent*, all the Rooms of State,   130
And *Emptiness* is Solemn there, and great;
No more Recesses of the sprightly Gay,
But a *Retreat* for Death, from Noise and Day:

Eccho's from Room to Room we may pursue,
Soft *sighs* may hear, but *Nothing* is in view;   135
Like Groves inchanted, where wreck'd Lovers ly,
And breath their Moans to all the Passers-by;
Who no kind Aids to their Relief can bring,
But Eccho back their *Pittying Sighs* agen.
But the mysterious *Sanctum* is conceal'd   140
To *vulgar Eyes* that must not be reveal'd;
To your *Alcove* your Splendours you confine,
Like a *Bright Saint* veil'd in a *Sable* Shrine;
As the *Chaste Goddess* of the *silent Night*,
You Reign alone, retir'd from *Gaudy* Light;   145
So Mourning *Cinthia* with her Starry Train,
Wept the sad Fate of her Lov'd sleeping *Swain*.

FINIS

A Pindarick Poem
ON THE
CORONATION

I.

Arise my Muse! Advance thy *Mourning* Head!
And *cease* lamenting for the *Mighty Dead!*
Quench all the *Funeral Tapers* in your *Tears,*
    And as the fainting flames expire,
    Let your soft falling Tides retire;
While you behold the *Prospect* that appears   5
    In the vast Glories of *succeeding years!*
    Advance! and throw thy sable weeds away!
    And string thy Lyre for some *Harmonious* Lay,
Worthy the *Celebration* of this *Mighty Day!*   10
  Come ye soft Angels all, and lend your aid,
    Ye little Gods that tun'd the Spheres,
    That wanton'd, sung, and smil'd and play'd,
When the *first World* was by your *Numbers* made;
And Danc'd to *order* by your *Sacred Ayrs!*   15
Such *Heavenly Notes* as *Souls* Divine can *warm,*
    Such wond'rous *touches* as wou'd move
And teach the *Blest* to *Sing* and *Love!*
And even the *Anger* of a *GOD* wou'd *Charm!*
O Tune it high, and strike with bold success,   20
    But sweet and gentle, every strain,
As that which once taught by the *Charming Swain,*
By its soft force the *Spirit disposest*
From the great *King* and *Prophets* raging Breast.

II.

Yet when thou woud'st the *Royal HERO* sing   25
Thy *Godlike* Patron, and thy *Godlike* King!
Rough as a *useful storm* make him appear!

33

Or as that welcome *Eastern* Wind,
　　By which th' *Almighty Pow'r* designed
Th' *Egyptian* Locust from the Land to bear.　　　　30
Resolv'd as the *first Messenger* of Heav'n,
　　To whom the great Command was giv'n
　　The first Born *Rebells* to chastise;
　　Who, while the flaming Sword he bore,
　　'Twas only to declare his Pow'r,　　　　35
And *unusurpt* maintain his *Paradice*,
Paint him like *Mars* when *Battails* were in *view*,
And no soft *Venus* cou'd his Soul *subdue*;
All bent for *nobler spoil* than *Beauties Charms*,
And loos'd a while from Sacred *LAURA's* Arms.　　　　40
LAURA! the Chast! the Pious! and the Fair!
Glorious, and kind as Guardian-Angels are,
Earths *darling Goddess*! and Heav'ns *tend'rest care*!

III.

But oh my Muse, when e're thou do'st presume
　　To touch on so *Divine* a *Theam*,　　　　45
Let it be *Nature* all, thou do'st indite,
That those who read in Ages *distant* hence
May *feel* the very *Zeal* with which I write;
And by th' *unlabour'd* Verse be *warm'd* to tender sense:
　　That *future Lovers* when they hear,　　　　50
　　Your *all-ador'd* and *wond'rous* character;
　　(For sure the mighty *LAURA's* Name will Live
　　As long as *Time* its self survive)
May find the *Holy Passions* you inspire,
　　Such *awful* flame, such *hopeless* pain,　　　　55
Wander and trill through every trembling Vein;
And *Bless* the *Charmer* that *Creates* the Fire!
　　Bless the *soft Muse* that cou'd express
Beauty and *Majesty* in such a dress,
As all the World *Adoring* shall confess!　　　　60
Oh *fond seducer* of my *Nobler part*,

Thou soft insinuating *Muse*,
If ever *inspiration* did impart
The *Soul* of *Musick* or *Poetick* Art;
    Teach me, oh teach me how to chuse   65
Fancy for so *Divine* a *Theam*, O thou inchanting Muse!

IV.

The Glorious Ides of *April* now were come,
    And Heav'n all open'd to survey
The *Mighty Triumphs* of the Blessed Day:
And *Earth* had drest her self in all her *Bloom*,   70
And sent abroad a *universal joy*!
Ten Thousand *Angels* fill'd the glitt'ring A*ir*;
    And all was *Harmony* above,
O're all the *Azure plains* the *Golden Cherubs* move;
    And *Seraphins* were chanting every where,   75
Gay Robes of *Light* the young Divinities put on,
    And spread their *shining Locks* to outvie the *Sun*.
    On *Pillows* form'd of *yielding Air* they lye,
    Plac'd in the mid-way Regions of the Sky;
    On *Jvry Lutes* and *Silver Harps* they play'd,   80
And gave the *Sacred PAIR* a Heav'nly *Serenade*:
    Call'd forth the *wond'ring* Crowd, the *Beaut'ous* throng,
While all the *Host of Heav'n* attended on the *Song*.

V.

Awake, Oh *Royal Sir*! Oh *Queen*, ador'd, awake!
    For whom our *Triumphs* and our *Songs* we make;   85
    The *sleepless Crowds* their *early duties* show,
    Th' attending Hierarchies of *Angels* bow;
    All *Heav'n* and *Earth* with one united joy
Expect the *mighty business* of this *coming Day*:
    All Languish for its blest approach—but You,   90
    You to whom *Glory's* can no *Luster* give,
        Whose *Beams*, like the expanded Sun,

Adorn what e're they deign to *shine* upon;
But no *exalt addition* can receive.
Thou *HERO* of th' *expecting world* arise!   95
Shake off the downy pleasures from thy eyes;
And from the softest Charms of LOVE, Arise!
From *joys* too fierce for *any* sense but *Thine*,
Whose *Soul*, whose *Faculty's* are all *Divine*;
So *Bodies* when *refin'd*, all Heav'n survey,   100
While *feebler* Mortals *faint* with ev'ry ray:
O rise from the *inchanting Ravisher*,
Nor listen to the *Musick* of Her *Tongue*;
Her *Angel* Eyes, and Voice, so *conqu'ring* are,
Love will make *humbler Glory* wait too long.   105

VI.

    And *Thou* bright *Goddess* of the *Day*!
For *whom* all longing *Eyes* and *Hearts* prepare;
These tender panting, *those* soft *Tears* of *Joy*,
And with impatient Murm'rings fill the Air;
O Charming *Goddess* of the Day appear!   110
Full of Thy *Blest Idea*, they disdain
    A *vulgar thought* to entertain;
Big with *Prophetick Joy*, they lab'ring wait
To utter Blessings *wonderful* and *great*;
This day no *rough Fatigues* of Life shall vex,   115
No more *Domestick Cares* the mind perplex;
All *common thoughts* are lost in the *vast crowd* of *Joy*,
    This *Jubilee*! this Sacred *Holy-day*!
    The *Soul* resolves for *Mirth* and *Play*.
    She leaves all *Worldly thoughts* behind,   120
And in Her hast out-strips the wanton Wind;
Wou'd ev'n her early vows *neglect* to pay,
    But that to Heav'n you *guide* the way;
When for *Your safety* all agree to *Pray*.
The *Poor Man* now forgets his *pressing needs*,   125
No Penury his exalted looks confess,

Neglects the *Body*, while the *Soul* he feeds
On *fancy'd pleasures* scarce arriv'd in *guess*.
   No sad *Complaints* ascend the Sky's,
     No Nymphs *reproach'd* in Lovers *sighs*,   130
Or Maid *forsaken*, *bends* her lovely eyes.
All with *erected Looks* salute the World!
None *bow* beneath the *Pressure* of a thought,
Unless where *Envy* has her *Vipers* hurl'd,
And raging *Malice* even to *Madness* wrought,   135
   They hate the *Light* that guides the *work Divine*;
And how'l and gnash their Teeth, and suffer Hell before their time.
The *Brave* are glad, and gay, the *young* rejoyce,
The *old* in Prayers and Blessings lift the Voice;
Virgins the wealth of Flow'ry *April* bring,   140
And all the *Muses*, and the *Angels* sing!

VII.

Behold the *HERO* the blest Voice obeys,
   And like the God of *Luster* gilds
   With early Beams the Eastern Hills,
And by degrees th' adoring World surveys: 145
   So the bright *Harness* he puts on,
And in his hand Divine he takes the *Reins*,
And with life-giving Rule the *God* maintains
   The *Glorious Empire* of the *Sun*.
With *ease* he guides the fiery *Coursers* round,   150
And *heat*, and *life*, and *light*, do still abound;
And all things *smile* and *thrive* that are in *Nature* found.
Now fiercer *Rays* of *Brightness* he assumes,
And ev'ry *Minute* do's *inlarge* his Beams;
Till to the farthest Poles their *Influence* spread,   155
And scatter *Plenty* where his *Glory's* shed.
While all the *guilty* fantôms of the *Night*
Shrink from the Piercing *terror* of his Light!
Each coming *vulgar* day, the MONARCH show'd,
But *this* more Sacred, views Him all a *GOD*!   160

New *youth* and *vigor* fill His *Royal Veins,*
His Glorious *Eyes,* young *flames* adorn;
A new *Divinity* in His looks, Proclames
That for *Eternal Empire* He was *Born!*
'Twas so He look'd in *Dunkirks* bloody field,   165
When the dull faithless *Belgians* He compell'd;
But when He saw th'ungrateful *British* Foe advance,
For whom *even yet* He had a *tender* sense,
Thus spoke! (When, mounted like a Conquering *God,*
From Rank to Rank the wond'rous *Hero* Rod!)   170
Before (said he) mixt Nations *We withstood*
Conquest, scarce worthy *our expence* of *Blood;*
Like Gallick *onsets, brisk* at first *they 'ppear,*
But dare not trust the event of fiercer *War:*
'Twas play *before, a game We* smiling *won,*   175
Now *'twill be* Toyl, *and work, not easily done;*
My dear lov'd Souldiers these are English Men!
Who though they're forc'd *to fly will* turn *agen;*
Stanch *to the* Scent *of* War, *inur'd to Blood!*
     Oh happy, if the expensive flood   180
Had been defus'd for wretched Englands good!
New Courage to the *fainting Troops* He gave,
And by His great *Example* taught 'em to be *Brave:*
Wonders the *Promis'd Monarch* did perform,
And dealt *Destruction* round like a resistless storm!   185

VIII.

Nor did His *forward Gallantry* in *War*
     Surmount his *Clemency in Peace,*
His *Captives* proudly their *soft Fetters* bear,
         And charm'd to an excess,
     Adore the *wonders* they beheld,   190
And kist the *Sacred Hand* that chast 'em ore the field.
     His *early Courage* did His Foes *convince,*
         Who now their *scorn'd Commissions* tear,
     No longer will the *Tyrants Ensigns* bear;

But Vow *Allegiance* to their *Native Prince*.   195
They saw the *God of War* in ev'ry Grace,
While soft *Adonis* revell'd in His face;
The Goddess here, might all her wish enjoy,
The *rough stern* HERO, in the *Charming Boy*!
Such *Looks* as after *Victory* He put on,   200
With *such* to day the Glitt'ring MONARCH shone;
Such *Grace* in Smiles, such *sweetness* in address,
Awfull as *Heav'n*, as easy of *Access*;
And *Merciful* as that, when e're he can redress!
    True *Representer* of the Pow'rs Divine!   205
        Such was the first Born-Man,
Heav'n did for an immortal Race design,
      E're the first bright deluded Maid
    To sense of Fear, the *Lord* of *All* betray'd;
So look'd the new-form'd *wonder*, so His *Reign* began!   210
    So the gay Beauties of His World survey'd,
While Heav'n look'd down and smil'd, well-please'd with what
    'thad made.

IX.

See the bright *QUEEN* forsakes her softer *joys*,
    And now prepares for *Pomp* and *Noise*;
That *necessary* Toyl of the *Illustrious Great*!   215
    Who rarely taste the *Bliss* of sweet *Retreat*,
Like *Heav'n* who neither sleep nor slumber knows,
Short *Dreams* of *Glory* make their whole *repose*:
Whatever *rest* soft Nature do's design,
    The *Sun*, and *They*, must still appear and shine!   220
      And now, the more surprising Light
    Breaks from the silent Empire of the Night;
      So *Venus* look't when from the Seas
      The rising Beauty view'd the world,
When amorous Waves around the Virgin curl'd,   225
And all the *wond'ring Gods* with awful pleasure gaz'd:
    All sigh with Love! all languish in their flame,

Yet none his pain presumes to name;
For oh! the *God-born Maid* from mighty *Neptune* came.

X.

And now the *Nymphs* ply all their Female arts   230
To dress Her for Her *victory* of hearts;
    A Thousand little *LOVES* descend!
Young waiting *Cupids* with officious care
    In smiling order all attend:
This, decks Her S*nowy Neck*, and that Her *Ebon Hair*.   235
    The Trophies which the *Conqueress* must adorn,
      Are by the *busie wantons* born;
Who at Her Feet the shining burdens lay,
    The GODDESS pleas'd to see their Toyls,
Scatters Ten Thousand *Graces* from Her *Smiles*;   240
While the wing'd Boys catch ev'ry *flying Ray*.
This bears the valu'd *Treasure* of the *East*,
And lugs the Golden casket on His Breast;
    Anothers little hand sustains
    The weight of *Oriental* Chains;   245
    And in the flowing jetty *curles*
    They weave and braid the luced *Pearls*;
Round Her bright *Face* their nimble fingers play,
And ev'ry *touch* gives the young *Gods* a *joy*!
They gaze and hov'r round Her wond'rous *Eyes*,   250
Where a vast Heav'n of *Wit* and *Beauty* lies;
They point their Darts, and make their Arrows fine,
From the eternal Rays with which they shine;
From Her fair rising *Breasts* soft sighs they take,
To keep young tortur'd *Lovers* still awake.   255
    From ev'ry *Charm* and *Grace* they bear,
    Uneasie wishes, and *despair*;
From Her alone the Bankrupt LOVES supply,
Their rifl'd Quivers with Artillery.
Fatal to *All* but Her Lov'd *Monarchs* heart,   260
Who of the *same* Divine Materials wrought;

Cou'd equally exchange the dart,
Receive the wound with Life, with Life the wound impart;
And mixt the Soul as gently as the thought:
So the Great THUNDERER *Semele* d'stroy'd,   265
Whil'st only JUNO cou'd embrace the *God!*

XI.

Behold Her now by *Loves* and *Graces* drest!
Like the Great Wife of *Jove* in *Venus Cest*;
Now She may ask whate're the *God* can grant,
If ought of Pow'r, or Glory, She can want;   270
But Heav'n has superseded all Her care,
And giv'n till it has left no *use* for Pray'r.
No wish for *Times* swift Coursers to run back,
    To catch one flying minute past;
    The co*ming* hours, new *pleasures* hast;   275
Fortune and *Nature* still agree to make
Each present minute gayer than the last:
This gives you *Empire!* while Three Nations pay
Their *willing homage* to your Scepters sway.
That gives you *Beauty!* which without the aid   280
Of feebler pow'r, *Commands* and is *obey'd!*
Bewitching *youth* do's over all appear,
So Flow'rs just blown, their noblest Luster shew,
    When shining in their Morning dew;
    All their fresh Fragrancies they wear.   285
Almighty *Wit* and *Vertue!* Crowns the whole,
In ev'ry look and Feature of your Face,
We may the well-known *Excellencies* Trace
        Of your Diviner Soul!
Though the soft Musick of your *Words* shou'd cease,   290
Your Charming *Eyes* wou'd Your great *Thoughts* confess!
Oh Blest are they that may at *distance* gaze,
And *Inspirations* from Your *looks* may take,
But how much more their happier Stars they Praise,
    Who *wait*, and *listen* when you *speak!*   295

41

Mine for no *scanted bliss* so *much* I blame,
    (Though they the *humblest* Portion destin'd me)
        As when they *stint* my *noblest Aim*,
        And by a silent dull obscurity
        Set me at *distance*, much too far   300
The *Deity* to *view*, or Divine *Oracle* to hear!
    So when the *Israelites* all wond'ring stood,
    With awful Rev'rence in the vale beneath,
    They saw from *far* the *Glory's* of the GOD;
    But to *approach* the Sacred *Mount* was *Death*!   305
    His *Dictates* by the *Holy Prophet* came,
    'Twas He *alone* that did the pow'r receive,
        To *hear* th'ALMIGHTY's voice and *live*;
It was enough for them below to *view* the Heav'nly flame.

XII.

Not the gay feather'd Chanters of the A*ir*   310
With earlier Songs salute the breaking Day,
Than crowding *Hero's*, who to Court repair,
Do hail, and bless the Kingdoms *Hope* and *Joy*!
    And now the gilded Barges wait
        The coming of th'*Illustrious Fraight*;   315
So *Rich* a Prize no Vessel blest before,
But *that* which the *Almighty SAVIOUR* bore!
Their Golden Streamers glitter in the *Air*,
        And rufl'd by the softer Wind,
        (That plays and wantons unconfin'd)   320
They gently waft the Worlds *Peculiar Care*.
        The sullen *Sea-Gods* wondr'ing rise,
        Rous'd by the *joyful* shouts and cry's;
Which from the crowded shores ascend the Sky's.
They shake Their Tridents and the Waves obey,   325
Dress their *Blew Locks* and flounce along the Sea,
To pay their Tributes to the *Greater* DEITY.
    Him, whome so *oft* with wonder they beheld,
    With slaughter dye the verdant watry field;

When o're the wild insatiate flood,   330
He darted *Thunder* like an *Angry God!*
While round Him 𝕯𝖊𝖆𝖙𝖍 in *horrid* Triumph lay,
Where storms of *winged ruine* forc'd their way.
Yet still the *saving Angel* guarded *Him*;
      The *Bloody* Signets which He wore   335
Made the *Avenger* pass the *sacred Dore*,
And still *Preserv'd* the faithful *guest* within.
Oh had *that Senate*, whose *Ingratitude*
The ROYAL HEIR indeavour'd to *Exclude*;
Beheld His *single* wonders of that Day,   340
When o're the liquid Plain He cut His way;
Through show'rs of *Death* and Clouds of dark'ning smoke,
Like fatal *Light'ning* the fierce *Victor* broke,
And *kill'd*, where e're He dasht th'*unerring stroke*;
Instead of *Votes* against His *Right* and *Fame*,   345
They'd rais'd *Eternal Altars* to His *Name*!
      Ador'd Him as a thing Divine,
And made a *God* of Him before His time!
But *they* Heav'ns mightiest Blessing did *disown*,
And strove (oh *base* reward!) in *vain* to blast His NAVAL CROWN.

XIII.

The *Titans* from the *Marvels* which they saw,
Did *Omens* of their *Future homage* draw;
They in the HERO view'd their *coming* KING,
And from Their *wonder* fell to *Worshipping*.
And what before was to the victor due,   355
They to the Monarch doubly here renew.
The *River Nymphs* forsake their native streams,
      And make their Court to happier *Thames*;
Their Pipes of Reeds and shelly Musick bring,
The *Tritons* play, while the young *Naieds* sing;   360
      And all the listening shore along,
      Of *Jove!* and *Juno!* was their Song.
Which oftentimes they did rehearse,

43

And *Iô peans* Crown'd the Verse!

XIV.

Jove *for whom our Alters smoke,*   365
Jove, *whom Gods and Men invoke;*
By whose sole power the laughing year
Rouls round the gilded Hemisphere;
Who do'st its easie paces move,
By the soft rule of Peace and Love: 370
Accept that we thy watery Subjects bring,
Oaken Garlands for our King,
Ever Green and flourishing!
Which Thy Empire shall Proclaim
O're the Tributary Main;   375
See the Triumphant wreath's are drest
With all the shining Trophies of the East;
Such as remotest shores afford,
With which they own and greet their Lord;
By this gay tenure 'tis they hold   380
Their Rocks of Diamonds, and their Hills of Gold:
And thus acknowledge thus we pay
Great Jove! *on this Thy solemn Holy-day.*

XV.

But what at Sacred Juno's *feet*
Shall the Adoring Nymphs present?   385
Juno *charming, chast and sweet,*
The refuge of the Innocent:
The business of our pious Theames,
Our waking Bliss, our joy in Dreams;
The President of Vertuous Wives,   390
The bright example of the fair,
Whence Virgins learn their modest lives,
And Saints their pure Devotion there:
And all the Goddesses of less degree

Take a peculiar *Majesty*.   395
The humble softness of a mortal mind,
(Where all the Graces are confin'd)
With every Grandure of a Deity!
The noblest Songs from You their Beauties take,
Divinely you restore our fainting skill,   400
  Inspire the chast and flowing quill,
Teach Poets how to sing! and Angels how to speak!
  Oh what to Juno shall we pay
  On this Her solemn Holy day!

XVI.

Ten Thousand Garlands from the stores   405
  Of flowr'y Aromatick shores;
  With shining Colours newly born
All blooming Beauties of the Morn!
Gather'd before the Delphick God,
  Or the soft Wind that gently breaths,   410
  Had kist the tender Virgin Bud,
  Had robb'd the sweetness from their leaves;
  In mystick order these shall spread
  The hollow'd ground, where Thou shalt tread,
And shed their Infant Odours round Thy Sacred head: 415
Ten Thousand Hearts all with soft wishes fill'd,
  Chast as Thy Bosom, pure as is Thy Fame,
  Ten Thousand Vows from Souls that yield
Eternal Adorations to Thy Name!
  Let the contending Merchant strive   420
  For Indian Pearls and Western Ore,
  Those raffl'd Toys by which They thrive,
  And sell their safties on the shore;
Unvalu'd trifles to a Power Divine,
  To whom a wounded Heart is more   425
Than all the Ransackt World has laid before
  Upon the Worshipt shrine!
These are the Tributes we devoutly pay

45

Great Juno *on Her solemn* Holy-day.

XVII.

While thus the Ravisht *Nerieds* Sung   430
    The Echoes from the crowded shore,
    Repeated the glad Musick o're;
And all the Banks with Acclamations rung,
Like well-tun'd Vollies with united Peals:
Which after rattle in the distant Sky,   435
Long live our Sacred *King* and *Queen!* they cry,
And all the vacant round with joyful murmer fills,
    Repeating still the grateful noise
As fast as e're they could recharge the Voice;
    The different shoutings of the Throng,   440
The Female Treble, and the Manly Base,
The dead flat Notes of the declining race,
    Tun'd to the sharp ones of the young,
Compleats the noblest Musick of the Day:
    And though each bore a different part,   445
'Twas all one Voice, and one united Heart,
Rejoyc'd, and blest the Monarch all the way.

XVIII.

Here let the *Royal Pair* a while repose
    Oh thou impatient Muse!
Though loth as are my Eyes the bliss to lose;   450
    Who never yet could satisfie their sight,
        Which do's new life infuse,
    When ever they repeat the true delight.
        How oft, how silently, alas!
I glide, and hover round the awful place,   455
    Like Fantoms, where their hidden Treasure lies;
    Or hoping Lovers who at distance gaze,

And watch the tender Moments of their Mistress Eyes.
How e're I toil for Life all day,
With what e're cares my Soul's opprest,   460
'Tis in that Sun-shine still I play,
'Tis there my wearied Mind's at rest,
But oh *Vicisitudes* of Night must come
Between the rising Glories of the Sun!

XIX.

And now the *Royal Robes* are on,   465
But oh! what numbers can express
The Glory of the Sacred Dress!
Not the gay *Planet*, when he's hasting down,
Flowing and ruddy to his *Thetis* Bed,
And guilds the Sky with dazling Red: 470
Nor the soft Rays of new-born Light,
Or Heav'n in fancy e're was formed so bright.
And now a vast Illustrious Train of Stars
Declares, great *CYNTHIA* first appears;
Those Stars who rule the Fortune, and the Fate,   475
Of all the Amorous, Brave, and Great:
For what e're Merit *Nature* gives,
'Tis by their influence alone it thrives;
So sparkling and so fair a Train,
Did ne're attend the Goddess o're the Aerial Plain;   480
The Conqu'ring Nymphs and Hero's there,
The Graces and the Worthy's mingled were;
Each would a noble Song require,
But I have Tun'd my joyful *Lyre*
Only for *Royal Theams;*   485
And the kind flatterer sooths my heart,
And will no trembling Note impart
To any Musick, but the Charming Names
Of Sacred *LAURA!* Sacred *JAMES.*

XX.

She Comes ——— ———   490
Beholde the Badge of Peace and Innocence!
The Ivory Scepter is in Triumph born,
    So do's the Milky way advance
      Before the Rising Morn;
      A *Hero* more than half a God,   495
Whom all the Graces and the Charms Adorn;
Whom ev'ry Muse, and Vertue do's inspire,
Whom all the Witty, Great, and Good, admire,
      Supports the awful Mystick Rod:
DORSET, whose Eyes with all the Beauties shone,   500
Which he in *Love*, and in *Success* puts on.
A careless Grandure, and a Generous Air,
Did over all the Lord of Hearts appear,
Eternal softness, and Eternal Wit:
His looks made good to day, all he e're spoke or Write.   505

XXI.

The Golden *Scepter* noble RUTLAND bore,
In whose rich Veins the *Royal* Purple Springs
From mighty *YORK!* whose conqu'ring Arms of yore
Could sway the Fortunes, and the Fates of *Kings:*
Still to the *juster* side they brought their *Swords*,   510
And many a Glorious *field* the wond'rous Name *Records.*

Next view a *Hero* in his propher Sphere,
While BEAUFORD do's the Sacred Circle bear,
A *Prince!* whom Heav'n and Nature form'd to move
The ill-maner'd World to *Reverence*, and to *Love.*   515
A *Prince!* so truly brave, so greatly good,
What when in after *Ages* men would *Fame*,
Some future *Hero* with the Noblest Name,
Whose constant *Loyalty* undaunted stood,

Preserv'd it self in its divinest forms   520
   Amidst a Thousand meeting *Storms;*
A second *BEAUFORD's* Name the youth shall Crown,
And over pay His *Glory* and *Renown.*

XXII.

And now loud *Admirations* fill the space,
   And *Hearts* with nimbler *Motions* beat,   525
Behold the QUEEN the Raptur'd Crowds repeat!
She comes! She comes with a Triumphant Grace,
And all Heav'n opens in her Angel Face;
Bright were her *Beams,* and all around they *Shone,*
And darted awful *Fire* to all the *lookers* on;   530
So heedless *Lovers* do with CUPIDS play
'Till the *Boys* shoot and spoil their fancy'd Joy:
Thus all adorn'd with Sacred Beauty's Charms
Through the vast *Christian* Camp the fair *INCHANTRESS* Rode,
   And where the noblest *Warriers* wond'ring stood,   535
Her killing eyes dealt their resistless *harms;*
Through the rough *Male* the subtle *Light'ning* plaid,
Who the stern *Heart* to tenderness betray'd:
Her *Love-drawn Chariot* mov'd with solemn State,
While round it the adoring *Princes* wait,   540
With *Sigh* and *Vows Petitioning* their *Fate;*
But with this difference, while that *Charmer* strove
To take *Revenge!* in the soft snares of *Love,*
Ours, all *Divine!* by *chance* her Beauty hurl'd,
And has without *design* subdu'd the World;   545
But oh! in vain is any *likeness* made,
'Tis Coppying of the *Day!* by *Gloom* and *Shade.*
The *wonder* that the PROPHET did unfold,
When Heav'n in Revelation he survey'd,
   And the Bright WOMAN did behold   550
In wond'rous *Garments* of the *SUN Aray'd,*
And underneath *her feet* the *Moon* subdu'd,
At this *Divine Appearance* seem'd *renew'd.*

XXIII.

A *NYMPH* the fairest ever shin'd in Courts,
    NORFOLK the *Generous, Gay*, and *Great*,   555
To whom each *Muse* officiously resorts,
And with their *Songs* their *Patron* Mistress Greet,
To make the Illustrious *Train* compleat;
    The Sacred ROBE supports.
Aided by young DIANA's all as fair   560
As the coy *Maid* the *amorous GOD* pursu'd,
    As *Chast* as *she*, as *unsubdu'd;*
Unsoyl'd even by the wanton wisp'ring *Air.*
    No *guilty* thought had ever spread
    Their lovely *Virgin* Cheeks with Red,   565
No *Lovers Sighs* had blown the *blushes* there,
For all their *Roses* in the *Bud* appear.

XXIV.

And now the ravisht *People* shout a new!
Their KING! their dear-lov'd MONARCH is in view;
The constant *AYLESBURY*, and the Loyal *GRAY*,   570
    Prepare the mighty Way.
This bears the *Marshall Staff*, and that the *Spur*,
Of blest *Saint EDWARD*, KING and CONFESSOR.
To whom Heav'n first the *Mystery* did unfold,
By Sacred *Touches*, and by *Hollow'd Gold*,   575
To *heal* that else *uncurable* Disease
That poses *Art*, and baffles all the *Wise.*

The faithful *PETERBOROW*, whose unmatch'd *zeal*,
Pursu'd his *Suffering Princes* adverse *Fate*,
Then *Factious Malice* that out-acted *Hell*,   580
Drove the submitting *Exile* to a Foreign State;
Deserv'd the Glory which that day he wore,
And dares defend the Treasure that he bore.

PEMBROOK! the thoughful *PEMBROOK* next surveys,
   All form'd for *Victory* and *Love*,   585
In whose fine *Eyes* a Thousand *Graces* move,
And little *sighing Gods* around *him* play,
Who watch each melancholy *look*, and bear
The pointed *Ruin* to some gazing *fair.*
His hand the SWORD adorn'd with equal Grace,   590
As *Wit* his softer *Tongue*, or *Love* his conqu'ring *Face.*

Great DARBY, and the long-fam'd *SHREWSBURY,*
Whose happless *Sires* in bright 𝕬𝖑𝖑𝖊𝖌𝖎𝖆𝖓𝖈𝖊 shone,
With *Toyl*, and *Wounds*, and many a *Victory,*
   Such *Trophies* for their *Heirs* have wone,   595
As this days *Triumphs* do their *Fames* reward,
The *Pointed* and more Honour'd *Broken* SWORD.

OXFORD the *Brave*, whose unexampl'd *Name,*
Was never tainted with *Rebellious* Crimes,
But 'mongst the vast *Records* of *deeds* and *times,*   600
Remains *unblemisht* in the Book of *Fame:*
Justly that 𝕾𝖜𝖔𝖗𝖉 of *State* in *Peace* he ought to bear,
Who knows so *Nobly* how to manage *it* in 𝖂𝖆𝖗.

XXV.

Upon the *Royal Charge* two *Princes* wait,
Youg(*sic*) GRAFTON, the *Illustrious* and the *Great,*   605
England's 𝕳𝖎𝖌𝖍 𝕮𝖔𝖓𝖘𝖙𝖆𝖇𝖑𝖊, for this blest *Day,*
Too large a *Power* to bear a longer *Sway.*
Beneath this *Change*, ah! sigh not *Royal Youth,*
Thy blooming *Vertues* still will *rise* and *Live;*
   As *Flowers* transplanted better *thrive,*   610
   And mend their *Luster*, and their *growth;*
Securely *thou* may'st *shine* beneath this *Sun,*
And in the *Path* of *Honour* thou'st begun,
May'st a long *Race*, of lasting *Glories* run:

Remaining as thou art, *brave, Loyal, true,*   615
Thou, in *thy* KING, will find the FATHER too.

NORFOLK! the greatest *Subject,* and the *best,*
Whose *Loyalty* indur'd the utmost test;
    A PRINCE! whose Glorious *Name* has stood,
    Belov'd at *home,* ador'd *abroad:*   620
Stedfast in all the *Vertues* of the *Brave,*
And to no *Vices* of the *Great* a slave;
    True to *his* KING, *his Honour,* and *his Word,*
MÆCENA of my *Muse,* my *Patron* Lord.

XXVI.

Great *ORMOND!* whom no *time* or *Age* can bow;   625
    But on his awful Reverend brow,
Serenely as the *Summer* of his years,
    Before the *Autumn* blasts bereaves
The goodly *Ceder* of his youthful *Leaves,*
    Full *blown,* nor *fading,* still appears.   620
    Who to *Command,* and to obey,
For a long *Race* of years has show'd the noblest way;
    Brave in the *Field,* in *Council* Wise,
Stedfast in *Loyalty,* in *Honour* nice;
Gracious in *Power,* unruffl'd in a *Storm,*   635
Humble in *Court,* and Glorious in a *Calm:*
This *Day,* the Sacred *Diadem* he bore,
Whose dear *defence* so long had been *his care,*
That *Diadem* that Grac'd his hand before,
Whose *Right,* so oft he did assert in 𝔚𝔞𝔯.   640

Great *SOMERSET,* that Name of high Renown,
Allied to *Kings,* though not of *Kingly Race,*
Guarded the Worlds great Treasure, *Englands* Crown,
While the Worlds *Emblim* did the *Hero* Grace;
His *Youth* and *Beauty* did Adorn *his* State,   645
And the young 𝔄𝔱𝔩𝔞𝔰 smil'd beneath *his* Glorious weight.

The n're to be forgotten *ALBEMARLE*,
Whose *Name* shall last when *Nature* is no more,
That *Name*, that did lost 𝔅𝔯𝔦𝔱𝔞𝔦𝔫's Joy *restore;*
Its *Worship'd* 𝔠𝔥𝔞𝔪𝔭𝔦𝔬𝔫 and its 𝔊𝔢𝔫𝔢𝔯𝔞𝔩.   650
The second *Guardian* of the CROWN was made,
And in *his hand* to *day* the *Peaceful* SCEPTER sway'd;
The true-born *English Bravery* of whose *mind*,
His Native *Loyalty*, and intrinsick *worth*,
    Shows *him* of that *Diviner* kind,   655
    When *Demi-Gods* with *Mortals* joyn'd,
And brought the *first-born Race* of *Hero's* forth.

XXVII.

And now, the *Earthly GOD* appears in *view*,
While the glad *Crowd* their lowder shouts renew,
Wild with their *joy*, even rudly they *express*   660
    Its vast *concern*, its vast *excess!*
All stretch themselves beyond their native height,
    At more advantage to behold the *Sight*;
That Sacred *sight!* which though each day we view,
'Tis every day all *Charming, Dear*, and *New!*   665
So on *Olympus* top the *GOD* appears,
    When of his *Thunder* he disarms,
And all his *attributes* of *mercy* wears
The sweetness of Divine *forgiving* Charms.
With Smiles he casts His *Gracious* Eyes around,   670
Inspiring FAITH from ev'ry *look* and *Grace*,
    No *Soul* so dull to humane *sense* was found
As not to read its *safety* in His *Face*.
    Where 𝔉𝔬𝔯𝔱𝔦𝔱𝔲𝔡𝔢 and 𝔅𝔯𝔞𝔳𝔢𝔯𝔶 sate
    In solemn Triumph over 𝔉𝔞𝔱𝔢,   675
Where 𝔗𝔯𝔲𝔱𝔥 in all her *honest* Glory shin'd,
That darling *vertue* of His *Godlike* mind;
    So well His *looks*, and *Soul* accord,
    The kind 𝔠𝔬𝔫𝔣𝔦𝔯𝔪𝔢𝔯𝔰 do confess

How like a *King!* he does profess   680
How like a GOD! maintain His *Word*!
O ye fond *hapless* unbelieving *few*,
Ye *Obstinate*, ye *Stubborn, stiff-neck'd crew;*
Who love your fears of *insecurity*:
And have like **Witches**, your infection hurl'd,   685
   To *torture* and *disease* the World;
Come and be *cur'd* of your blind **Sorcery**,
That *Hell-born* **Malice** which you have *exprest*,
And *Damn'd* your selves meerly to *Damn* the rest;
You, whom no *word of King*, or *GOD!* can calm,   690
But wrest'em both to your *convenient* sense,
   Who like *Land Pirates* bless the *Storm*,
When the rich *Ship-wrack* proves your *recompence.*
By different *Kings* your *Vertues* have been try'd,
The *Pious, Peaceful*, and the *Brave* were given,   695
But still that *Hypocrite* (*self-interest*) sway'd,
And *you dislik'd*, because the choice of *Heav'n!*
So the fond *Jews* their *Faithless* murmerings show'd,
Rebell'd for *change*, though *Govern'd* by their *GOD.*

As a bright *Evening* Crowns a Glorious *Day*,   700
NORTHUMBERLAND brought up the *Reer*,
NORTHUMBERLAND the *Lovely, Young*, and *Gay*,
Blest by the *Crowds*, and to the *Souldiers* dear;
   A charming *Youth* of *Royal Race*,
His God-like *Father* pictured in *his face*,   705
With a soft *mixture* of *his* Beautious *Mothers Grace.*

XXVIII.

Thus the great *charge* they to the *Temple* bring
There, not to *make*, but to *confirm* the *King!*
So the Triumphant *Ark* with *Songs* was *born*,
And *sanctify'd* the place it did *Adorn!*   710
And Lo——— ———
The opening *Scene* of the third *Heav'n* appears,

Where *Glory* sits Enthron'd above the *Stars*;
Where no faint *Mortal* object meets the *Eye*,
 But ev'ry where 'tis all *Divine*,   715
All Raptur'd *Joy!* all perfect *Extasie*;
 Where *Angels* and *Dominions* joyn,
 Where *Principalities* and *Powers* combine,
And round the Sacred *Throne* in wond'rous order *shine*.
Where every *sense* receives the full *delight*;   720
Seraphic Musick Charms the *Ear*:
The *Eyes* are Ravisht with incessant *Light*,
And Hallow'd *Incese* fills the perfum'd Air.
 The *Soul* with Noblest *touches* blest,
 Disdains the scanty confines of the *breast*,   725
 And flatters where emencer *Glories* play,
 And greedily it feeds on *Heav'nly* joy!

XXIX.

Mistaken *School-men*, you who vainly strive
Just Notions of *Eternal Bliss* to give,
 By dull comparison with *things* below,   730
Saphers, and *Diamonds*, *Chrystals*, *Gold*, and *Light*;
By lessening *Objects*, *time*, and *pains* bestow
To *Paint*, what cannot be conceiv'd by *sight*.
Henceforth the Sacred Mansion to display,
 (And tell us what you *mean*, by what ye *say*)   735
Describe Great *JAMES*, and *LAURIA's Coronation Day!*
Tell, how they sate *Enthron'd* with Rays of *light*,
What *Hosts* of *Angels* did Adore the *sight*.
Describe the *Hallelujah's* of the *Crowd*,
When thrice with joyful cries they gave *Assent* aloud: 740
 Tell, how the awful MONARCH Mounted stood,
And by the best of *Mortals* make us guess the *GOD*.
Tell us, that so Mount *SINAI's* top *He* blest;
 VVhen to his *People* he dispenc'd the *Law*,
 VVhen shining *Glories* all the *God-head* drest   745
And all below *ador'd* the wonder that they *Saw!*

And when the *Ministering Powers* yea would express,
Describe the *Reverend* Clergy in *Pontifick* dress.
And who would tell us how th'Almighty speaks,
When *Angels* bow with awful list'ning down!   750
From Ely's *Sermon*, the best *Rhetorick* takes;
Ely, that Ornament of the still Loyal *Gown:*
And when *Heav'ns* brightness ye would make appear,
Behold the *QUEEN*, and copy it all from *Her.*

XXX.

All *Hail!* thou *born* of more than *Kingly Race*,   755
Monarchs and Poets did thy *Lineage* Grace!
        At once the *Crown* and *Lawrel* drest,
        The *Royal* Family of the *ESST.*
Great *ARIOSTO* from Thy Race did *spring*,
That taught his *Hero's* how to *Love* and *Sing!*   760
May all the *Joys* Triumphant *Beauties* Bless,
And all Chast *Lovers* fancy in *Success:*
May all the *Glory* that on *Empires* wait,
        With ev'ry *quiet* of *retreat*,
Crown your soft *hours*, and be in *Heav'n* confirm'd,   765
While to secure you Blest, the adoring *Worlds* concern'd.

Great Prince of *wonders*, and welcome to that *Throne*,
Both to Your *Vertues*, and Your *Sufferings* due,
        By *Heav'n* and *Birth-right* all Your own,
You shar'd the *Danger*, share the *Glory* too;   770
Whom *Providence*, (by Numerous *Miracles* wrought)
Through all the mazes of *Misfortunes* brought!
You mount the unruly *World* with easie *force*,
Reward with joy, but *Punish* with remorse;
The wanton *Beast Restive* with ease has lain,   775
And 'gainst the *Rider* lifts the sawcy *heel;*
But now a skillful *hand* assumes the *Rein*,
        He do's the *experienc'd Conquerour* feel,
And finds his head-strong D*isobedience* vain,

Proud of his *Glorious load*, he *leaps*, and *bounds*   780
Becomes the *Beauty* of the neighbouring *Plains*,
New *Life* and new *Activity* he gains,
And through the *Groves* his cheerful *Neigh* resounds;
Lives *Glad* and *Gay*, beneath that Generous *Rule*
That ne're will let his *useful* Mettle *cool*.   785

FINIS

ÆSOP'S FABLES

[The Life of Æsop – Captions to the Plates]

1 [The lying slaves vomit the figs they said Æsop had eaten]

So thrive false witnesses, and perjur'd Lyes
Confounded by the innocent, and wise,
Tho hid like thought the guilded Treason rest,
The Mask pul'd off, the villain is confest.

2 [Æsop shares his food with the priests who pray for him]

See here a Proverb crost, the shape tho foule,
Retaines a Beauteous, and Generous Soule,
While Cinthias Priests, accept, his rustick treat,
They grace his vile, deformity, with witt.

3 [Xanthus offers only a few pence for Æsop]

Women and Fooles, I grant, may disesteeme
Aesop's uncharming forme, ungraceful mien,
But Xanthus to refuse for that pretence,
Shows even Philosophers want judging sense.

4 [Æsop carries bread and it is eaten during the journey]

All laugh at Aesop's choyce of Loads while he
Has secrett reasons for his Policie
Th'unthinking Rable thus wise States-men blame
When ere they act beyond their duller aime

5   [*Xanthus buys Æsop*]

> How poore's the price the Jewells vallu'd at,
> When Ignorance sells, and dull contempt shall rate,
> No woman could, a vallew set so base,
> Who meanely traffick for a shape and face.

6   [*Xanthus' wife protests at the ugliness of their new slave;*
>   *Æsop explains that he will not cuckold his master*]

> Was this a Slave a gay young Wife t'appease
> Whom Age in thee, dull scoole-man, could not please,
> Ill does that Spark a woman's pleasure fitt
> Whose person is not finer, then his witt.

7   [*Æsop explains the properties of herbs*]

> No more you learned fops, your knowledge boast,
> Pretending all to know, by reading most,
> True witt by Inspiration wee obtaine
> Nature, not Art, Apollo's wreath must gaine.

8   [*Æsop gives the wife's dinner to the dog*]

> A Wife, or Dog as certaine reasons prove
> May fawne, & wag the tayle, but never love,
> Yet of the two, this story has confest,
> That 'tis the Dog, deserves the Present best.

9   [*The wife returns when Xanthus threatens to take another*]

> Insulting women while their slaves obey,
> Admitt no bounds to their tyranick sway;
> But let the nobler Captive break his noose,
> To keep her Cully she'l her Empire loose.

10 [*Æsop serves a meal comprising nothing but tongues*]

> The maryed men afronted at the jest,
> Seeing nought but Tongues presented for a feast,
> Spare S^r your Treat cry they, we need not come
> Abroad for these, we're too well stor'd at home.

11 [*Æsop serves nothing but tongues again*]

> If tongues (quoth Xanthus) be thy best of meat,
> Prethee buy us the worst, at night to eat,
> The willing Slave, repeating o're the jest,
> Cryd — as you use 'em they are worst or best.

12 [*Xanthus tries to shock a torpid peasant by threatening to burn his wife*]

> When Xanthus seeming angry, strove to prove,
> How far he could a certaine Rustick move,
> Condemnd his wife to flames, hold quoth the clowne,
> To bear her company, I'll fetch my owne.

13 [*Æsop says there is only one man in the bath, because
all the others tripped on a stone, but did not move it*]

> In Aesop's sense (of human Race) none can
> Deserve the glorious Title, of a man,
> But he, who prudently him selfe can free,
> From all outrages of Injury.

14 [*Æsop asked where he is going says he does not know
and is clapped in prison for his insolence*]

> How vaine are mens designes, since all their houres
> Are guided by the more inconstant powers,
> None ought to say, he will do this or that,
> One unexpected minute, turnes his fate.

15 [*Xanthus in wine wagers that he can drink the sea*]

> In heat of Love, and Wine, we often make
> Contracts wch in our sober thoughts we break,
> Philosophers in high debauch, beware,
> You'l want an Aesop when you rashly swear.

16 [*Xanthus tells Æsop he will be beaten unless he sees two crows; he does but one flies away and he is beaten after all*]

> Philosophers like Fortune tellers thrive,
> Those by false notions, these by false flateries liive
> And those as oft true vertue do mistake,
> As these false auguries, and predictions make.

17 [*Æsop exposes Xanthus' wife's 'unlovely parts' as she sleeps*]

> Oft for a jest we expose our modesty,
> And to assume a vertue, tell a ly,
> But here deceiveing fair thou'dst small pretence,
> Thy Taile wants all but the kind feeling sense.

18 [*Æsop admits only those who have understood his joke*]

> Of all the vertues which the wise admitt,
> There's none so nicely ūderstood, as witt,
> But he who aptly answers to a jest,
> In Aesop's sense, is worthy of the feast.

19 [*Æsop deciphers the riddle that leads his master to treasure, but Xanthus refuses to pay his reward*]

> How poore is man whom sordid intrest sways,
> He flatters even his slave, protests and prays,
> But once attain'd his beastly Lust of Powre,
> Th'ingrate remembers his false vows no more.

20 [*Æsop construes the augury of the eagle and the ring*]

> In vaine the learned do their knowledge boast,
> Witt is not allways gain'd, by reading most,
> Women do oft those hights of Glory reach,
> Which even the scooles, have wanted power to teach.

21 [*Æsop before Croesus*]

> Of all the graces, Heaven in man designd,
> None charmes us like the beautyes of the mind,
> The fickle forme, each accident destroys,
> But witt deverts with new and lasting joys.

22 [*Aesop embarks on his travels*]

> When Eloquence the stuborne powers assailes,
> It oft beyond dull brutall force prevailes,
> But Aesop not content with home bread fame,
> Spre^{a}ds o're the habitable world his name.

23 [*Æsop is calumniated by Ennus, his adopted son*]

> To what vast hights had Aesop's glory run,
> If unbetray'd by an adopted sone,
> Ennus, thou pilyed (*sic*) Tipe, of modern lust,
> How happy hadst thou liv'd, hadst thou been just.

24 [*Æsop is imprisoned*]

> So pitty'd falls the Innocent accus'd,
> By perjury, and too much faith abus'd;
> An Evidence a Title is so base,
> It brands the villaine on the noblest Race.

25 [*Æsop is released from prison*]

> Tho' vertue, like the Sun whom clouds confine,
> Or veild in night, may sometimes cease to shine,
> Yet when at length its beames around are hurl'd,
> It pleases, and instructs the duller world.

31 [*Æsop's statue is completed.*]

> Thus did not our ungratfull Brittish brood
> To expiat, for guiltless Royall blood,
> Had we thy sacred name great Charles imortal made,
> Wee'd shund those Plagues the wiser delphians stayd.

THE FABLES

3 [F2]   I [*The Cock and Gem.*]

A Cock who to a neighbouring Dunghill tries,
Finding a gemme that 'mongst the Rubish lyes.
Cry'd he — A Barly corne woud please me more
Then all the Treasures on the eastern shore.
                Morall
Gay nonsense does the noysy fopling please,
Beyond the noblest Arts and Sciences.

5 [G]   II *The Wolf and Lamb.*

A Wolf who at the Rivers head did drink,
Seeing a trembling Lambe upon the brink,
Disdaining that shoud tast what he injoys,
First quarrels, then the innocent destroys.
                Morall
Thus the proud great by lawless might opress
While the complaining poore find no redress.

7 [G2]   III [*The Lyon and Four Bulls*]

The Lyon saw three Bulls securely feed,
By murmuring springs, in a large flowery mead,
First by perswasive power the friends diuide,
Then makes 'em fall, the Ravage of his Pride.
           Morall
Thus mighty states, are to Confusion hurld,
Which when united woud subdue the world.

9 [H]   IV *The Fox and Frog.*

A Bog borne Frog a Doctor would commence,
And the dull Heard trust his false Eloquence,
But the more subtile Fox in scorne replyes,
To give me faith, cure thy owne Maladyes.
           Morall
Vaine are the precepts they to others give,
Who do themselves, in ill Examples live.

11 [H2]   V *The Ass eating Thistles.*

A sordid Ass, while on his back he bore,
Of choicest delicates, a plenteous store;
His courser Appetite with Thistles treats,
And starves beneath his load of nobler meats.
           Morall
Profuseness is a farr less dangerous vice
Than the Ill natur'd damning Avarice.

13 [I]   VI *The Lark's Nest in the Corn*

When the old Lark did heare ye neighbouring swaines,
Would joyn to cutt the corne she still remains,
But when she heard the owner and his sone,
Woud do't themselves, she cry'd — then let's be gone.
           Morall
Services done by friends come slowly on,
He acts himselfe, who has his work well done.

15 [I2]   VII *The Fox and Cock in a Tree.*

The Fox perswades the Cock, to quit his shade,
Since betweene Birds, and Beasts, a truce was made.
But he secur'd amidst the hinder boughs,
Reply'd, I'll first be certaine of your news.
       Morall
The wise from publick fame no judgments make,
But such as they from righter reasoning take.

17[K]   VII *The Fox in the Well.*

The Fox in a deep well implores the aid,
Of a grave Wolfe; who many questions made,
How he came there, the Fox halfe drowd replyes
Oh cease vaine words, & help thy friend that dyes
       Morall
Men of good Counsell can bestow in griefe,
But with no reall good will bring reliefe.

19[K2]   IX *The Wolves and Sheep.*
                    was
A truce concluded 'twixt wolves and sheepe,
The wolves, their dogs as a firm hostage keepe,
The Sheepe, their whelps, who with design complaine,
Their Dames break in and slaughter o're the plaine.
       Morall
Those who with foes too mighty make a peace
Give 'em but power to hurt 'em with more ease.

21 [L]   X *The Eagle's Nest.*

A Foxes cub the kingly Eagle prest,
And bore the trembler to her royall nest,
The Fox inrag'd, the sacred Pile will burne
To save her throne the prise she does reture.
       Morall
The haughty great with caution should oppress,
Since Slaves provok'd deep injuryes may redress.

23 [L2]   XI *The Wolf in Sheep's Clothing.*

A subtile Wolfe, more safly to betray,
In a sheepes Clothing does himselfe aray,
And unexpected now whole flocks destroys,
Till a kind halter ends his stoln joys.
Morall
The zealous Cheat has wrought the land more woe,
Than bare fac'd villainie coud ever doe

25 [M]   XII *The Ringdove and Fowler.*

While the young fouler sought with eager skill,
A Ring Dove in a neighbouring Tree to kill,
An Adder in the floury mead beneath,
Stung the unhappy youth, and stung to death.
Morall
The young usurper who design'd t'invade,
An others right, himselfe the victim made.

27 [M2]   XIII *The Sow and her Pigs.*

The Wolf intreats the Sow, that he might be,
A guard to keep her Pigs from injury.
The Sow, who knew the nature of the Beast,
Replyd, when absent, S^r you'l guard 'em best.
Morall
Belive not those who often Friendship swear,
Least they som privat Intrest woud prefer.

29 [N]   XIV *The Horse and Ass.*

A Horse, whom guilded Equipage made gay,
Commands a Drudging Ass to yield the way,
But when diseas'd, and to a Cart condemn'd,
The Ass lookt big, and his owne forme esteem'd.
Morall
The great are often lost in stormes of State,
While the poor Cottager despises fate.

31 [N2]   XV *The Wolf and Goat.*

The Wolf endeavor'd to perswade the Lamb,
To leave her Gardian Goat, and to her Damm
To trust her selfe with him, but she reply'd,
I know his friendship, yours I never try'd.
        Morall
He that old Loves and Friends forsakes for new,
Deserves no Mistress, nor a friend that's true.

33 [O]   XVI *The Doves and Hawk.*

Twixt Doves and Kites a Combatt rose while they
The Sparhawk chose for King beneath whose sway
The Doves with greater rage opprest complaine
And wish lesse Tyrant Kite woud reigne againe.
        Morall
We nere are pleas'd with what the Gods bestow
To worse we change when ere we change for new.

35 [O2]   XVII [*The City Mouse and Country Mouse.*]

The City Mouse invites her Country Guest,
To tast the daintyes of a Citty feast.
But oft disturb'd by interupted noys,
They hide, and fear his appetite destroys.
        Morall
The great the Hurry of the world indure,
And 'tis the country life alone's secure.

37 [P]   XVIII *The Swallow and other Birds.*

The Swallow saw pernicious Hempseed sowne,
And vow'd to spoyle the Tillage of the Clowne,
The Birds are summon'd, but they being slow
Permite that weed that ruins 'em to grow.
        Morall
They that neglect the Councell of the wise,
Suffer small faults to grow past remedies.

67

39[P2]   XIX *The Hunted Beaver.*

The hunted Beaver knowing what sweet Prise,
Would make him to the dogs a sacrifise,
Bites of the prey, and ends the eager strife,
And with the loss of treasure bailes his life.
Morall
Who woud not part with momentary Toys
To purchass to themselves eternall joys.

41 [Q]   XX *The Fox and Cat.*

The Fox pretends a thousand shifts t'ave found,
To save him from the hard persuing Hound.
The Catt but one, who climes the Tree amaine,
Anon the dogs persue, and Renard's slaine.
Morall
One Action where discretion is its guide
Transcends all the results of noys and pride.

43 [Q2]   XXI *The Cat and Mice* .

The Mice consult, how to prevent their fate
By timely notice of th'aproaching Catt,
We'll hang a Bell about her neck, cryd one,
A third replyd — but who shall putt it on.
Morall
Good Councells easy given, but ye effect
Oft renders it uneasy to transact.

45[R]   XXII *The Lyon and other Beasts.*

Hunting, the beasts agree to share the Prey
One part the Lyon claimes as bearing sway,
An other for his strength, a third his toyle,
The last in gratitude they ought to make his spoile.
Morall
Proud Senatts thus by easy Monarchs thrive
Incroaching on their whole prerogative.

68

47 [R2]   XXIII *The Lyon and Mouse.*

The Royall Beast intangl'd in a snare,
Coud not with teeth and claws the ambush tear,
When a kind humble Mouse the Cord untwind,
And broke that Mase the Forest King confind.
Morall
Doe not despise the Service of a Slave,
An Oak did once a glorious Monarch save.

49 [S]   XXIV *The Lyon and Mouse.*

The Mouse for his late service fil'd with pride,
Demands the Royall virgin for his bride,
The match agreed while he in flames admir'd,
He unawares crusht by her paw expird.
Morall
To false ambition if thy thoughts are bent,
Reflect on a late pittye^d president.

51 [S2]   XXV *The Dog with a Clog.*

A Dog whose fierceness was with fetters checkt,
Fancyd himselfe with some new honour deckt,
Thy folly's great, the wiser currs replye,
For glory, to mistake thy infamie.
Morall
Thus dareing debauchee (*sic*) do often boast
In those loose vices men dishonour most.

53 [T]   XXVI *The Ox and Toad.*

The Toad woud needs the Oxes size attaine,
And with fell poyson puffs up every veine,
Then askd her sone if equall were their size,
Then swells againe, and with her penome (*sic*) dies.
Morall
The woud-bee witts to Lawrrells woud aspire,
And write till damn'd they shamefully retire.

55 [T2]   XXVII *The Lion and Fox.*

When first the Fox the forest monarch saw,
He gaz'd with trembling feare, & reverend awe,
But by degrees more boldly he adrest,
Than holds a Parly with the Royall Beast.
              Morall
Vertues seem rigid to the wild and loose
But grow familiar by their constant use.

57 [U]   XXVIII *The Ape and Fox.*

The Ape implord, the fox her bum woud vaile
With a proportion of his useless Taile,
But he replyd — tho me no good it do,
I will not spare an Inch to favour you.
              Morall
Thus the Ill naturd Rich reserve their store,
And please themselves to see their nighbours poor.

59 [U2]   XXIX *The Dog and Oxe.*

An Envious Dog in a full manger lay,
Nor eats himselfe, nor to the Ox gives way,
Who griev'd reply'd — ah grudge not me that meat,
Which (cruell) thou thy selfe disdainst to eate,
              Morall
Thus aged Lovers with young Beautys live,
Keepe off those joys they want the power to give.

61[X]   XXX *The Birds and Beasts.*

Twixt birds and beasts a fatall warr is held,
The winged powers are conquers o're the field.
The Batt is captive tane whom all detest
For she forsook her nation and her nest.
              Morall
A Traytor all behold with just disdaine,
Who basely quitts his cause, and soveraigne.

63[X2]   XXXI *The Tygre and Fox*

The Tyger boasts to guard the Beasts from harme,
Since his tough hide so well his vitals arme,
Which the young hunter heareing sent a dart,
That pearc'd the fancy'd victor to the heart,
                    Morall
So the young Hero on his strength relying
Renderd him more remark'd and worthyer dying.

65 [Y]   XXXI *The Lionness and Fox.*

The Fox will with the Lyoness compaire,
For noble Reace, cause she does numbers bear.
Who thus reply'd — tho' I but one do bring,
That one shall rule thy numbers as their King.
                    Morall
'Tis not a gawdy title formes the great
Who shoud with nobler vertue be repleat.

67 [Y2]   XXXIII *The Oak and Reed.*

The wind bore downe a mighty Oake that stood,
To shade the margent of a silver flood,
Who seeing the Reed unruffl'd by the storme,
He dying, wisht that he'd beene humbly borne.
                    Morall
He that to elivated hights arrives
Is oft in stormes and still in danger lives.

69 [Z]   XXXIV *The Wind and Sun.*

Opprest with wind the Traveller girts on,
His warm Surtout anon the rageing Sun,
With his fierce beames does incomode him more,
Then all the ill supported storme before.
                    Morall
In every passion moderation chuse,
For all extreames doe bad effects produce.

71

71 [Z2]   XXXV *The Kite, Frog and Mouse.*

The Frog and Mouse themselves to armes betake,
To fight for the Dominion of the Lake,
But while in field the boasting Champions dare,
The Kite makes both her prey, so ends the Warr.
                    Morall
The fond aspiring youth who empire sought
By dire ambition was to ruine brought.

73 [Aa]   XXXVI *Jupiter and the Frogs*

The Frogs implore a king, and Iupiter
To please the Rable does king Log preffer,
But too unactive he— again they implore
Iove sends the Stork who does the fooles devour.
                    Morall
If Kings be mild they'r dull, if active they
We blast 'em with the guilt of Tyrant sway.

75 [Aa2]   XXXVII *The Old Woman and her Maids*

When the shrill Cock told that the morn was nigh,
The good-wife calls her maids to Housewifry,
But they too soone awackt the telltale kill,
And now their Dame calls earlier with a Bell.
                    Morall
He who to cure his love to drinking ruñes
Contracts a greater evill than he shuns

77 [Bb]   XXXVIII *The Lyon and Bear.*

The Bear and Lyon on a Summers day,
A combate held for the divided pray,
When both grown faint with fatigues of warr,
Suffer the fox the prize away to beare.
                    Morall
Thus nations oft by Civill Conflicts torne
By a third power away the scepter's borne.

79 [Bb2]   XXXIX *The Crow and Pot*

A thirsty Crow the medow did survey
But found no streame her faintings to allay,
Till in the Bottom of a Pott, whose drink
She boys with Pebles to the kinder brink.
           Morall
One wisely man^ag'd pleasure brings more joys,
Than all dull fancy can create with noys

81 [Cc]   XL *The Porcupines and Adders*

The Adders had the Porcupines deceivd
Of their warm Nest which coud not be retrieu'd.
By subtillty possession first was gain'd,
But now by force the title is mentain'd.
           Morall
Crownes got by force are often times made good,
By the more rough designes of warr, and blood.

83 [Cc2]   XLI *The Hares and Storm*

The Hares in storms to close recesses hye,
And thro' a scanted breach themselves convey,
But when they find a Lake they must wade thro'
Forward they dare not, backward can not goe.
           Morall
When counsell'd thus by a more prudent Hare
What can't be remedied with patience bear.

85 [Dd]   XLII *The Fox and Wolf*

A Fox does to a Hunters rage betray
A Lambe gorg'd wolf who close in kenelld lay,
The conquering Swain his Iustice to evince
First kills the wolf, and then the Evidence.
           Morall
From this that certaine truth we may inferr,
Who loves the guilt, heats the discoverer.

87 [Dd2]   XLIII *The Dog and Sheep*

The Dog impeacht a Sheep of Crimes unthought,
And the false wolf, and Kite for wittnes brought,
The innocent by perjury betray'd
Is to the black caball a victim made.
Morall
He that woud search for presidents so base,
Let him survey our home bread perjur'd Race.

89 [Ee]   XLIV *The Crane and Peacock*

The gay plumd Peacock wth a nice disdaine
Scornd the cheap clothing of ye humbler crane,
But she replyd, my wings can reach ye skye,
Thy duller beautys do but please the eye.
Morall
Scorn not the courser sort whose mind may be
Richer than thou, with all thy pedigree.

91 [Ee2]   XLV *The Viper and File*

An hungry Viper neare a Black Smiths forge
Snatcht at a file his eager maw to gorge,
But the tough steele his feebler teeth repels,
Its dinted force his Jaws with anguish fills
Morall
Contend not with a power too great t'orecome
Least toyle and shame become thy certaine doome

93 [Ff]   XLVI *The Lion, Ass and Cock*

The Lyon meets the Cock, whose early straynes
Frights the rough forest monarch ore the plaines,
The Asse who thought his presence made him scowre,
Persuing, falls a victim to his power.
Morall
The forward spark who thinks his noys may pass
Incountering sense perceives himselfe an Ass.

95 [Ff2]   XLVII *The Jay and Peacock*

The Jay woud for a gawdy Peacock pass,
And with their borowed plumes her tayle dos grace
But when from thence each had his feathers torne,
By her own Birds she is receiv'd with scorne.

        Morall

Tis the gay Dress that makes the Lover doat,
Not the fine Soule, but the fine Petticoat.

97 [Gg]   XLVIII *The Ant and Fly*

The Fly thus to the Ants — poore humble things,
You live in Dunghills, while I feast with Kings,
The Ant reply'd —thy feasts by thift are gaind,
Mine tho' with toyle, are with repose mayntaind.

        Morall

The humble life the Rurall Swain injoys
Exceeds High Birth with all its pomp & noys.

99 [Gg2]   XLIX *The Ant and Grasshopper*

The wanton Grashopper implores the Ant
In winter season to relive her want,
But she replyd — thou all the plentious spring
Tookst care for nought, but how to dance and sing.

        Morall

He that his helpless age from want woud free
Must in his youth learn Industry of me.

101 [Hh]   L *The Countryman and Snake*

Even dead with winters cold, a pittying Swain
Finds an expiring Snake upon the plaine,
Which home he brought, and scares wth heat reviv'd
He then persues his life by whom he livd.

        Morall

Mercy extended to ungratfull men
Does but impower em to rebell agen.

103 [Hh2]   LI *The Sick Lion*

The Lyon (past his hunting youth) pretends
He's sick, and begs the visitts of his friends,
All but the Fox obey, who thus bespake
Footsteps to's Den I find, but none turn'd back.
Morall
Of Specious overtures lett all be ware
'Twas fair pretences rais'd the western warr.

105 [Ii]   LII *The Wanton Calf*

A Calf who ne're the presures felt of yoakes
Saucily triumph'd ore a labouring Oxe,
At length with Garlands crown'd the Scorners led
And by a Priest a sacrifise is made.
Morall
Labour in rustick Swaines dull Life supports
Longer than all the Luxuries of Courts.

107 [Ii2]   LIII *The Clown and Cart*

A Clowne whose Cart in a deep quagmire stuck,
For speedy aid did Hercules invoke
Who thus replyd — first your owne strenght essay,
Without your Industry in vain you pray.
Morall
Lazy Devotion's not enough to live,
Add Dilligence to prayer and then you'll thrive.

109 [Kk]   LIV *The Belly and Members*

The hands, and feete the Belly do upbraid,
And will no more the useless Slugard aid,
Who fainting all the members share its fate,
And now thy'd work, but it is now too late.
Morall
In states all Intrests must each other prop,
Which if they clash will into ruine drop.

111 [Kk2]   LV *The Horse and Lion*

The Lyon Age'd does now in Ambush ly,
And to secure his prey setts up for Surgery,
The Hors pretends a thorne his foot opprest,
And asking Cure spurns the deceining (*sic*) beast
                Morall
T'has been a Maxim that the world belives
That 'tis no sin to cuzen who deceives.

113 [Ll]   LVI *The Stork and Geese*

A Clown an Ambush spread for Cranes, & Geese,
Whose Ravage wasted his sowne field of pease.
A Stork surprisd did for his life request,
No quoth ye Clowne thou dy'st for heading wth ye rest
                Morall
He that adheres but to a villainie,
(As well as he that acts) deserves to dye.

115 [Ll2]   LVII *The Cat and Cock*

The Catt does on the Cock with fury fly
And many reasons urg'd that he must dy,
The Cock denys the fact, in vaine thou pleadst,
Reply'd the Catt, for right or wrong thou bleedst
                Morall
So a luxurious power Oft makes its will
The only cause of an oppression still.

117 [Mm]   LVIII *The Leopard and Fox*

The Leopard for the splender of his hide
Boasts himself Lord of Beasts, the Fox replyd
Tho thou the fairest are of all beast kind,
Other excell in beauties of the mind.
                Morall
Not the gay spark that in guilt Coach does roule
Can form the Hero, but the nobler soule.

119 [Mm2]   LIX *The Shepherd's Boy*

A wanton rurall boy with false alarms,
Oft frights the shepherds with approaching harmes
But when indeed ye Wolf surpris'd a Lambe
Deceiv'd before, none to his rescue came.
Morall
Deceitfull tongues no creditt can infuse
An tho' even truths they tell, they pass for lyes.

121 [Nn]   LX *The Goat in the Well*

The Goat implores the Fox (since he was freed
From the deep well) to help his friend wth speed,
But he replyd, ah foole did thy witt bear
Proportion with thy beard, thoudst ne're been there.
Morall
Try friends before you of their kindnes boast,
Least they decline you when you need 'em most.

123 [Nn2]   LXI *Cupid and Death*

Cupid and Death by dire mistake chang'd Darts
Death shot young flames into the Aged hearts.
From Cupids Bow deaths fatall arow flyes,
And when the Youth shoud only languish dyes.
Morall
Tis death to youth by age to be imbrac'd,
And winters Snow woud Junes gay Roses blast.

125 [Oo]   LXII *The Old Man and his Sons*

The Father does a heap of Osiers take
And bids his jarring sons the boundle break,
They strive in vaine, at last the Rods devide
And then they broke with ease — the Sire reply'd
Morall
Lo thus my sones by concord things obtaine
New vigour, which by discord break in twaine.

78

127 [Oo2]   LXIII *The Old Deer and Fawne*

Says the young Fawne my father why do ye dread
The Howndes since nature so well armes your head
When he reply'd, my Child when Dogs I heare,
My hornes can not secure my heart from feare.
        Morall
Cowards by nature, by no magic Art
Can be incourag'd with a Heros heart.

129 [Pp]   LXIV *The Old Hound*

The Hownd grown old no more persues ye game,
But bends beneath the Huntmans weighty Cane,
And being opprest, does thus his cace bemone,
O spare my age for what in youth I've done.
        Morall
Old servants when their labour's past are scorn'd,
And out of favour and of Service turn'd.

131 [Pp2]   LXV *Jupiter and the Camel*

For hornes the Camell Iupiter implord,
With which so many beasts so well were stord
The God inrag'd reply'd, thy forehead weares
Hence forth no horns, and what is worse no eares.
        Morall
With what kind heaven bestowes be thou at rest
For that knows where to place its bounty best.

133 [Qq]   LXVI *The Tailless Fox*

The Fox (who lost her Tayle) perswades the rest
To bob their traines, as most commod, and best,
When one replyd — we more discreet disdaine
To buy convenience with publict shame.
        Morall
He that grave Councell for your good pretends
Fifty to one, promotes his private ends.

135 [Qq2]   LXVII *The Fox and Crow*

The Crow with laden beak the tree retires
The Fox to gett her prey her forme admires
While she to show her gratitude not small
Offering to give her thanks, her prize lets fall.
            Morall
Shun faithless flatterors, Harlots jilting tears
They are fooles hopes, and youhs (*sic*) deceitfull snares.

137 [Rr]   LXVIII *Of the Dove and the Hawk*

A Sparohawk being taken in a traine
For life thus did implore the seizing swain,
Those that devour thy Corne I make my food,
The Lad replyd thou'rt worse that lives by blood.
            Morall
Many pretend in Warr their King to aid
When they in Blood for private interest trade.

139 [Rr2]   LXIX *The Nurse and Wolf*

A Nurse, to make her Bantling cease to cry
Told it, the Wolf should eat it instantly,
This heard the Wolf, and for his prey he waits
But the Child slept, and all his hopes defeats.
            Morall
Trust not a womans vows, her fickle mind
Is far less constant than the seas, and wind.

141 [Ss]   LXX *The Tortoise and Hare*

The Hare and Tortois being to run a Race,
The Hare first slept, depending on his Pace,
The Tortois still krept on with motion Slow
And won the Victory from her swift heeld foe.
            Morall
Mean parts by Industry have luckyer hitts,
Then all the fancy'd power of lazyer witts.

143 [Ss2]   LXX *The Young Man and his Cat*

A Youth in Love with Puss, to Venus prayd
To change the useless Beauty to a maid
Venus consents, but in the height of Charmes
A Mouse she cry'd and leaves his ravisht armes.
                    Morall
Ill principles no mercy can reclaime,
And once a Rebell still will be the same.

145 [Tt]   LXXI *The Ass in a Lion's Skin*

The Ass puts on the Lyons feirce disguise
And does the heard with awfull feare surprise,
But when the master came, the asses eares
Betray'd the Cheat, and rid them of their fears.
                    Morall
A hott braind Statesman once sett up for wise
But knave and foole was plaine thro the disguise.

147 [Tt2]   LXXIII *The Birth of the Mountains*

The Mountaine grones and some prodigious birth
The wondering Crowd expect her to bring forth,
A second Alps at least, her time being come,
A litle Mouse starts from her teeming Wombe.
                    Morall
Our most aspiring hopes abortive are
And fall like Towers whose bases are the air.

149 [Vv]   LXXIV *The Satyr and Clown*

The Satyr sees the Clowne whom Cold assailes
To heate his hands, by breathing on his nailes,
Finding him blow his broath the cause demands,
Cryd he, that cooles my broath that warmes my hands.
                    Morall
The Sycophant with the same breath can praise
Each faction, and whats upermost obeys.

151 [Vv2]   LXXV *The Young Kite and his Mother*

The sick Kite begs his mother to apply
Her self to Heaven for some kind remedy,
But she reply'd in health you heaven blasphemd,
And can not hope (in pain) to be redeemd.
        Morall
He that tho late woud to the Gods repair
Must seeke their blest abodes with early prayr.

153 [Xx]   LXXVI *The Nightingale and Hawk*

The eager Hawk surpris'd the Nightingall
Who with soft notes her foe did thus assaile,
Ah lett me go I'm nought but song, cryd she
There is a Bird just by worth two of me.
        Morall
Tho ne're so small loose not an intrest gain'd
Which industry or meritt has obtain'd.

155 [Xx2]   LXXVII *The Peacock and Nightingale*

The Peacock to the wife of Jove complaines
The Nightingall outcharm'd her in her straines,
Juno reply'd — tho' she in voice excell
She cannot thy bright beauties parallell.
        Morall
Envy not others good since Providence
Guifts fitted to each genious does dispence.

157 [Yy]   LXVIII *The Angler and Little Fish*

The little fish implores he may be throwne
Back to the stream till he were bigger growne
And then he'd come to's angle, no quoth he
While thou art here small friend I'm shure of thee
        Morall
Let no false flatterers have it in their power
To make thee quite what gone is thine no more.

82

159 [Yy2]   LXXIX *The Geese in the Corn*

The Geese, and Cranes a field of Corn do wast
And being surpris'd the Cranes wth nimble hast
Out fly revenge, the geese whome bulk and weight
Made slow of flight, for all must expiate.
       Morall
In Civel broyles the Indigent are freed,
And he thats rich most likly is to bleed.

161 [Zz]   LXXX *The Dog and Piece of Flesh*

The Dog who with his prey the River swam
Saw his owne laden Image in the streame,
The wishing Curr growne covetous of all
To catch the Shadow letts the Substance fall.
       Morall
So fancy'd Crownes led the young Warriour on,
Till loosing all he found himselfe undone.

163 [Zz2]   LXXXI *The Ass and little Dog*

With a fine Dog his Masters care and joy
The Ass with anguish oft had seen him play,
With the same grace he thinks he may carress,
And with an awkward onsett makes address.
       Morall
The worne out Beauty for eighteē woud pass,
And nautiously acts youth with fullsome grace.

165 [Aaa]   LXXXII *The Wolf and Crane*

In vaine the tortourd wolfe to all complaine,
Till meeting with the Crane in hope of gaine,
She gives him ease, when asking to be paid
Fond foole cryd he go thank me for thy head.
       Morall
Well meaning love is often paid with heat,
And a good natures lost on an ingrate.

167 [Aaa2] LXXXIII *The Covetous and Envious Man*

The Miser heard what ere his friend did crave
From Iove, a doble portion he shoud have,
There stood mute — the envious man replyes,
Iove I'll spare one so he may loos both eyes.
Morall
The sin of Envy nought can equalize,
But the ungenerous sensless Misers vice.

169 [Bbb] LXXXIV *The two Pots.*

Two Potts (of Earth and Brass) at distance swim,
The first of lighter burden cuts the stream,
The Brass intreats her stay, but she replyd
No, thines too rough to touch my tender side.
Morall
Mix not with those whose wealths for thine too great,
To keepe an equal pace with them thou't break.

171 [Bbb2] LXXXV *The Fox and Stork*

The Crane in pure revenge the Fox invites
To dinner, and dispos'd her delicates
In a glass violl, which her beak alone
Coud reach, the Fox asham'd went empty home.
Morall
Fraud is by fraud but justly paid againe,
And to deceive the Cusener is no shame.

173 [Ccc] LXXXVI *The Bear and Bee-hives*

A Bees keene sting a Bear did so inrage,
That with the Hives a war he does ingage,
The numbers joyne and on the foe do fall,
Who grieues, his private feud prov'd nationall.
Morall
So petty feuds by the Rout persu'd
Have often mighty common wealths subdu'd.

175 [Ccc2]   LXXXVII *The Bear and two Travellers*

A Bear approcht two Travellers one fled
To a safe tree, the other lay still as dead,
The Bear but smelling to his face retird,
The friend descends and laughing thus inquird
                    Morall
What was't he whisperd in his eare quoth he
He bad me shun a treacherous friend like thee.

177 [Ddd]   LXXXVIII *The Captive Trumpeter*

A Trumpiter implores for life, and said
His harmless sounds alass no victims made,
But you designd, cryd they, for greater ill
Who men each other do excite to kill.
                    Morall
Those that by secrett ways do ills contract
Will be as guilty found, as those that act.

179 [Ddd2]   LXXXIX *The Fighting Cocks and Partridge*

The Patridge grieus the Cock shoud use her ill,
But when she found they did each other kill,
She sighing cryd, no wonder me th'annoy
Who do maliciously themselves destroy
                    Morall
Mallice in men breeds to themselves more wo
Than their ill nature can in others do.

181 [Eee]   XC *The Fowler and Partridge*

The Partridge caught for life the man woud bribe
By whedeling to his Netts her heedless tribe,
No, thou deserv'st said he, a Double Doom
Who woudst betray thy friends to martyrdom.
                    Morall
Traitors who men impeach a life to gaine
If they be honest, 'tis against the graine.

183 [Eee2] XCI *The Eagle and Crow*

The Crow who saw an Eagle seize a Lamb,
Thinks with like force to bear away a Ram,
The Shepherd takes him captive, prunes his wings,
And him in scorn t'insulting children flings.
Morall
Ambition shoud to mighty parts be borne
Least wanting sense it fall the vulgar scorne

185 [Fff] XCII *The Lion, Ass and Fox*

The Ass claimes part o'th'prey, for wch shees killd,
But the wise Fox does his proportion yield,
The Lyon asks the reason — he replyes
The Asses fate has taught me to be wise.
Morall
That prudent man is circumspect alone
Who by an others fall declines his owne.

187 [Fff2] XCIII *The Fox and Grapes*

The Fox who longd for Grapes, beholds wth paine
The tempting Clusters were too high to gaine,
Grieu'd in his heart, he forc'd a carless smile,
And cry'd, Theyr sharp, & hardly worth my toyle.
Morall
Young Debauchees to Beauty thus ingrate,
That vertue blast, they cannot violate.

189 [Ggg] XCIV *The Horse and Hart*

The Horse unable to out-race the Hart,
Implores the aid of man to take his part,
Then won the prize, but hence his fate began
For ever since he'as been inslavd by man.
Morall
He who by th'Rables power a Crowne does weare
May be a King, but is a Slave to feare.

191 [Ggg2]   XCV *The Young Man and Swallow*

The spend thrift seeing the Swallow yet to fly,
Sells all his cloaths, and dreames not winte^{r}s nigh
Deceivd the killing frost he does behold,
And with the flattering bird even dyes with cold.
        Morall
Each little hope cajoles the prodigall,
And fancying miracles, he looses all.

193 [Hhh]   XCVI *The Man and his Goose*

The Man whose Goose vends dayly golden ore,
Belives her paunch containes a wonderous store,
So kills her, but alas his vaine desire
And greedy hope doe with his Goose expire.
        Morall
He that too soone vast Riches woud attaine,
Oft missing of the mark comes off with shame.

195 [Hhh2]   XCVII *The Wolf and Dog*

A Dog who boasts of luxury, and ease
Was by the Wolf demanded, what bald crease
Was that about his Neck, replyd the Dog
To civilize me, S^r I wear a Clog.
        Morall
Reply'd the Wolf, in Woods I'd rather range,
Then my rouh (*sic*) freedom for Court slavery change.

197 [Iii]   XCVIII *The Wood and Clown*

The Clowne implord the tree, that he woud spare
A butt of Wood, his Hatchett to repair,
The tree Consent, but the false Clowne betryd
The generous Stock, and all in ruins layd.
        Morall
Ungratefull People thus on Princes fall,
And given some liberties rebell for all.

199 [Iii2]   XCIX *The Old Lion*

The Lyon sick, the beasts do all agree,
To take revenge for past injury,
He beares with royal patience, till he feeles,
The dull Ass spurne him, with his sawcy heeles.
                    Morall
Then dying cryd, let the proud great be warn'd
For when they'r falne by kneaves, and fooles, they'r scorn'd.

201 [Kkk]   C *The Horse and Loaded Ass*

The laden Ass implord the Horse woud bear,
Of her unconscionable load a share,
Which he disdaining the poore Ass falls dead,
Then on the scorners back they place the load.
                    Morall
They who do men contemn whom griefs oppress,
Will in like circumstance find like success.

203 [Kkk2]   CI *The Old Man and Death*

An aged Man whose shoulders bowd beneath
Almighty load, in anguish wisht for death,
Death straight approcht, and asking his command,
Cry'd — only S^r to lend your helping hand.
                    Morall
Tho wrackt with various paines yet life does please
Much more then death, which all our pressures ease.

205 [Lll]   CII *The Boar and Ass*

While the dull Ass the sturdy Boar derides,
The Boar whom moderation wisely guides,
Replyd — Iest on thou dull insipid thing,
Fooles cannot move, their railiery wants sting
                    Morall
Be not concerned when Coxcombs witty grow
Least others think their pert aspersions true.

207 [Lll2]   CIII *The Dolphin and Tunis*

The Tunis to escape the Dolphin's shock
Flying for safty to a fatall Rock
There lay insnar'd, as was her foe beneath
Who to behold him perish, welcomes death.
Morall
The injur'd innocent is pleas'd to see
His treacherous friend opprest as well as he.

209 [Mmm]   CIV *The Peacock and Pie*

The Birds woud chuse a King, the Peacockes claime
By all confirm'd, they chuse him soveraign,
But the wise Pye reprocht his forward pride
And to the listening Sennat thus reply'd.
Morall
Elective Monarchs shoud not be indu'd
With a gay form alone, but fortitude.

211 [Mmm2]   CV *The Forrester and Lion*

The Image of a Man the Lyon spy'd
Conquering the Royal Be^ast, When he reply'd,
Coud we but paint, youd find less victorys won
O're us by men than we o're feebler man.
Morall
So Bullys boast when they pretend to've don
Acts, which they never durst adventur on.

213 [Nnn]   CVI *The Stag looking into the Water*

The Stag admires the beauty of his hornes
But the ill graces of his legs he scornes,
The Dogs aproach, and with those legs he'ad fled
Had he not been intangled by the head.
Morall
That which ^we vallue most may help us least
And often we despise what serves us best.

215 [Nnn2]   CVII *The Stag in the Ox-stall*

A Stag whom Hounds pursu'd to an Oxstall flyes,
Where Straw secures him from dull heards mens eyes,
But when the Master comes, he was betryd,
And the poor weeping prize his victm made.
        Morall
Our ruin oft does from those acts begin,
Our fears at first contriv'd to shield us in.

217 [Ooo]   CVIII *The Dove and Pismire*

A Pismire once sav'd by a gentle Dove,
Who seing her like to be insnar'd, she strove
With her keene sting the Fowlers heele to frett,
The Dove perceiv'd it, and avoids the nett.
        Morall
Behold unthinking man the pious Ant
Can teach you gratitude, and industry in want.

219 [Ooo2]   CIX *The Lion in Love*

A Maid who by a Lyon was adord
Consents to love, but first she him implord
To quitt his nailes, and teeth, the Monarch yields
Which done with ease she her fond Lover kills.
        Morall
Almighty love asailes with powerful charmes
And both our Prudence, and our strength disarmes.

221 [Ppp]   CX *The Tortoise and Eagle*

The Tortois begs the Eagle her to beare
To search for Iewells in a Rock oth'Ayr,
But having ransackt all the distant skyes,
He finds the cheat, and makes his load the prize.
        Morall
Promise not princes what you never meant,
Least death, or worse deserv'd be the event.

TO THE
MOST ILLUSTRIOUS PRINCE,
CHRISTOPHER,
DUKE OF
ALBEMARLE
ON HIS
VOYAGE
TO HIS
GOVERNMENT of *JAMAICA*

It is resolv'd! His Word and Honour's past!
  We must submit, and let the *Heroe* go:
  This Scanty Isle He long has Serv'd and Grac't,
And distant Worlds expect Him now.
  No Grateful Laurels this allows,   5
  To Crown the Noble Victor's Brows:
Supinely here His Generous Youth was lost,
Which shou'd more memorable Glories boast;
  Such as shou'd more Renown His Name,
And still maintain aloft His spreading Fame.   10
His Soul by Nature Bravely Rough and Great,
Scorns the Confinement of a Home-Retreat;
  But soft Repose, that Court-Disease,
  Infectious to the Great and Young,
  Subdu'd His Martial Mind to Ease,   15
  And Charm'd Him with her Pleasures long.
Born for Great Action, but compell'd to Sloth,
He yields to all the Splendid Baits for Youth.

II.

So the Young Victor did at *Capua* lie,
  Tamely unnerv'd in Luxury;   20
While all his gilded Arms hung Useless by:
In daz'ling Riots wanton'd with his Fair,

Despising Conquests, and renouncing War,
Till Glory wak'd him from th'Inchanting Dream,
And pointing out his Youth a Nobler Theam.   25
He rowses now and puts his Armour on,
   Gives Order for his Warlike Steeds;
In vain the Lovely Charmer Weeps and Pleads,
He'll be no more by Idle Love undone;
In vain the shining Goblets take their Round,   30
   And with Obliging Healths are Crown'd,
The Ivory Tables bending with the Weight
   Of Costly Fare, in O're-charg'd Plate:
He now for Fame Ignoble Ease disdains;
Bravely Resolv'd, he breaks the Lazy Chains.   35

III.

   Well did Great *Caesar* know,
   His Grandeur and Magnificence
To New-found Worlds He cou'd not shew
   So greatly to His Fame, as now,
     In so Renown'd a Prince: 40
Already to the utmost Bounds of Shore
   His Mighty Name is gone before.
Great ALBEMARLE the Sea-born *Nereids* sung,
   Upon that Memorable Day,
When all the Floods let loose their joyful Throng,   45
And bore the MARTYR'S SONS in Triumph o'er the Sea:
   And still between the Monarchs Praise
   The Fame of ALBEMARLE they raise,
Crowns to the Royal Youth they brought, and to the Victor Bays.

IV.

How must that Wondring World rejoyce to see   50
Their Land so Honour'd, and themselves so Blest,
When on their Shores (*Great Prince)* they Welcom Thee,
Whose Brave Hereditary Loyalty

Has been so many generous ways exprest:
What Homage must Your Ravisht Subjects pay   55
For the vast Condescention You have shewn?
What Treasures offer, how enough Obey,
      Their Humble Gratitude to own,
      When they behold a Prince so Great
      From an Illustrious Court retreat,   60
To render all their Happiness compleat?
A Prince whom no Ignoble Interest sways,
To trust his Fortune with the Fickle Seas,
Altho' its Tributary Waves before
      Allow'd Him so immense a Store,   65
As if the Wonders of the Deep till now,
      Of which we have so oft been told,
      Did never yet its meaning shew,
Till yielding up the Miracle in Gold:
      And 'tis Great ALBEMARLE alone   70
Has found the Secret of the Philosophic Stone.

                              V.

With Him, His Princess, whose High Birth
      Must Adoration claim
      O're all the Habitable Earth
That ever heard the Great *Newcastle*'s Name.   75
How justly is our Verse a Tribute due,
      Illustrious Patroness, to You!
Descended from a Prince and Poet too!
That Honour which no Mortal Pow'r can give,
And is alone the Gods Prerogative;   80
Like that bright Vertue which do's in You shine,
And, more than Mortal, renders You Divine.
Prepare, ye Sun-scorch'd Natives of the Shore,
Prepare another Rising Sun t'adore,
Such as has never blest your Horizon before.   85
And you the Brave Inhabitants of the Place,
Who have by Conquest made it all your own,

Whose Generous and Industrious Race
Has paid such Useful Tribute to the Crown;
See what your Grateful King for you has done!   90
Behold a Prince high in His Favor plac'd,
By Fortune Blest, and lavish Honour grac'd,
Lov'd by the Great, and Worshipp'd by the Crowd,
Of whom the Nation has so long been proud,
The Souldiers Honour, and the Brave Mans Friend,   95
   The Muses best-lov'd Theme,
To whom their Noblest Verse they Recommend,
And to whose Vertues pay their Noblest Flame.

VI.

This Prince thus Lov'd, we do resign to you,
   Yet must but lend Him for a space: 100
   Fond Parents lose their Darling so,
   To Dangers thus they let him go,
With tender Tears, and many a soft Embrace;
Loth to forego the Treasure of their Heart,
   And yet wou'd have him Honour share,   105
With trembling Doubts and Fears at last they part,
With Vows and Pray'rs commit Him to Heav'ns Care.
We lend Him to eternize you a Fame,
That to the Coming Age your Land may boast,
Of all that e're Obey'd great CÆSAR's Name,   110
   He Honour'd yours the Most.
Prepare your Triumphs, and your Songs of Joy,
   Let ALBEMARLE's Great Name resound
To all your Happy Shores, and let the Sea
To the glad Echo's and the Nymphs convey   115
   The grateful Tidings all around,
   While the soft Breezes prune their Wings,
   And gather all their Gentlest Air,
(In the Rich Groves, drest with Perpetual Springs)
To Fan and Entertain the *Hero* there.   120
   Let all your World be Glad and Gay,

To make His Joy Compleat,
Eternal *Zephires* round Him play,
And Flowers beneath His Feet.
Thus for Our Honour, and for your Repose,   125
We are content Our Happiness to lose:
But, like the Souls to Bodies newly Born,
He is but Lent, more Glorious to Return.

FINIS

A
CONGRATULATORY
POEM
TO HER MOST
Sacred Majesty
ON THE
UNIVERSAL HOPES
OF ALL
LOYAL PERSONS
FOR A
PRINCE OF WALES.

The Mighty *BLESSING* is *at last* arriv'd,
Heav'n has, *at last* the Wond'rous *WORK* achiev'd.
Long did th'*ALMIGHTY* pause, and long debate;
For *MONARCHS* are not fashion'd at a Heat.
So the first *Nations*, that were bless'd by *Heaven*,   5
Had the Eternal *WORD* by *Promise* given.
The *Faithful* did the Coming *GOD* believe,
And ev'n that *Faith* alone had Pow'r to *save*.

   If *Gods* we may with Humane Things compare,
(For *Gods* and *Kings* ally'd most nearly are)   10
This is the Second *Birth* the World e'er knew,
So long expected, so much Wanted too.

   Like the first Sacred *Infant*, this will come
With Promise laden from the *Blessed* Womb,
To call the wand'ring, scatter'd Nations home.   15
Adoring *PRINCES* shall arrive from far,
Inform'd by *ANGELS*, guided by his Star,
The New-born *Wonder* to behold, and greet;
And *Kings* shall offer Incense at his Feet.

Hail, Royal *BOY!* whose Coming is design'd   20
To calm the Murmurs of all Humane Kind.
On thy great *Birth,* Depending *Monarchs* wait:
From thee the *Universe* expects its *Fate.*
This glorious *PROSPECT,* like the sacred *Law,*
Stints factious *Crouds,* and keeps the World in awe;   25
Breaks their consulted Measures, and o'erthrows
All the Designs aspiring *STATES* propose;
Arrests the *Wheel,* in spight of *Fortune's* Hand,
And leaves the World's vast Bus'ness at a Stand.

And you, bless'd *QUEEN,* to whom *ALL HAIL* belongs   30
From *Angels,* rather than from Mortal Tongues;
Whose Charms of *Beauty, Wit* and *Vertue* join'd
To chuse you Second *Bless'd* of *Woman-kind.*

ALL HAIL,———
    O Sacred *VESSEL,* fraught with *England's STORE,*   35
(A *PRIZE* more valu'd, *ATLAS* never bore;)
Guard safe our *TREASURE* to the wish'd for *Shore* .
And you, Immortal *Pow'rs,* who have begun
Your Noblest *FABRICK; let your* WORK go on:
The Royal *YOUTH* with all those Charms adorn,   40
The World adores in his bright *MOTHER'S* Form:
His Soul, by his, by his Illustrious *SIRES,* compleat:
All *Hero,* all *Resolv'd,* Divinely *Great.*

    Where are ye, O ye once officious NINE,
That on a *Theam* so glorious, and sublime,   45
Your Voices are not tun'd to noblest *Song?*
But, Oh! your *Lutes* are on the Willows hung
Your lov'd *BRITANIA* listens now no more ;
MARS frights her from the soft *Castalian* Shore;
Upon whose Banks, beneath your Shades, each Day,   50
The ravish'd *Nymph,* charm'd with your Numbers, lay.
But from your *Groves* the fickle *Maid* is gone,
And all your boasted *Harmony* undone.

But once more tune your *Lutes* and Voices high;
Your tenderest Strains, and noblest Numbers try: 55
Raise those dejected Eyes, in Sorrow dress'd,
And view the *PROSPECT* of the dawning *East*.

  A young *APOLLO*, rising from the Gloom,
Dress'd in his Father's brightest *Rays*, shall come;
(Dispersing lall the baneful Mists of Night)   60
And bless the Earth with New-*created LIGHT*;
Make all the Face of *Nature* sweet and gay,
Revive her *Birth*, and triumph o'er the Day.
Beneath *his* Feet Eternal Spring shall spread,
And blossom from the Lustre round his Head.   65
He the faint *Muses* shall a-new inspire,
And from *his Beams*, kindle their useful Fire;
His Right Hand *Crowns*, his Left shall *Lawrels* give,
And *POETS* shall by *Patron-PRINCES* live;
On all shall scatter *Plenty, Joy,* and *Peace*,   70
Unite the World and make *Dissention* cease.

  And you, Dread *Monarch!* ne'er to be confin'd,
In any glorious *Act* you have design'd,
Who, like wise *Heaven*, need but decree alone,
And with the Thought, the mighty *Task* is done;   75
Who for a stubborn *Nation's* Glory toil,
And court her to be Great against her Will.
When you esteem'd her worth your Royal Care,
You gave her this last Blessing, of an *HEIR*.
O happy *KING!* to whom a Son is born!   80
What more can *Fortune, Heaven* and *You* perform?

  Behold, with Joy three prostrate *Nations* come:
ALBION, HIBERNIA and old *CALEDON*
Now join their *Int'rests*, and no more dispute,
With sawcy Murmurs, who is *Absolute*;   85
Since, from the Wonders of your Life, 'tis plain,
You *will*, you *shall*, and *must* for ever Reign.

A
CONGRATULATORY
POEM
TO THE
King's Most Sacred Majesty,
on the Happy BIRTH of the
PRINCE of WALES

Joy to the *Greatest MONARCH* of the Earth!
As many Joys as this *Illustrious BIRTH*
Has Elevated HEARTS! As Endless too,
As are the VOWS we Offer up for You.
"Oh Happy *KING!* to whom a *SON* is Born! 5
"What more cou'd *Heaven* for this Bless'd Land perform?

Long with *Prophetick Fire*, Resolv'd and Bold,
Your *Glorious FATE* and *FORTVNE* I foretold.
I saw the *Stars* that did attend Your *REIGN*,
And how they Triumph'd o'er Great *Charles's Wain*. 10
Far off I saw this *HAPPY DAY* Appear;
This *Jubilee*, not known this *Fifty Year.*
This Day foretold, (*Great SIR!*) that gives you more
Than even Your *Glorious Virtues* did before.

No *MONARCH's Birth* was ever Usher'd in 15
With Signs so Fortunate as this has been.
(a) Trinity Sunday. The *(a) Holy Trinity* his *BIRTH-DAY* claims,
Who to the World their best *Lov'd Blessings* sends.
Guarded he comes, in Triumph over *FATE*,
And all the *Shining HOST* around him wait. 20
Angels and *Saints*, that do his *Train* Adorn,
In Hallelujahs Sing, *A KING IS BORN!*
(b) St. Margaret's Day. *Blest (b) MARGARET, Scotlands* Royal *Saint* and *Queen*,
The last *Great Branch* of all the *Saxon Line*,
Waits on this *HAPPY BIRTH*; and does Declare 25

99

He, in her Right to *Saxons*, is the *HEIR*.
In the *Fam'd* Room, by happy Fate brought forth,
(c) Charles II. Where *(c)* Two *Illustrious KINGS* receiv'd their *Birth*.
James II.

    The *LESSONS* for *This Day*, by Chance *Divine*,
The Morn-   Appear'd as they were Order'd by Design.   30
ing Lesson
for the Day. The *First*, the *Holy PROPHET* did Unfold
When he the *Birth* of the *MESSIAH* told.
(d) Matt. The Words are These; *(d) His Fan is in his Hand,*
3. 12.   *And he shall throughly purge the Floor or Land,*
Gathering the Wheat into the Granary: 35
Then all *One FAITH*, at least *One SOUL* shall be.
The Evening
Lesson Gen.   "The *ANGEL* next the *PATRIARCH* did Inform,
18.10.   "That *ISAAC*, Chosen *ISAAC*, shou'd be *Born*.

    ASTROLOGERS Divine! that when the *Sun*
Is Mounted to his Full Meridian,   40
'Tis lucky to be Born; and does Portend
Long Life, that can by no Misfortune end.
This, in his Summer-*Solstice* views the Light,
Breaks out, and makes our *Longest Day* more *Bright*.

    Methinks I hear the *Belgick LION* Roar,   45
And Lash his *Angry Tail* against the Shore.
Inrag'd to hear a *PRINCE OF WALES* is *Born:*
Whose BROWS his *Boasted Laurels* shall Adorn.
Whose *Angel FACE* already does express
His Foreign *CONQUESTS*, and *Domestick PEACE*. 50
While in his *Awful little EYES* we Fin'd
He's of the *Brave*, and the *Forgiving KIND*.

    All Joy *Great QUEEN!* — *if to your* Happy Store
Our *Grateful Pray'rs*, and *Wishes* can add more.
Your *Blest DELIVERANCE* to Congratulate,   55
The *Adoring World* is Prostrate at your *Feet*.
Where *TEARS* of *Joy*, and *Humble VERSE* I lay

Too mean a *Trophy* for this *GLORIOUS DAY:*
Inspir'd by Nothing but *Prophetick Truth,*
They boast no other *Fire*, no other *Worth.*   60
Full of the *JOY*, no *LINES Correct* can write,
My *Pleasure's* too Extream for *Thought* or *Wit.*
Charm'd to Excess, alass! I strive in *Vain,*   ⎫
In *Scanty VERSE* my Transports to Explain   ⎬
Too *Vast* for *Narrow NUMBERS* to Contain.   ⎭   65

UPON THE
POET BAVIUS

A Labouring *Muse*, that full Nine Months had been
In Painful thro's *Pregnant*[1] at last became.
Nine Months[2] *a Loyal Zeal had Fir'd my Breast,*
Which for Nine Muses cou'd not be at rest.
Tell me, vain hard'ned *Scribler,* what Pretence   5
Have those two Lines, to Kindred, or to Sense?
The Luckey gingle of the *Nine* and *Nine,*
Produc'd 'em without Thinking or Design.
The first thy L*oyalties* short date Rehearses:
The next, how Damnably thou Pumpst for Verses.   10
But Duty did my desperate Ray Controule[3]:
'Tis false, thy *Muse* was Tame, as is thy Soul;
Thou hast no Rage, no Fire, no Spirit or Power,
But Feeble Rancor, for the Happy Hour.
Some could not Bridle their Officious Rhime[4],   15
But must bestow an Heir before the Time.
While thou dull Faithless Scribling Infidel,
Cou'd not Believe till thou cou'dst See, and Feel:
We like the Joyful P*atriarchs* of Old,
Believ'd the good to Come, when but Fore told.   20
But thou, as scanted in thy *Faith* as *Sense,*
Wanted the Courage to Trust *Providence.*
It was enough, we saw a *Pregnant Queen!*
To Inspire our *Muse,* tho' we no more had seen.
Where each well-wisher Honestly intends,   25
Good Will for Paltry Lines must make amends:
And why so sharp Squire *Bavius* on your Friends?

---

1. *First in* Labour *and then* Pregnant
2. *So long* loyal
3. *But for* Duty *he had been inraged at the Birth of the* Prince
4. *Nor more cou'd* Bavius, *who proffer'd his Poem to* Bentley *two months before the Prince was born; but had not the Courage to venture it till he saw indeed 'twas a Son.*

Thou who hast been this *Fifteen Years* at least,
Thro' all the *Town* the most *Notorious Jest;*
E're (to Increase thy *Foppery*) thou hadst *Writ:*   30
The Scorne o'th'*Boxes,* Laughter of the *Pit.*
Famous in *Julians* Song, till Vile Lampoon
Discarded thee for a too dull *Buffoon.*
But once a *Poet,* our Diversion fail'd;
Thou fellest below, even being Redicul'd,   35
And had not thy Unlucky *Rhiming Spirit,*
Writ *Satyr* now instead of *Panygerick:*
Vile Pointless *Satyr,* thou might'st still have been
A poor forgotten Drone without a Sting:
And without notice follow'd still the King.   40
His Couchees, and his Levies, wait, and get
As much, as by thy ever failing Wit.

　　VVhile with Abortive Lines¹ the Land you fill,
And make the Consort hear your Nonsense still.
Such Sawcy Puns, with an irreverend S*he*——   45
And World of *Do's* makes up thy Poetry:
Below thy Native Dulness sinks thy *Rhimes*
And are a Woful Libel on the Times.
Maces *and* Furrs², *their Princes Favour gone,*
Neglected, look like Roses *after* June: 50
Or, like Fop *Bavius* Verse, quite out of Tune.
Why does the Trading City look so Blew?³
Unless by Trusting Sharping *Bavius* like you.
And why, a Body that no Soul can Boast⁴
Or why have they their Princes Favour lost?   55
The King no Thanks will give your Misplac'd Zeal,

---

1. *Then with Abortive Joy the Nation fill, And make the Consort bear the Burden still–*
Bavius *Poem.*
2. On the City
3. Query, *he says the City looks Bleak.*
4. *He calls it a Body without a Soul, and tells 'em they have lost the King's favour.*

To judge his Sentiments t' the *Commonweal*.

If *Roses* after *June*; are *Roses* still;
Retain their Colour, Beauty, and their Smell:
The Novelty begets 'em more Esteem,   60
Than if they Bloom'd the common Month of *June*.[1]
So while the City keeps her *Loyalty*,
She's still in Favour; and deserves to be,
Inspight of all thy ill-tim'd Poetry.
And who, but Rhiming *Bavius*, could suppose   65
Maces, and *Furrs*, so very like a *Rose*.
Or think, because the *Judges* Chaines is gone,[2]
The gaudy Triffle lost, the Mans undone:
Dull Fool, that ne're to Merit gave its due,
But thinks all Vertue to consist of Show: 70
As if the Man, once Worth his Prince's Grace,
Must with his short-liv'd Frown become an Ass,
A Prince's Favour, then, by the same Rule,
Should make him Lov'd, or VVise that is a Fool.

But now the bitter *Robe*; the Reverend Gown,[3]   75
Doom'd by his Nations Scandal, must go down:
First tell us, that thou art a *Renigade*,
E're to thy Mother thou turn Retrograde:
If of the *Primitive Roman Church* thou be,[4]
(Heaven guard her from so great an Infamie)   80
Stick to that Point, and then we Pardon Thee.
But thou who still the *Establish'd Faith* Profest,
Like an Ungrateful Bird, Bewrayst thy Nest:
Or like the Amphibious Batt, that shuns the Light,
VVith *Beast* canst walk, and with the Fowles take flight.   85

---

9. *Upon his Simily of the* Rose *confuted*.
10. *His Jerk for the turned-out Judges*.
11.*Witty on the Bishops*
12.*He pretends to be of the Church of* England

The next high Jest, is the Discarded stuff;
Now *Bavius* hand is in, he claws it off.
And like *Almanzor* when Inrag'd he grows,
Promiscuously he falls on Friends and Foes.
Tho' with substantiall Limbs and brisk in Walking   90
Without your Staff, you are but lame and Halting.[1]
O Luckey hit! what strange Prodigious skill
Thou hast in Clinching, Quibling, Doggeril.

The *Colonels*[2] next; but by unhappy Chance,
No *Puns* the value of these Lines Advance: 95
But *Dids*, and *Does*, and a quant *Simely*,
Which must the Place of smarter Clinch supply.
He tells you here, *That loss of a Commission,*
Is very much like a Death-Bed Contrition:
Nay, what is worse, so wretched is their Fate,   100
No Galloon-Coats their Levires now must wait;[3]
In *Bavius* Sense, VVit, Honour, Vertue lyes
In the *Lac'd-Coat* and *Gay-Embroaderies.*
Nor is the *Garter* from his Rage exempt,
Turn'd off, he adds the weight of his Contempt: 105
Unhappy *Peers*, when once you're in Disgrace;
Your Ribban's dirty and your Stars are brass:
VVorse than *Beau Bavius* Belt all set with *Glass.*
The suck-blood Vermin of the Robe *alone*
Can smile to see Men every day undone.[4]   110

If by *Permissu Superiorum*,[5] this
Dull, Sawcy Libel, thro' the Town must pass:
VVhere Reverend Bishops, *Ravenous Wolves* are deem'd;

---

1. *A Bob for the Controllers that are out.*
2. *a notable Pun*
3. *A great Misfortune*
4. *Here he is Civil to all of the* Robe *in General.*
5. *His Book so* Licens'd

And all the Judges, *Bloody Knaves*, esteem'd:
White Staves, Blew Garters, all within his reach; 115
His *Evidence Muse*, must of some Crime Impeach.
Then farewell all Good Manners, Sense, and VVit,
If *Superiorums* will such Stuff admit.
But this was slyly meant, like all the rest;
Upon the *Reverend Fathers* for a Jest. 120
No Order, Honour or High Place, can be
From his immortal Nonsense *Satyr* free.
Hadst thou not better in a few dull Lines,
Plain honest *Meeter*—— tag'd with gingling *Rhimes*;
In thy *Coronation Stile*, and usual Sense, 125
Hamer'd some Hearty Welcome to the *Prince*:
Kept to thy *Theam*, and his just Praises Sung;
And not have took this time for publick wrong
Lybel, this great Occasion, cou'd not bear;
All Love, and Softness, was the Business here: 130
Malice shou'd here be banish'd from thy Quill, ⎫
Then we'd excus'd thy barely writing ill; ⎬
And for bad Lines have taken thy good Will. ⎭
VVe are content thou shouldst in *Scoundrel Verse*,
Put into *French* the famous *Hudebras*; 135
Or Nobler *Boileau* into *English* turn,
And move at once our Laughter and our Scorn.

   Thy dull Advice too, we with Patience read,
VVhich tells us, how *Young Monarchs* shou'd be Bred;
('Tis pitty, but thou wert a Tutor made.) 140
And who that see the *Politiques* that shine,
Thró' all the *Nonsense* of each *strugling* Line:[1]
Thy exact *Grammar*, and Coherence views,
VVith the good Nature of thy Railing *Muse*:
Thy VVit, thy Parts, thy Conduct, Mien and Grace, ⎫ 145
Thy *Presence*, Cringes, and thy Court *Grimarce*; ⎬
But Swears Heaven meant thee for a perfect —As— ⎭

---

1. *See* Bavius

A
POEM
TO
Sir Roger L'Estrange
ON HIS
THIRD PART
OF THE
HISTORY of the TIMES
Relating to the
DEATH
OF
Sir *EDMUND BURY-GODFREY*

In what loud Songs of everlasting *Fame*,
Shall we adore the great *L'Estrange's Name*;
Who like a pitying God, does *Truth* advance,
Rescuing the *World* from stupid Ignorance.
Truth, which so long in shameful Darkness lay,   5
Raises her shineing Head, and views the Day.
Truth, the *First-born* of *Heaven!* and *Being* had,
E'r the vast World was from the *Chaos* made!
'Twas *That* form'd *Souls*; and by a *Power* sublime,
Was *all in all*, the very *Word* Divine: 10
Till Man by *Vice* and *Villany* betray'd,
By *Perjury* and false *Ambition* sway'd,
Banisht the Noble *Vertue* from its Seat,
As *Vseless* in the Politick, and Great.
Then Fraud and Flattery first in *Courts* began,   15
And thence assum'd by all the *Race* of *Man*:
Grave *Judges*, *Church-men*, and whole *Senates* now,
Ev'n *Laws* and *Gospel*, were corrupted too.
By *these* misled, the restless People Range
Into a Thousand *Errors*, New and Strange;   20

To every *God*, to every *Idol-Change*.
  Unknown *Religions* first their *Poyson* hurl'd,
And with *New Lights* Debauch'd the giddy World;
Not the *Rebellious, Stubborn Hebrew Race*,
More false forbidden *Worships* did Embrace.   25
Hence Universal *Feuds* and *Mischiefs* rose,
And *Friends* to *Friends, Parents* to *Sons* were Foes.
The Inspir'd *Rabble*, now wou'd *Monarchs* Rule,
And *Government* was turn'd to Ridicule:
No *Magistrates*, no *Order*, was Obey'd;   30
But new *Club-Laws*, by *Knaves* and *Villains* made.
From *Wapping-Councils*, all *Decrees* went out,
And *manag'd* as *they* pleas'd the Frantick *Rout*:
Then *Perj'ries, Treasons, Murthers*, did ensure,
And total *Dissolution* seem'd in View.   35
For safety *Gods Anointed* found no *Place*;
And 'midst his *Senate*, most in danger was.
The *Lord* of *Life*, his *Image* rudely torn,
To *Flames* was by the *Common-Hangman* born.
Here Noble *Stafford* fell, on *Death's* great *Stage*,   40
A *Victim* to the Lawless Peoples rage.
Calm as a *Dove*, receiv'd a shameful Death, ⎫
To Undeceive the *World*, resign'd his *Breath*; ⎬
And like a *God*, dy'd to redeem *Our Faith*.   ⎭

  At *Golgatha, they glut thee'r Insatiate *Eyes*   *Tyburn 45
With *Scenes* of *Blood*, and *Humane Sacrifice*,
Men Consecrate to Heaven, were *piece-meal* hew'd
For Sport and Pastime, to the brutal Crowd.
The *World* ran *Mad*, and each distemper'd *Brain*
Did *strange* and *different Frenzies* entertain: 50
Here *Politick Mischiefs*, there *Ambition* sway'd;
The Credulous *Rest*, were *Fool* and *Coward-Mad*.
The Wiser *few*, who did th'*Infection* shun,
Were *those* most lyable to be *undone*:
Honour, as *Breach* of *Priviledge*, was detected;   55
And *Common Sense*, was *Popishly Affected*.

Thus bashful *Truth* was *Victim'd* on our *Shore*,
And none the frighted *Virtue* durst restore:
No *Perseus* found, the *Monster* to Out-brave,
And from the *fatal Rock*, the *Virgin* save.   60
No *Curtius* the vast *Precipice* would leap,
That *Rome* might from the dire *Contagion* scape;
Till like a *saving Angel* o're the Land,
You, *Mighty Sir*, stretch'd your all *Conquering Hand*.
You tun'd your *Sacred Lyre*, and stopt the Rage,   65
Of this abandon'd, this distemper'd Age.
By the soft force of *Charming Eloquence*,
You eas'd Our *Fears*, and brought us back to *Sense*.

By You the *fatal Riddle* was reveal'd,
Which *Hell's* Dark *Malice* long had keep't conceal'd.   70
You pointed out the *Hand* that did the *Deed*,
For which so many *Innocents* did *Bleed*.
'Tis plain! and he denies the Noon-day light,
Who questions the vast Reason which you write.
'Tis brave! 'Tis Noble *Truth, Divinely spoke!*   75
Detecting Knaves, who willingly mistook;
It shews the *Source* from whence the Mischief broke.

The Melancholly *Self-Murtherer* You trace
Thro' his *Death-searching Paths* e'n to the fatal *Place:*
The *Picture* you have drawn so Just, so True,   80
We have the very *Fact* it self in view.
And with a just Disdain those *Authors* hate,
Who on the *Innocents* transferr'd his *Fate*;
A *Sacrifice* to save a *vile Estate*.
'Tis you alone these Truths to be admir'd   85
Have writ, as with a *Fiery Tongue* Inspir'd.
This *Crowns* your *Labours*, makes your *Works* compleat;
Which, like your *self*, are eminently Great.

FINIS

OF
PLANTS.

BOOK VI.

SYLVA

Cease, O my Muse, the soft delights to sing
Of flowry Gardens in their fragrant Spring;
And trace the rougher Paths of obscure Woods,
All gloom aloft, beneath o'rgrown with Shrubs:
Where *Phœbus*, once thy Guide, can dart no ray   5
T'inspire thy flight, and make the Scene look gay.
　　Courage, my Huntress, let us range the Glades,
And search the inmost Grotto's of the Shades:
Even to the lone Recesses let us pass,
Where the green Goddess rests on Beds of Moss.   10
Let loose, my Fancy, swift of foot to trace
With a sagacious scent the noble chase,
And with a joyful cry pursue the Prey;
'Tis hidden Nature we must rouse to day.
Set all your Gins, let every Toil be plac'd,   15
Through all her Tracks let flying Truth be chas'd,
And seize her panting with her eager hast.
Nor yet disdain, my Muse, in Groves to range,
Or humbler Woods for nobler Orchards change.
Here Deities of old have made abode,   20
And once secur'd Great *Charles* our earthly God.
The Royal Youth, born to out-brave his Fate,
Within a neighbouring Oak maintain'd his State:
The faithful Boughs in kind Allegiance spread
Their sheltring Branches round his awful Head   25
Twin'd their rough Arms, and thicken'd all the Shade.
　　To thee, belov'd of Heaven, to thee we sing

Of sacred Groves blooming perpetual Spring.
Mayst thou be to my Rural Verse and Me,
A present and assisting Deity.   30
Disdain not in this leafy Court to dwell,
Who its lov'd Monarch did secure so well.
Th'Eternal *Oak* now consecrate to thee
No more thy Refuge, but thy Throne shall be.
We'll place thee Conqueror now, and crown thy brows   35
With Garlands made of its young gayest boughs:
While from our oaten Pipes the world shall know
How much they to this sacred shelter owe.
   And you, the soft Inhabitants of the Groves,
You Wood-Nymphs, Hamadryades and Loves,   40
Satyrs and Fauns, who in these Arbors play.
Permit my Song, and give my Muse her way.
She tells of ancient Woods the wondrous things,
Of Groves long veil'd in sacred darkness sings,
And a new Light into your Gloom she brings.   45
Let it be lawful for me to unfold
Divine Decrees that never yet were told:
The Harangues of the Wood Gods to rehearse,
And sing of Flowry Senates in my Verse.
Voices unknown to Man he now shall hear,   50
Who always ignorant of what they were,
Have pass'd 'em by with a regardless ear;
Thought 'em the murmurings of the ruffled Trees,
That mov'd and wanton'd with the sporting Breeze.
But *Daphne knew the Mysteries of the Wood   55
And made discoveries to her amorous God;
Apollo me inform'd, and did inspire
My Soul with his Divine Prophetic fire:
And I, the Priest of Plants, theirs sense expound.
Hear, O ye Worlds, and listen all around.   60
   'Twas now when Royal Charles that Prince of peace,

---

* *Daphne* being turn'd into a laurel.

III

(That pious Off spring of the Olive Race)
Sway'd *Englands* Sceptre with a God-like hand,
Scattering soft Ease and Plenty o'r the Land,
Happy 'bove all the neighbouring Kings, while yet   65
Unruffled by the rudest storms of Fate,
More fortunate the People, till their Pride
Disdain'd Obedience to the Sovereign Guide,
And to a base Plebeian Senate gave
The Arbitrary Priv'lege to enslave;   70
Who through a Sea of Noblest Blood did wade,
To tear the Diadem from the Sacred Head.
Now above Envy, far above the Clouds
The Martyr sits triumphing with the Gods.
While Peace before did o'r the Ocean fly   75
On our blest Shore to find security:
In *British* Groves she built her downy nest,
No other Climate could afford her rest:
For warring Winds o'r wretched *Europe* range,
Threatning Destruction, universal Change.   80
The raging Tempest tore the aged Woods,
Shook the vast Earth, and troubl'd all the Floods.
Nor did the fruitful Goddess brood in vain,
But here in safety hatch'd her golden train.
Justice and Faith one *Cornucopia* fill.   85
Of useful Med'cines known to many an Ill.
Such was the Golden Age in *Saturn*'s sway,
Easie and innocent it pass'd away:
But too much Luxury and good Fortune cloys
And Virtues she should cherish she destroys.   90
What we most wish, what we most toil to gain
Enjoyment palls, add (*sic*) turns the Bliss to pain.
Possession makes us shift our Happiness,
From peaceful Wives to noisie Mistrisses.
The Repetition makes the Pleasure dull;   95
'Tis only change that's gay and beautiful.
O Notion false! O Appetite deprav'd,
That has the nobler part of Man enslav'd.

Man born to Reason, does that Safety quit,
To split upon the dangerous Rock of Wit. 100
Physicians say, there's no such danger near,
As when, though no signs manifest appear,
Self-tir'd and dull, man knows not what he ails,
And without toil his Strength and Vigor fails.
  Such was the State of *England*, sick with Ease, 105
Too happy, if she knew her Happiness.
Their Crime no Ignorance for Excuse can plead,
That wretched refuge for Ingratitude.
'Twas then that from the pitying Gods there came ⎫
A kind admonishing Anger to reclaim   ⎬ 110
In dreadful Prodigies; but, alas, in vain.   ⎭
So rapid Thunder-bolts before the Flame
Fly, the consuming Vengeance to proclaim.
I. then a Boy, arriv'd to my tenth year,
And still those horrid Images I bear.* 115
The mournful Signs are present to my Eyes.
I saw o'r all the Region of the Skies,
The History of our approaching Wars
Writ in the Heav'ns in wondrous Characters.
The vaulted Firmament with Lightning burns, 120
And all the Clouds were kindled into Storms,
And form'd an Image of th'infernal Hell;
(I shake with the portentous things I tell)
Like sulph'rous waves the horrid Flames did roll,
Whose raging Tides were hurl'd from Pole to Pole; 125
Then suddenly the bursting Clouds divide,
A Fire-like burning mounts on either side,
Discovering (to th'astonish'd World) within
At once a dreadful and a beauteous Scene:
Two mighty Armies clad in Battle-array 130
Ready by Combat to dispute the day:
Their waving Plumes and glittering Armour shone,

---

* This relation of Prodigies, Mr. *Cowley* assures to be true; *Veram esse in me recipio.*
In the margin to the Original.

Mov'd by the Winds and guilded by the Sun.
So well in order seem'd each fearless Rank,
As they'd been marshall'd by our Hero, *Monk*,   135
Monk, born for mighty things and great command,
The glorious Pillar of our falling Land.
Perhaps his Genius on the Royal side
One of those Heav'nly Figures did describe,
Here pointed out to us his noble force,   140
And form'd him Conqueror on a flaming Horse.
We hear, or fancy'd tht we heard, around,
The Signal giv'n by Drum and Trumpet sound,
We saw the fire-winged Horses fiercely meet,
And with their fatal Spears each other greet.   145
Here shining brandish'd Pikes like Lightning shook,
While from Ethereal Guns true Thunder broke.
With gloomy Mists th'involv'd the Plains of Heaven,
And to the Cloud-begotten men was given
A memorable Fate ——   150
By the dire Splendor which their Arms display'd,
And dreadful Lightning that from Cannons play'd,
We saw extended o're the Aereal Plain
The wounded Bodies of the numerous slain.
(Their Faces fierce with anger understood)   155
Turning the Sky red with their gushing Blood,
At last that Army we the Just esteem'd,
And which adorn'd by noblest Figures seem'd
Of Arms and Men, alas! was put to flight;
The rest was veil'd in the deep Shades of Night,   160
And Fates to come secur'd from humane sight.
  But stupid *England* touch'd with no remorse,
Beholds these Prodigies as things of course.
(With many more, which to the Just appear'd
As ominous Presages.) Then who fear'd   165
The Monsters of the *Caledonian* Woods,
Or the hid ferments of Schismatic Crowds?
Nor had the impious *Cromwel* then a Name,
For *England's* Ruin, and for *England's* Shame.

Nor were the Gods pleas'd only to exhort   170
By signs the restive City and the Court.
Th'impending Fates o'r all the Thickets reign'd,
And Ruin to the *English* Wood proclaim'd,
We saw the sturdy Oaks of monstrous growth,
Whose spreading roots fix'd in their native Earth,   175
Where for a thousand years in peace they grew,
Torn from the Soil, though none but Zeph'rus blew.
But who such violent Outrages could find
To be th'effects of the soft Western wind?
The *Dryads* saw the right hand of the Gods   180
O'rturn the noblest shelters of the Woods.
Others their Arms with baneful leaves were clad,
That new unusual Forms and Colours had,
Whence now no *Aromatic* moisture flows,
Or noble *Misseltoe* enrich the boughs.   185
But bow'd with Galls, within whose boding hulls
Lurk'd Flies, diviners of ensuing ills.
Whose fatal buz did future slaughters threat,
And confus'd murmurs full of dread, repeat,
When no rude winds disturb'd the ambient Air,   190
The Trees, as weary of repose, made war.
With horrid noise grappling their knotty Arms,
Like meeting Tides they ruffle into Storms;
But when the VVinds to ratling Tempests rise,
Instead of warring Trees we heard the Cries   195
Of warring Men, whose dying Groans around
The VVoods and mournful Echo's did resound.
    The dismal Shades with Birds obscene were fill'd,
Which, spight of *Phoebus*, he himself beheld.
On the wild Ashes tops the Bats and Owls,   200
With all night, ominous and baneful Fowls
Sate brooding, while the Scrieches of these Droves
Prophan'd and violated all the Groves.
If ought that Poets do relate be true,

The strange Spinturnix[1] led the feather'd crew.   205
Of all the Monsters of the Earth and Air
Spinturnix bears the cruellest Character.
The barbarous Bird to mortal Eyes unknown
Is seen but by the Goddesses alone:
And then they tremble; for she always bodes   210
Some fatal Discord, even among the Gods.
But that which gave more wonder than the rest,
Within an Ash a Serpent built her nest,
And laid her Eggs; when once, to come beneath
The very shadow of an Ash, was death:[2]   215
Rather, if Chance should force, she through the Fire
From its faln Leaves so baneful, would retire.
But none of all the *Sylvan* Prodigies
Did more surprise the Rural Deities,
Than when the Lightning did the Laurel blast,   220
The Lightning their lov'd Laurels all defac'd:
The Laurel, which by *Jove's* Divine Decree
Since ancient time from injuring Tempests free;
No angry threats from the celestial powers
Could make her fear the ruin of her Bowers: 225
But always she enjoy'd a certain Fate,
Which she cou'd ne'r secure the Victor yet.
In vain these Signs and Monsters were not sent
From angry Heav'n; the wise knew what they meant.
Their coming by Conjectures understood,   230
As did the *Dryads* of the *British* wood,
    There is an ancient Forest[3] known to fame
On this side separate from the Cambrian Plain
By wandering *Wye*; whose winding Current glides,
And murmuring Leaves behind its flowry sides.   235

1. What this Bird truly was, is not known, but It was much dreaded by the *Aruspices. Plin. Servius, &c*
2. For the truth hereof take *Pliny's word, l.*16, 13
3. The Forest of *Dean.*

On that, 'tis wash'd by nobler *Severn's* streams
Whose Beauties scarce will yield to famous Thames.
Of yore 'twas *Arden* call'd, but to that great Name,
As like her self diminish'd, into *Dean*.
The cursed Weapons of destructive War   240
In all their Cruelties have made her share;
The Iron has its noblest Shades destroy'd,
Then to melt Iron is its Wood employ'd;
And so unhappy 'tis as it presents,
Of its own Death the fatal Instruments.   245
With Industry its ruin to improve
Bears Minerals below, and Trees above.
Oh Poverty! thou happiness extreme,
(When no afflicting want can intervene)
And oh thou subtle Treasure of the Earth,   250
From whence all Rapes and Mischiefs take their birth;
And you, triumphing Woods, secur'd from spoil
By the base blessing of your barren Soil.
Here, unconsum'd, how small a part remains
Of that rich store that once adorn'd the Plains.   255
Yet that small part that has escap'd the Ire
Of lawless Steel, and avaritious Fire,
By many Nymphs and deities possest
Of all the *British* shades continues still the best.
Here the long Reverend *Dryas* (who had been   260
Of all the shady verdant Regions Queen,
To which by Conquest she had forc'd the Sea
His constant tributary Waves to pay)
Proclaim'd a general Council through her Court
To which the *Sylvan* Nymphs shou'd all resort.   265
   All the Wood-Goddesses do strait appear,
At least who cou'd the *British* Climate bear,
And on a soft ascent of rising Ground
Their Queen, their charming *Dryas* they surround.
Who all adorn'd was in the middle plac'd,   270
And by a thousand awful Beauties grac'd.
These Goddesses alike were drest in Green,

The Ornaments and Liveries of their Queen.
Had travellers at any distance view'd
The beauteous Order of this stately Crowd,   275
They wou'd not guess they'd been Divinities,
But Groves all sacred to the Deities.
Such was the Image of this leafy Scene,
On one side water'd by a cooling Stream,
Upon whose brink the *Poplar* took her place,   280
The *Poplar* whom *Alcides* once did grace,
Whose double colour'd shadow'd Leaves express
The Labours of her Hero *Hercules*:
Whose upper sides are black, the under white
To represent his Toil and his Delight.   285
    The *Phaetonian Alder* next took Place,
Still sensible of the burnt Youths disgrace,
She loves the purling Streams and often Laves
Beneath the Floods, and wantons with the Waves.
    Close by her side the Pensive *Willows* join'd,   290
Chast Sisters all, to Lovers most unkind.
*Olesicarpians call'd, in Youth severe
Before the VVinter age had snow'd their Hair.
In Rivers take delight, whose chilling Streams,
Mixt with the native coldness of their Veins;   295
Like *Salamanders* can all heat remove,
And quite extinguish the quick fire of Love.
Firm lasting Bonds they yield to all beside,
But take delight the Lovers to divide.
    The *Elders* next, who though they Waters love   300
The same, from Humane Bodies yet remove,
And quite disperse the humid Moisture thence,
And parly with the *Dropsie* in this sense.
"Why do you linger here, O lazy Flood?
"This Soil belongs to Rivolets of Blood.   305
"Why do you Men torment, when many a shade,

---

*That is a Tribe which early drops its Seed; or which is an Enemy to Venery.

"And honest trees and Plants do want your Aid?
"Begon, from humane Bodies quick begon,
"And back into your native Channels run
"By every Pore, by all the ways you can.   310
The Moisture frightned, flies at the command,
And awful terror of her powerful wand.
    The Hospitable *Birch* does next appear,
Joyful and Gay on hot or frigid Air,
Flowing her Hair, her Garments soft and white,   315
And yet in Cruelty she takes delight,
No wild Inhabitant of the Woods can be
So quick in Wrath, and in Revenge as she;
In Houses great Authority assumes,
And's the sole punisher of petty Crimes.   320
But most of all her Malice she employs
In Schools, to terrifie and awe young Boys,
If she chastise, 'tis for the Patients good,
Though oft she blushes with their tender Blood
    Not so the generous *Maples*; they present   325
What e'r the City Luxury can invent,
Who with industrious Management and Pains
Divide the Labyrinth of their curious Grains,
And many necessary things produce,
That serve at once for Ornament and Use.   330
But thou, O *Pteleas*[1], to the Swain allows
Shades to his Cattel, Timber for his Plows,
Ennobled thou above the leafie Race
In that an Amorous God does thee embrace.[2]
    Next the *Oxias*[3] of her self a Grove,   335
Whose spreading Shades the Flocks and Shepherds love,
Whether thy Murmurs do to sleep invite,
Or thy soft noise inspire the rural Pipe;

---

1. *The Elm*

2. *Bacchus,* or the *Vine.*

3. The *Beech.*

Alike thou'rt grateful, and canst always charm,
In Summer cooling, and in Winter warm.   340
Tityrus of yore the Nymph with Garlands hung,
And all his Love-lays in her shadow sung.
When first the infant-World her reign began,
Ere pride and Luxury had corrupted Man,
Before for Gold the Earth they did invade,   350
The useful Houshold-stuff of *Beech* was made;
No other plate the humble Side board drest,
No other Bowls adorn'd the wholesom Feast,
Which no voluptuous Cookery cou'd boast,
The home-bred Kid or Lamb was all the cost.   355
The Mirth, the Innocence and little Care,
Surpast the loaded boards of high-priz'd Fare.
There came no Guest, for interest or Design,
For guilty Love, fine Eating or rich Wine.
The *Beechen*-Bowl without Debauch went round,   360
And was with harmless Mirth and Roses crown'd:
In these — the Ancients in their happy state
Their Feasts and Banquets us'd to celebrate.
Fill'd to the Brim with uncorrupted Wine,
They made Libations to the Powers divine   365
To keep 'em still benign, no Sacrifice
They need perform the angry Gods t'appease.
They knew no Crimes the Deities to offend,
But all their care was still to keep'em kind.
No Poyson ever did those Bowls infest,   370
Securely here the Shepherd quench'd his thirst;
'Twas not that any Vertue in the Wood
Against the baneful Liquor was thought good,
But Poverty and Innocence were here
The Antidote against all Ills and Fear.   375
    Such was the *Ash*, the Nymph was *Melias* nam'd,
For peaceful Use, and liberal Virtues fam'd:
But when *Achilles* Spear was of her Wood
Fatally form'd, and drank of *Hector's* Blood,
O wretched Glory! O unhappy Power,   380

She loves the Rain, and neighbouring Floods no more,
No more the falling Showers delight her now,
She only thirsts to drink of bloody Dew.
   Phylira[1], not Inferior to her Race,
For her *Bel-taille*, good Mien and handsom Grace,   385
For pious use, and noble studies fit,
Minerva here might exercise her wit,
And on the lasting Vellum which she brings
May in small Volumes write Seraphic things;
'Mongst all the Nymphs and Hamadryades,   390
There's none so fair, and so adorn'd as this.
All soft her Body, Innocent and White,
In her Green flowing Hair she takes delight,
Proud of her perfum'd Blossoms far she spreads
Her lovely, charming, odoriferous Shades.   395
Her native Beauties even excelling Art;
Her Vertues many Medicines still impart;
The dowry of each Plant in her does rest,
And she deserv'dly triumphs o'er the Best.
   Next her *Orcimelis* and *Achras*[2] stood,   400
Whose Off-spring is a sharp and rigid Brood,
A Fruit no Season e'er cou'd work upon,
Not to be mellow'd by th' all ripening Sun.
   Hither the fair Amphibious Nymphs resort,
Who both in Woods and Gardens keep their Court,   405
The *Ouas*[3], but of no ignoble Fame,
Though she bears a base and servile Name,
Sharp *Oxyacantha*[4], next the *Mulberry* stood,
The *Mulberry* dy'd in hapless Lovers[5] blood.
   Craneia[6], a nymph too lean to be admir'd,   410

---

1. *The Lime-Tree.*
2. *Wood-pear* and *Crab-apple.*
3. *Service-tree*
4. *Barberry*
5. Pyramus and Thisbe
6. Cornelian-berry

But hard-grain'd *Carya*¹ is by all desir'd,
The pretty *Corylus*² so neat and trim,
And *Castanis* with rough ungrateful Skin.
These Nymphs of all their Race live rich and high,
They taste the City Garden Luxury, 415
And Woods their Country *Villa*'s do supply.
   Nor was the *Hawthorn* absent from this place,
All Soils are native to her harden'd Race,
Though her the Fields and Gardens do reject,
She with a thorny Hedge does both protect. 420
*Helvetia*³ rough with Cold and Stones first bred
The Nymph who thence to other Climates fled,
Of her a warlike sturdy Race was born,
Whose dress nor Court nor City can adorn,
But with a faithful hand they both defend 425
While they upon no Garrison depend.
No show, or noisie Grandeur they affect,
But to their Trust they'r constant and exact:
Should you behold 'em rang'd in Battel-array,
All muster'd in due order, you wou'd say, 430
That no *Militia* were so fine and gay.
Let none the Ancients rashly then reproach,
Who cut from hence the Hymeneal Torch.
Since they such safeguards were 'gainst Thieves and Beasts,
Which with an equal force their charge molests. 435
And 'twas commanded they should always bear
Their watchful Twigs before the married Pair.
   With the *Helvetian* Nymph, a pretty Train,
All her Companions to the Circle came.
The fruitful *Bullace* first, whose Off-spring are, 440
Though harsh and sharp, yet moderately fair.
   The prickly *Bramble*, neat and lovely *Rose*

---

1. Wall-nut.
2. Small *Nuts*
3. *Switzerland.*

So nice and coy, they never will dispose
Their valu'd Favours, but some wounds they give
To those who would their guarded Joys receive.   445
   No less a Troop of those gay Nymphs were seen,
Who nobly flourish in Eternal Green,
Unsubject to the Laws o'th'changing Year.
They want no Aids of kindly Beams or Air.
But happy in their own peculiar Spring,   450
While the Pole weeps in showers, they laugh and sing.
The generous *Pyxias* who a Conquest gains
O'r armed Winter with her Host of Rains,
All Ages she sudued (*sic*): devouring Time
In vain endeavours to destroy her prime;   455
Still in her Youth and Beauty she survives,
When all the Spring is dead, she smiles and lives:
Yet though she's obstinate to time and storms,
She's kindly pliable to all curious Forms;
To artful Masters she Obedience lends,   460
And to the ingenious hand with ease she bends.
Into a thousand True-loves knots she twines,
And with a verdant Wall the Flowers confines,
Still looking up with gay and youthful Love
To the triumphing Flow'rs that reign above.   465
Or if you please, she will advance on high,
And with the lofty Trees her stature vie,
And chearfully will any figure take,
VVhether Man, or Lyon, or Bird you make,
Or on her Trunk like a green Parrot show,   470
Or sometimes like a *Hercules* she grow:
And hence *Praxiteles* fair Statues forms,
When with Green Gods the Gardens he adorns.
Nor yet being dead does of less use appear
To the Industrious Artificer: 475
From her the noblest Figures do arise,

---

*The *Box-tree*.

And almost are Immortal Deities;
Of her the *Berecynthian* Pipe is made,
That charms its native Mountain and its shade,
That in such tuneful Harmonies express   480
The Praises of their Goddess *Cibeles*.
VVith this the lovely Females dress their Hair,[1]
That not least powerful Beauty of the Fair,
Their noblest Ornament and th'Lovers snare.
This into form the beauteous Nets still lay   485
That the poor heedless Gazer does betray.
   Agrias[2] is content with easier spoils,
Onely for silly Birds she pitches toyls.
The wanton Bird she stops upon the wing,
And can forbid the insolence of Men.   490
With a Defence the Garden she supplys,
And does perpetually delight the Eyes:
Her shining Leaves a lovely green produce,
And serve at once for Ornament and Use.
Deform'd *December* by her Posie-boughs   495
All deck'd and drest like joyful *April* shows
Cold Winter days she both adorns and chears,
While she her constant springing Livery wears.
   Camaris[3], who in *Winter* give their Birth
Not humbly creeping on the servile Earth,   500
But rear aloft their nobler fruitful heads,
Whose *Sylvan* food unhappy *Janus* feeds.
His hungry Appetite he here destroys,
And both his ravenous Mouths at once destroys.
   Phillyrea, here and *Pyracantha*[4] rise,   505
Whose beauty onely gratifies the Eyes
Of Gods and Men, no Banquets they afford

---

1. Combs made of its Wood.
2. The *Holly*, Hereof Bird-Lime is made.
3. *Strawberry* Tree
4. Evergreen *Privet* and Prickly *Coral*-Tree.

But to the welcome though unbidden Bird,
Here gratefully in *Winter* they repay
For all the Summer Songs that made their Groves so gay.   510
    Next came the melancholy *Yew*, who mourns
With silent Languor at the Warriers Urns,
See where she comes all in black shadow veil'd,
Ah too unhappy Nymph on every side assail'd!
Whom the *Greek* Poets and Historians blame,   515
(Deceiv'd by easie faith and common fame)
Thee as a guilty poisoner they present;
Oh false Aspersers of the Innocent!
If Poets may find credit when they speak,
(At least all those who are not of the *Greek*)   520
No baneful Poison, no Malignant dew
Lurks in, or hangs about the harmless *Yew*,
No secret mischief dares the Nymph invade,
And those are safe that sleep beneath her shade.
    *Nor thou *Arceuthis*,[1] art an Enemy   525
To the soft Notes of charming Harmony.
Falsly the chief of Poets would persuade
That Evil's lodg'd in thy Eternal shade,
Thy Aromatic shade, whose verdant Arms
Even thy own useful fruits secures from harms;   530
Many false Crimes to thee they attribute,
Wou'd no false Virtues too, they wou'd to thee impute.
    But thou *Sabina*,[2] my impartial Muse
Cannot with any honesty excuse,
By thee, the first new sparks of Life, not yet   535
Struck up to shining flame to mature heat,
Sprinkled by thy moist Poison fade and die,
Fatal *Sabina* Nymph of Infamy.
For this the *Cypress* thee companion calls,
Who piously attends at Funerals: 540

---

1. *Juniper* Tree.
2. *Savin*

125

But thou more barbarous, dost thy pow'r employ,
And even the unborn Innocent destroy.
Like Fate destructive thou, without remorse,
While she the Death of even the Ag'd deplores.
   Such *Cyparissus* was, that bashful Boy,   545
Who was belov'd by the bright God of Day;
Of such a tender mind, so soft a Breast,
With so compassionate a Grief opprest,
For wounding his lov'd Dear, that down he lay
And wept, and pin'd his sighing Soul away.   550
Apollo pitying it, renew'd his fate
And to the *Cypress* did the Boy translate,
And gave his hapless life a longer Date.
Then thus decreed the God— and thou oh Tree,
Chief Mourner at all Funerals shall be.   555
And since so small a cause such grief cou'd give,
Be't still thy Talent (pitying youth) to grieve.
Sacred be thou in *Pluto's* dark abodes,
For ever sacred to th'Infernal Gods!
This said, well skill'd in truth he did bequeath   560
Eternal life to the dire Tree of Death,
A substance that no Worm can e'r subdue
Whose never dying Leaves each Day renew,
Whose Figures like aspiring flames still rise,
And with a noble Pride salute the Skies.   565
   Next the fair Nymph that *Phaebus* does adore,
But yet as nice and cold as heretofore:
She hates all fires, and with aversion still
She chides and crackles if the flame she feel.
Yet though she's chast, the burning God no less   570
Adores, and makes his Love his Prophetess.
And even the Murmurs of her scorn do now
For joyful Sounds and happy Omens go.
Nor does the Humble, though the sacred Tree
Fear wounds from any Earthly Enemy;   575
For she beholds when loudest storms abound,
The flying thunder of the Gods around,

Let all the flaming Heav'ns threat as they will
Unmov'd th'undaunted Nymph out-braves it still.
   Oh thou! ———   580
Of all the woody Nations happiest made
Thou greatest Princess of the fragrant shade,
But should the Goddess *Dryas* not allow
That Royal Title to thy Vertue due,
At least her justice must this truth confess   585
If not a Princess, thou'rt a Prophetess,
And all the Glories of immortal Fame
Which conquering Monarchs so much strive to gain;
Is but at best from thy triumphing Boughs
To reach a Garland to adorn their Brows,   590
And after Monarchs, Poets claim a share
As the next worthy thy priz'd wreaths to wear.
*Among that number, do not me disdain,
Me, the most humble of that glorious Train.
I by a double right thy Bounties claim,   595
Both from my Sex, and in *Apollo's* name:
Let me with *Sappho* and *Orinda* be
Oh ever sacred Nymph, adorn'd by thee;
And give my Verses Immortality.
   The tall *Elate* next, and *Peuce* stood   600
The stateliest Sister-Nymphs of all the wood.
The flying Winds sport with their flowing Hair,
While to the dewy Clouds their lofty heads they rear.
As mighty Hills above the Valleys show,
And look with scorn on the descent below,   605
So do these view the Mountains where they grow.
So much above their humbler Tops they rise,
So stood the Giants that besieg'd the Skies,
The terror of the Gods! they having thrown
Huge *Ossa* on the Leafy *Pelion*,   610
The *Firr* with the proud *Pine* thus threatening stands
Lifting to Heav'n two hundred warring hands,

---

*The Translatress in her own Person speaks

127

In this vast prospect they with ease survey
The various figur'd Land and boundless Sea,
With joy behold the Ships their timber builds,   615
How they've with Cities stor'd once spacious Fields.
   This grove of *English* Nymphs, this noble train
In a large Circle compass in their Queen,
The Scepter bearing *Dryas* ————
Her Throne-arising Hillock where she sat   620
With all the Charms of Majesty and State,
With awful Grace the numbers she survey'd,
Dealing around the favours of her shade.
   If I the voice of the loud winds cou'd take
Which the re echoing Oaks do agitate,   625
'Twou'd not suffice to celebrate thy Name
Oh sacred *Dryas* of Immortal Fame.
If we a faith can give Antiquity
That sings of many Miracles, from thee
In the worlds Infant Age Mankind broke forth,   630
From thee the noble Race receiv'd their Birth;
Thou then in a green tender Bark wert clad,
But in *Deucalion's* Age a rougher covert had,
More hard and warm, with crusted white all o'r,
As noble Authors sung in times of yore;   635
Approv'd by some, condemn'd and argu'd down
By the vain troop of Sophists, and the Gown,
The scoffing Academy, and the Schools
Of *Pyrrho*; who Traditions over-rule:
But let 'em doubt, yet they must grant this truth   640
Those Brawny Men that then the Earth brought forth,
Did on thy Acorns feed, and feast and thrive
And with this wholsom Nourishment survive
In health and strength an equal Age with thee,
Secur'd from all the Banes of Luxury.   645
Oh happy Age! oh Nymph Divinely good!
That mak'st thy shade Man's house, thy fruit his food.
When onely Apples of the Wood did pass
For noble Banquets spread on beds of grass.

Tables not yet by any Art debauch'd, 650
And fruit that ne'r the Grudgers hand reproached.
Thy Bounties *Ceres* were of little use,
And thy sweet food ill Manners did produce:
Unluckily they did thy Virtues find
With that of the wild Boar and the hunted Hind; 655
With all wild Beasts on which their Luxury prey'd,
While new Desires their Appetites invade.
The Natures they partake of what they eat,
And salvage they become as was their Meat.

Hence the Republick of the world did cease, 660
Hence they might date the forfeit of their peace.
The common good was now peculiar made,
A generous Int'rest now became a Trade,
And Men began their Neighbour's rights t'invade.
For now they measur'd out their common ground 665
And outrages commit t'inlarge their Bound:
Their own seem'd despicable, poor and small;
Each wants more room and wou'd be Lord of all.
The Plowman with disdain his Field surveys,
Forsakes the Land, and plows the faithless Seas. 670
The Fool in these deep furrows seeks his gain,
Despising Dangers, and induring pain.
The sacred Oak her peaceful Mansion leaves
Transplanted to the Mountains of the Waves.

Oh *Dryas*, Patron to th'industrious kind, 675
If Man were wise and wou'd his safety find;
What perfect Bliss thy happy Shade wou'd give?
And Houses that their Masters wou'd out-live.
All necessaries thou afford'st alone
For harmless Innocence to live upon, 680
Strong yokes for Oxen, handles for the Plow,
What Husbandry requires thou dost allow;
But if the madness of desiring Gain,
Or wild Ambition agitate the Brain,
Straight to a wandering Ship they Thee transfer, 685
And none more justly serves the Mariner.

Thou cutst the Air, dost on the Waves rebound,
Wild Death and Fury raging all around,
Didsdaining to behold the manag'd Wood,
Out-brave the Storms and baffle the rude Flood.   690
    To Swine, O richest Oak, thy Acorns leave,
And search for Man what e'er the Earth can give,
All that the spacious Universe brings forth,
What Land and Sea conceals of any worth,
Bring Aromaticks from the distant East,   } 695
And Gold so dangerous from the rifl'd West,
What e'er the boundless Appetite can feast.
    With thee, the utmost bounds of Earth w'invade,
By thee the unlockt Orb is common made.
By thee——   700
The great Republique of the World revives,
And o'er the Earth luxurious traffick thrives;
If *Argos* Ship were valued at that rate
(Which Ancients Poets so much celebrate,
From Neighbouring *Colchos* only bringing home   705
The Golden Fleece from Seas whose Tracts were known:
If of the dangers they so much have spoke
(More worthy smiles) of the *Cyanean* Rock,
What Oceans then of Fame shall thee suffice?
What waves of Eloquence can sing thy Praise?   710
O sacred Oak, that great *Columbus* bore   }
IO! thou bearer of a happier Ore,
Than celebrated *Argo* did before.
    And Drake's brave Oak that's past to World unknown,
Whose Toils, O *Phebus*, were so like thy own;   715
Who round the Earths vast Globe triumphant rode,
Deserves the celebration of a God.
O let the *Pegasean* Ship no more
Be worshipt on the too unworthy Shore,
After her watery life, let her become   720
A fixt Star shining equal with the Ram.
Long since the Duty of a Star she's done,
And round the Earth with guiding Light has shone.

Oh how has Nature blest the British land,
Who both the valued *Indies* can command!   725
What tho thy Banks the Cedars do not grace
Those lofty Beauties of fam'd *Libanus*.
The Pine, or Palm of *Idumean* Plaines,
Arabs rich Wood or its sweet smelling Greens,
Or lovely Plantan whose large leafy boughs   730
A pleasant and a noble shade allows.
She has thy warlike Groves and Mountains blest
With sturdy Oaks, ore all the World the best,
And for the happy Islands sure Defence.
Has wall'd it with a Mote of Seas immense,   735
While to declare her Safety and thy Pride,
With Oaken Ships that Sea is fortifi'd.
   Nor was that Adoration vainly made,
Which to the Oak the Ancient Druids paid,
Who reasonably believed a God within.   740
Where such vast wonders were produc'd and seen.
Nor was it the dull Piety alone,
And superstition of our *Albion*,
Nor ignorance of the future Age, that paid
Honours Divine to thy surprising shade.   745
But they foresaw the Empire of the Sea,
Great *Charles*, should hold from the Triumphant Thee.
   No wonder then that Age should thee Adore,
Who gav'st out sacred Oracles heretofore,
The hidden Pleasure of the Gods was then   750
In a hoarse Voice deliver'd out to Men.
So vapors from *Cyrrhean* Caverns broke
Inspir'd *Apollo*'s Priestess when she spoke.
While ravisht the fair Enthusiastic stood,
Upon her *Tripos*, raging with the God.   755
So Priest Inspir'd with sacred fury shook,
When the Winds ruffld the *Dodonian* Oak,
And tost their branches, till a dreadful sound
Of awful horror they proclaim around.
Like frantic Bacchanals; and while they move   760

Possess with trembling all the sacred Grove.
Their rifl'd leaves the tempest bore away,
And their torn Boughs scatter'd on all sides lay.
The tortur'd thicket knew not that there came
A God Triumphant in the Hurricane, 765
Till the wing'd winds with an amazing cry,
Deliver'd down the pressing Deity.
Whose thundering voice strange secrets did unfold,
And wondrous things of Worlds to come he told.
But truths so veil'd in obscure Eloquence, 770
They 'muze the Adoring Crowd with double sense.
 But by Divine decree the Oak no more,
Declares security as heretofore,
With words, or voice, yet to the listening Wood,
Her differing Murmurs still are understood: 775
For sacred Divinations, while the sound,
Informs, all but Humanity, around
Nor e'er did *Dryas* Murmur awful truth
More clear and plain, from her Prophetic mouth,
Than when she spoke to the *Chaonian* Wood, 780
While all the Groves with eager silence stood.
And with erected Leaves themselves dispose,
To listen to the Language of her Boughs.
 You see (oh my companions) that the Gods,
Threaten a dire Destruction to the Woods, 785
And to all human kind— the black portents
Are seen, of many sinister Events;
But lest their quick Approach too much should press,
(Oh my astonish'd Nymphs) your Tenderness,
The Gods command me to foretel your Doom, 790
And prepossess ye with the Fate to come.
With heedful Reverence then their Will observe,
And in your Barks deep Chinks my Words preserve:
Believe me, Nymphs, nor is your Faith in vain,
This Oaken Trunk in which conceal'd I am 795
From a long honored Ancient Lineage came,
Who in that *Dodonian* Grove first spoke,

When with astonish'd awe the Sacred Valley shook.
'Know then that *Brutus* by unlucky Fate
'Murdering his Sire, did bear an immortal Hate   800
  'To his own Kingdom, who's ungrateful shore
'He leaves with Vows ne'er to revisit more.
'Then to *Epirus* a sad Exile came,
'(Unhappy Son who hast a Father slain,
'But happy Father of the *British* Name.)   805
'There by victorious Arms he did restore
'Those Scepters once the Race of *Priam* bore.
'In their paternal Thrones his Kindred plac'd,
'And by that Piety his fatal Crime defac'd.
  'There *Jupiter* disdain'd not to relate   810
'Thorough an Oaken Mouth his future Fate.
'Who for his Grandsire's, great *Æneas*, sake
'Upon the Royal Youth will pity take:
'Whose Toils to his shall this Resemblance bear
'A long and tedious Wandring to endure.   815
''Tis said the Deity-retaining Oak
'Bursting her Bark, thus to the Hero spoke,
'Whose Voice the Nymphs surpriz'd with awful Dread,
'Who in *Chaonian* Groves inhabited.
'Oh noble *Trojan* of great *Sylvia*'s Blood,   820
'Haste from the Covert of this threatening Wood.
'A Mansion here the Fates will not permit,
'Vast Toils and Dangers thou'rt to conquer yet,
'Ere for a murder'd Father thou canst be
'Absolv'd, tho innocently slain by thee,   825
'But much must bear by Land, and much by Sea.
'Then arm thy solid Mind, thy Virtues raise,
'And thro' thy rough Adventures cut new Ways,
'Whose End shall crown thee with immortal Bays.
'Tho *Hercules* so great a Fame atchiev'd,   830
'His Conquests but to th'Western *Cales* arriv'd:
'There finish'd all his Glories and his Toils,
'He wish'd no more, nor sought more distant Spoils.
'But the great Labors which thou hast begun

133

'Must, fearless of the Oceans Threats go on.   835
'And this remember, at thy lanching forth,
'To set thy full spread Sails against the North.
'In *Charles's Wain* thy Fates are born above
'Bright Stars descended from thy Grandsire *Jove*,
'Of motion certain, tho they slowly move.   840
'The *Bear* too shall assist thee in thy course
'With all her Constellations glittering Force.
'And as thou goest, thy Right Hand shall destroy
'Twice six *Gomerstish* Tyrants in thy way.
'Tho exil'd from the World, disdain all Fear,   845
'The Gods another World for thee prepare,
'Which in the Bosom of the deep conceal'd
'From Ages past. shall be to thee reveal'd.
'Reserv'd, O *Brutus*, to renown thy Fame,
'And shall be bless'd still with thy Race and Name,   850
'All that the Air surrounds, the Fates decree   ⎫
'To *Brutus* and *Æneas* Progeny,   ⎬
'*Æneas* all the Land, and Brutus all the Sea.   ⎭
This said the God, from the prophetick Oak,
Who stretching out her Branches further spoke: 855
'Here fill thy hands with Acorns from my Tree,   ⎫
'Which in thy tedious Toils of use may be,   ⎬
'And Witnesses of all I promise thee.   ⎭
'And when thy painful wand'ring shall be o'er,
'And thou arriv'd on happy *Britain*'s shore,   860
'Then in her fruitful Soil these Acorns sow,
'Which to vast Woods of mighty use shall grow.
'Not their *Chaonian* Mother's sacred Name
'Shall o'er the World be sung with greater F'ame.
'Then holy Druids thou shalt consecrate,   865
'My Honor and my Rites to celebrate.
'*Teutates* in the Sacred Oak shall grow,
'To give bless'd Omens of the *Misseltoe*.
Thus spake the Oak— with reverend Awe believ'd,
And in no one Prediction was deceiv'd.   870

My Lineage from *Chaonian* Acorns came,
I two Descents from that first Parent am;
And now Oraculous Truths to you proclaim.
My Grandam Oak her Blooming Beauties bore,
When first the *Danish* Fleet surpriz'd our Shore.　　　875
When *Thor* and Tuisco and the *Saxon* Gods
Were angry with their once belov'd Abodes,
Her Age two hundred years; a small Account
To what our long-lived Numbers do amount,
Such Prodigies then she saw as we behold,　　　880
And such our Ruins, as their signs foretold.
Now from the *Caledonian* Mountains came
New risen Clouds that cover'd all the Plain,
The quiet *Tweed* regards her Bounds no more,
But driv'n by Popular Winds usurps the Shore;　　　885
In her wild Course a horrid Murmur yields,
And frightens with her Sound the *English* Fields.
Nor did they hear in vain, or vainly fear
Those raging Prologues to approaching War.
But Silver Showers did soon the Foe subdue,　　　890
Weapons the Noble *English* never knew.
The People who for Peace so lavish were,
Did after buy the Merchandise more dear.
Curst Civil War even Peace betray'd to Guilt,
And made her blush with the first Blood was spilt.　　　895
O cruel Omens of those future Woes,
Which now sate brooding in the Senate House!
That Den of Mischief, where obscur'd she lyes,
And hides her purple Face from human Eyes.
The working Furies there, lay unreveal'd　　　900
Beneath the Privilege of the *House* conceal'd.
There, by the Malice of the Great and Proud,
And unjust Clamors of the frantick Crowd,
The Great, the learned *Strafford* met his Fate;
O Sacred Innocence! what can expiate　　　905
For guiltless Blood, but Blood? and much must flow

Both from the Guilty and the Faultless too.
O *Worcester*, condemn'd by Fate to be
The Mournful Witness of our Misery,
And to bewail our first Intestine Wars: 910
By thy soft *Severn*'s Murmurs, and her Tears;
Wars that more formidable did appear
Even at their End, than their Beginnings were.
   Me to *Kintonian* Hills[1] some God convey,
That I the horrid Valley may survey;   915
Which like a River seem'd of human Blood,
Swell'd with the numerous Bodies of the Dead.
What Slaughters makes fierce *Rupert* round the Field,
Whose Conquests Pious *Charles* with Sighs beheld;
And had not Fate the Course of Things forbade,   920
This Day an End of all our Woes was made.
   But our Success the angry Gods controul,
And stopt our Race of Glory near the Goal.
Where e'er the *British* Empire did extend,
The Tyrant War with Barbarous Rigor reign'd,   925
From the remotest Parts it rifled Peace
From the *Belerian Horn[2] even to the Orcades.
The Fields opprest, no joyful Harvests bear,
War ruin'd all the Product of the Year,
Unhappy *Albion!* by what Fury stung?   930
What Serpent of *Eumenides* has flung
 His Poison thro' thy Veins? thou bleed'st all o'er,
Art all one Wound, one universal Gore.
Unhappy *Newberry*, I thy fatal Field,
(Cover'd with mighty Slaughters, thrice beheld.)   935
In horrors thou *Philippi*'s Fields outvi'd
Which twice the Civil Gore of *Romans* di'd.
Long mutual Loss, and the alternate Weight
Of equal Slaughters, pois'd each others Fate.

---

1. Keinton-Field. Edge-Hill.

2. * *S.Burien*,the uttermost Point of *Cornwal*.

Uncertain Ruin waver'd to and fro,   940
And knew not where to fix the deadly Blow;
At last in *Northern* Fields like Lightening broke;
And *Naseby* doubl'd every fatal Stroke.
But, Oh ye Gods, permit me not to tell
The Woes that after this, the Land befel: 945
Oh, keep 'em to yourselves, lest they shou'd make
Humanity your Rites and Shrine forsake:
To future Ages let 'em not be known,
For wretched *England*'s credit, and your own.
   And take from me, ye Gods, Futurity,   950
And let my Oracles all silent lye,
Rather than by my Voice they shou'd declare
The dire Events of *England*'s Civil War.
And yet my Sight a confus'd Prospect fills,
A *Chaos* all deform'd, a Heap of Ills;   955
Such as no mortal Eyes cou'd e'r behold,
Such as no human Language can unfold.
But now————
The Conquering evil Genius of the Wars,
The impious Victor all before him bears;   960
And oh, —behold the Sacred Vanquish'd flies,
And tho in a *Plebean*'s mean Disguise,
I know his God-like Face; the Monarch sure
Did ne'er dissemble till this fatal hour.
But oh he flies, distrest, forlorn he flies,   965
And seeks his Safety 'mong his Enemies.
His Kingdoms all he finds hostile to be,
No place to th'vanquish'd proves a Sanctu'ry.
Thus Royal *Charles*————————-
From his own People cou'd no safety gain,   970
Alas, the King! (their Guest) implores in vain.
The Pilot thus the burning Vessel leaves,
And trusts what most he fears, the threatning Waves.
But oh the cruel Flood with rude Disdain
Throws him all struggling to the Flames again: 975
So did the *Scots*, alas, what shou'd they do,

That Prize of War (the Soldiers Interest now)
By Prayers and Threatnings back they strive to bring,
But the wise *Scot* will yield to no such thing;
And *England* to retrieve him buys her King.   980
Oh shame to future Worlds! who did command,
As powerful Lord of all the Sea and Land,
Is now a Captive-Slave expos'd to Sale;
And Villainy o'er Virtue must prevail.
The Servant his bought Master bears away,   985
Oh shameful Purchase of so glorious Prey.
But yet, O *Scotland*, far be it from me,
To charge thee wholly with this Infamy;
Thy Nations Virtues shall reverse that Fate,
And for the Criminal Few shall expiate: 990
Yet for these Few the Innocent Rest must feel,
The dire Effects of the avenging Steel.
    But now by Laws to God and Man unknown,
Their Sovereign, Gods anointed they dethrone,
Who to the *Isle of Wight* is prisoner sent: 995
What Tongue, what cruel Hearts do not lament?
That thee, O *Scotland*, with just Anger moves,
And Kent who valued Liberty so loves;
And thee, O *Wales*, of still as noble Fame,
As were the ancient *Britains* whence ye came.   1000
But why should I distinctly here relate
All I behold, the many Battels fought
Under the Conduct still of angry Stars:
Their new-made Wounds, and old ones turn'd to Scars;
The Blood that did the trembling *Ribla* dy,   1005
Stopping its frighted Stream that strove to fly.
Or thou, O *Medway*, swell'd with Slaughters, born
Above the flowery Banks that did thee once adorn.
Or why, O *Colchester*, shou'd I rehearse
Thy brave united Courage and thy Force,   1010
Or Deaths of those illustrious Men relate,
Who did with thee deserve a kinder Fate.
Or why the miserable Murders tell

Of Captives who by cooler Malice fell.
Nor to your Griefs will this Addition bring,   1015
The sad Idea's of a Martyred King.
A King who all the Wounds of Fortune bore,
Nor will his mournful Funerals deplore,
Lest that celestial Piety (of Fame
O'er all the World) should my sad Accents blame.   1020
Since Death he still esteem'd how e'er 'twas given,
The greatest Good, and noblest Gift of Heaven.
But I deplore Man's wretched Wickedness,
(Oh horrid to beheard (*sic*), or to express.)
Whom even Hell can ne'er enough torment   1025
With her eternal Pains and Punishment.
    But oh what do I see! alas they bring
Their Sacred Master forth, their God-like King,
There on a Scaffold rais'd in solemn State,
And plac'd before the Royal Palace Gate,   1030
'Midst of his Empire the black Deed was done,
While Day, and all the World, were looking on.
By common Hangman's Hands—Here stopt the Oak,
When from the bottom of its Root there broke
A thousand Sighs, which to the Sky she lifts,   1035
Bursting her solid Bark, into a thousand Clefts.
Each Branch her Tributary sorrow gives,
And Tears run trickling from her mournful Leaves;
Such numbers after rainy Nights they shed,
When showering Clouds that did surround her Head,   1040
Are by the rising Goddess of the Morn
Blown off, and flie before the approaching Sun.
At which the Troop of the Green Nymphs around
Ecchoing her Sighs, in wailing Accents groan'd,
Whose piercing sounds from far were understood,   1045
And the loud Tempest shook the wondering Wood:
And then a cruel Silence did succeed,
As in the gloomy Mansions of the Dead.
But after a long awful Interval
Dryas assum'd her sad Prophetick Tale.   1050

Now *Britany* o'erwhelm'd with many a Wound,
Her Head lopt off, in her own Blood lies drown'd:
A horrid Carcase, without Mind or Soul,
A Trunk not to be known, deform'd and foul.
And now who wou'd not hope there shou'd have been   1055
After so much Death, a quiet Scene,
Or rather with their Monarch's Funeral
Eternal Sleep shou'd not have seis'd 'em all.
But nothing less, for in the room of One,
Who govern'd justly on his peaceful Throne,   1060
A thousand Heads sprung up, deform'd and base,
With a tumultuous and ignoble Race;
The vile, the vulgar Off-spring of the Earth,
Insects of poisonous kinds, of monsterous Birth,
And ravenous Serpents now the Land infest;   1065
And *Cromwel* viler yet than all the rest.
That Serpent even upon the Marrow preys,
Devouring Kingdoms with insatiate Jaws.
Now Right and Wrong (mere Words confounded ly)
Rage sets no bounds to her Impiety;   1070
And having once transgrest the Rules of Shame,
Honor or Justice counts and empty Name.
In every Street, as Pastime for the Crowd,
Erected Scaffolds reek'd with Noble Blood.
Prisons were now th'Apartments of the Brave,   1075
Whom Tyranny commits, and only Death retrieve;
Whose Paths were crowded ere the Morning dawn,
Some to the Dungeons, some to Gibbets drawn.
But tir'd-out Cruelty pauses for a while,
To take new Breath amidst her Barbarous Toil.   1080
So does not Avarice, she unwearied still,
Ne'er stops her greedy Hand from doing ill;
The Warrior may a while his Spear forsake,
But Sequestrators will no Respit take.
What a long Race of Kings laid up with Care,   1085
The Gifts of happy Peace, and Spoils of War,
What ever liberal Piety did present,

Or the Religion (all magnificent)
Of our Fore-fathers to the Church had given,
And consecrated to the Pow'rs of Heav'n,   1090
Altars, or whatso'er cou'd guilty be
Of tempting Wealth, or fatal Loyalty,
Was not enough to satisfie the Rage
Of a few Earth-begotten Tyrants of the Age.
The impious Rout thought it a trivial thing   1095
To rob the Houses of their God and King,
Their Sacrilege admitting of no Bound,
Rejoyc'd to see 'em levell'd with the Ground;
As if the Nation (wicked and unjust)
Had even in Ruin found a certain Lust,   1100
On every side the labouring Hammers sound,
And Strokes from mighty Hatchets do rebound:
On every side the groaning Earth sustains
The ponderous weight of Stones and wonderous Beams.
Fiercely they ply their Work, with such a noise,   1105
As if some mighty Structure they wou'd raise
For the proud Tyrant; no, this clamorous Din
Is not for building but demolishing.
—When (my Companions) these sad things you see,
And each beholds the dead Beams of her parent Tree,   1110
Long since repos'd in Palaces of Kings,
Torn down by furious Hands as useless things;
Then know your Fate is come; those Hands that cou'd
From Houses tear dead Beams, and long hewn Wood,
Those cruel Hands by unresisted Force,   1115
Will for your living Trunks find no remorse.
   Religion, which was great of old, commands,
No Woods shou'd be profaned by impious Hands,
Those noble Seminaries for the Fleet,
Plantations that make Towns and Cities great: 1120
Those Hopes of War, and Ornaments of Peace
Shou'd live secure from any Outrages,
Which now the barbarous Conqueror will invade,
Tear up your Roots, and rifle all your shade,

For gain they'll sell you to the covetous Buyer,   1125
A Sacrifice to every common Fire.
  They'll spare no Race of Trees of any Age,
But murder infant Branches in their Rage:
Elms, Beeches, tender Ashes shall be fell'd,
And even the Grey and Reverend Bark must yield: 1130
The soft, the murmuring Troop shall be no more,
No more with Musick charm as heretofore,
No more each little Bird shall build her House,
And sing in her Hereditary Boughs,
But only *Philomel* shall celebrate   1135
In mournful Notes a new unhappy Fate;
The banish'd *Hamadryads* must be gone,
And take their flight with sad, but silent Moan;
For a Celestial Being ne'er complains,
Whatever be her Grief, in noisie Strains.   1140
The Wood-Gods fly, and whither shall they go,
Not all the *British* Orb can scarce allow,
A Trunk secure for them to rest in now.
  But yet these wild Saturnals shall not last,
Oppressing Vengeance follows on too fast;   1145
She shakes her brandish'd Steel, and still denies
Length to immoderate Rage and Cruelties.
Do not despond, my Nymphs; that wicked Birth
Th'avenging Powers will chase from off the Earth;
Let 'em hew down the Woods, destroy and burn,   1150
And all the lofty Groves to Ashes turn;
Yet still there will not want a Tree to yield
Timber enough old *Tiburn* to rebuild,
Where they may hang at last; and this kind one
Shall then revenge the Woods of all their Wrong.   1150
In the mean time (for Fate not always shows
A swift complyance to our Wish and Vows)
The Off-spring of great *Charles* forlorn and poor,
And exil'd from their cruel native Shore,
Wander in Foreign Kingdoms, where in vain   1160
They seek those Aids, alas, they cannot gain;

For still their pressing Fate pursues 'em hard,
And scarce a place of Refuge will afford.
O pious Son of such a holy Sire!
Who can enough thy Fortitude admire?   1165
How often tost by storms of Land and Sea,
Yet unconcern'd thy Fate thou didst survey,
And her Fatigues still underwent with Joy.
Oh Royal Youth, pursue thy just Disdain,
Let Fortune and her Furies frown in vain,   1170
Till tir'd with her Injustice she give out,
And leave her giddy Wheel for thee to turn about.
   Then that great Scepter which no human Hand
From the tenacious Tyrant can command,
Scorning the bold Usurper to adorn,   1175
Shall ripe and falling to thy Hand be born.
   But oh, he rowzes now before his time!
Illustrious Youth, whose Bravery is a Crime,
Alas, what wilt thou do? Ah, why so fast?
The Dice of Fate, alas, not yet are cast.   1180
While thou all fire, fearless of future Harms,
And prodigal of life, assumest thy Arms.
And even provoking Fame he cuts his way
Through hostile Fleets, and a rude Winters Sea.
But neither shall his daring Course oppose,   1185
Even to those Shores so very late his Foes,
And still to be suspected; but mean while
The *Oliverian* Demons of the Isle,
With all Hells Deities, with Fury burn,
To see great *Charles* preparing to return;   1190
They call up their Winds of dreadful Force
In vain, to stop his sacred Vessels course.
In vain their Storms a Ruine do prepare,
For what Fate means to take peculiar care;
And trembling find great *Cesar* safe at Land,   1195
By Heav'n conducted, not by Fortunes Hand.
   But *Scotland*, you your King recal in vain,
While you your unchang'd Principles retain;

But yet the time shall come, when some small share
Of Glory, that great Honor shall confer,   1200
When you a conquering Hero forth shall guide,
While Heaven and the Stars are on his side,
Who shall the exiled King in Peace recal,
And *England*'s Genius be esteem'd by all:
But this, not yet my Nymphs,—but now's the time,   1205
When the illustrious heir of *Fergus* line,
From full a hundred Kings, shall mount the throne,
Who now the Temple enters, and at *Scone*,
After the ancient manner he receives the Crown;
But, oh, with no auspicious Omens done,   1210
The Left Hand of the Kingdom put it on.
  But now th'insulting conqueror draws nigh,
Disturbing the August Solemnity;
When with Revenge and Indignation fir'd,
And by a father's Murder well inspir'd,   1215
The brave, the Royal Youth for War prepares,
O Heir most worthy of thy hundred Scepter'd Ancestors:
With Thoughts all Glorious, now he sallies forth;
Nor will he trust his Fortune in the North,
That Corner of his Realms, nor will his haste   1220
Lazily wait till coming Winter's past;
He scorns that Aid, nor will he hope t'oppose
High Mountains 'gainst the Fury of his Foes,
Nor their surrounding Force will he engage,
Or stay the Pressures of a shameful Siege;   1225
But boldly further on resolves t'advance,
And give a generous Loose to Fortunes Chance.
And shut from distant *Tay* he does essay
To *Thames*, even with his Death to force his way.
Behind he leaves his trembling Enemies,   1230
Amaz'd at this stupendous Enterprise.
  And now the wish'd for happy Day appears,
Sought for so long by *Britain*'s Prayers and Tears;
The King returns, and with a mighty Hand,
Avow'd Revenger of his Native Land.   1235

And through a thousand Dangers and Extremes,
Marches a Conqueror to *Sabrina*'s Streams;
(Ah, wou'd to Heaven *Sabrina* had been *Thames*.)
So wish'd the King, but the persuasive Force
Of kind mistaken Councils stopt his Course.   1240
   Now, warlike *England*, rouze at these Alarms,
Provide your Horses, and assume your Arms,
And fall on the Usurper, now for shame,
If Piety be not Pretence and Name;
Advance the Work Heaven has so well begun,   1245
Revenge the Father, and restore the Son.
No more let that old Cant destructive be,
Religion, Liberty, and Property.
No longer let that dear-bought Cheat delude,
(Oh you too credulous, senseless Multitude,)   1250
Words only form'd more easily to enslave,
By every popular and pretending Knave.
But now your bleeding Land expects you shou'd
Be wise, at the expence of so much Blood;
Rouze then, and with awaken'd Sense prepare   1260
To reap the Glory of this Holy War,
In which your King and Heaven have equal share.
His Right Divine let every Voice proclaim,
And a just Ardor every Soul inflame.
   But *England*'s evil Genius watchful still   1265
To ruin Virtue, and incourage Ill;
Industrious, even as *Cromwel*, to subvert
Honor and Loyalty in every Heart;
A baneful Drug of four-fold Poison makes,
And an infernal sleepy Asp he takes   1270
Of cold and fearful Nature, adds to this
Opium that binds the Nerves with Laziness,
Mixt with the Venom of vile Avarice:
Which all the Spirits benum, as when y'approach
The chilling wonderful *Torpedo*'s Touch.   1275
Next drops from *Lethe*'s Stream he does infuse,
And every Brest besprinkles with the Juice,

Till a deep Lethargy o'er all *Britain* came,
Who now forgot their Safety and their Fame.
Yet still Great *Charles*'s Valour stood the Test;   1280
By Fortune tho forsaken and opprest,
Witness the Purple of *Sabrina*'s Stream,
And the *Red Hill*, not call'd so now in vain.
And *Worster* thou, who did the Misery bear,
And saw'st the End of a long fatal War.   1285
  The King, tho vanquish'd, still his Fate outbraves,
And was the last the captiv'd City leaves;
Which from the Neighbouring Hills he does survey,
Where round about his bleeding Numbers lay.
He saw 'em rifled by th'insulting Foe,   1290
And fights for those he cannot rescue now.
But yet his Troops will rally once again,
Those few escap'd, all scatter'd o'er the Plain;
Disdain and Anger now resolves to try
How to repair this Day's Fatality,   1295
The King has sworn to conquer, or to dye.
Darby and *Willmot*,Chiefs of mighty Fame,
With that bold lovely Youth, great *Buckingham*,
Fiercer than Lightening; to his Monarch dear,
That brave *Achates* worth *Æneas* Care,   1300
Applaud his great Resolve! there's no delay
But toward the Foe in haste they take their way,
Not by vain hopes of a new Victory fir'd,
But by a kind Despair alone inspir'd.
This was the King's Resolve, and those great Few   1305
Whom Glory taught to die, as well as to subdue,
Who knew that Death and the reposing Grave
No Foes were to the Wretched or the Brave.
  But oh this noble Courage did not rest
In each ungenerous unconsidering Brest,   1310
They fearfully forsake their General,
Who now in vain the flying Cowards call,
Deaf to his Voice will no Obedience yield;
But in their hasty Flight scowr o'er the dreadful Field.

Oh vainly gallant Youth, what pitying God   1315
Shall free thee from this Soul-oppressing Load
Of Grief and Shame; abandon'd and betray'd
By perjur'd Slaves, whom thou hast fed and pay'd.
Prest with more Woes than mortal Force could bear,
And Fortune still resolv'd to be severe.   1320
But yet that God————
To whom no Wonders are impossible
Will to preserve thee, work a Miracle.
And for the sacred Father's Martyrdom
Will with a Crown reward the injur'd Son,   1325
While thou, great *Charles*, with a prevailing Pray'r
Dost to the Gods commend the safety of thy Heir;
And the Celestial Court of Powers Divine
By one Consent do in the *Chorus* joyn.
But why, oh why must I reveal the Doom,   1330
(Oh my Companions) of the years to come;
And why divulge the Mysteries that lye
Inroll'd long since in Heav'ns vast Treasury,
 In Characters which no Dreamer can unfold,
Nor ever yet Prophetick Rapture told;   1335
Nor the small Fibres of the victim'd Beast,
Or Birds which sacred Auguries have exprest;
No Stars, nor any Divination Shows
Made Mystick by the Murmurs of the Boughs.
Yet I must on, with a Divine Presage,   1340
And tell the Wonders of the coming Age.
In that far part where the rich *Salop* gains
An ample View o'er all the Western Plains,
A Grove appears, which *Boscobel* they name,
Not known to Maps; a Grove of scanty Fame,   1345
Scarce any human thing does there intrude,
But it enjoys it self in its own Solitude.
And yet henceforth no celebrated Shade,
Of all the *British* Groves shall be more Glorious made.
Near this obscure and destin'd happy Wood,   1350
A Sacred House of lucky Omen stood,

White Lady call'd; and old Records relate
'Twas once————
To Men of Holy Orders consecrate;
But to a King a refuge now is made, 1355
The first that gives a wearied Monarch Bread.
Oh Present of a wonderous Excellence!
That can relieve the Hunger of a Prince.
Fortune shall here a better Face put on,
And here the King shall first the King lay down; 1360
Here he dismisses all his Mourning Friends,
Whom to their kinder Stars he recommends,
With Eyes all drown'd in Tears, their Fate to see,
But unconcern'd at his own Destiny:
Here he puts off those Ornaments he wore 1365
Through all the Splendor of his Life before;
Even his Blew Garter he will now discharge,
Nor keep the Warlike Figure of Saint George ,
That holy Champion now is vanquish'd quite;
Alas, the Dragon has subdu'd the Knight; 1370
His Crown, that restless weight of Glory now
Divests a while from his more easie Brow:
And all those charming Curls that did adorn
His Royal Head — those Jetty Curls are shorn;
Himself he cloaths in a coarse Russet Weed, 1375
Nor was the poor Man feign'd, but so indeed;
And now the greatest King the World e'er saw
Is subject to the Houses ancient Law.
(A Convent once, which Poverty did profess,
Here, here puts off all worldly Pomp and Dress,) 1380
And like a Monk a sad Adieu he takes
Of all his Friends, and the false World forsakes.
But yet ere long, even this humble State,
Alas, shall be denied him by his Fate;
She drives him forth even from this mean Abode, 1385
Who wanders now a Hermit in the Wood,
Hungry and tir'd, to rest and seek his Food.
The dark and lonely Shade conceals the King,

Who feeds on Flowers, and drinks the murmuring Spring;
More happy here than on a restless Throne,   1390
Cou'd he but call'd those Shades and Springs his own:
No longer Fate will that Repose allow,
Who even of Earth itself deprives him now.
A Tree will hardly here a Seat afford
Amidst her Boughs, to her abandon'd Lord.   1395
   Then (O my Nymphs) you who your Monarch love,
To save your Darling, hasten to that Grove;
(Nor think I vain Propheticks do express)
In silence let each Nymph her trunk possess;
O'er all the Woods and Plains let not a Tree   1400
Be uninhabited by a Deity;
While I the largest Forest Oak inspire,
And with you to this Leafy Court retire.
There keep a faithful Watch each night and day,
And with erected Heads the Fields survey,   1405
Lest any impious Soldier pass that way:
And shou'd profanely touch that Pledge of Heaven,
Which to our guarding Shade in charge was given:
Here then, my Nymphs, your King you shall receive,
And safety in your darkest Coverts give.   1410
   But ha, what rustick Swain is that I see
Sleeping beneath the Shade of yonder Tree,
Upon whose knotty Root he leans his Head,
And on the Mossy Ground has made his bed?
And why alone? Alas, some Spy I fear,   1415
For only such a Wretch would wander here,
Who even the Winds and Showers of Rain defies,
Out-daring all the Anger of the Skies.
Observe his Face, see his disordered Hair
Is ruffl'd by the Tempest-beaten Air.   1420
Yet look what Tracts of Grief have ag'd his Face,
Where hardly twenty years have run their Race,
Worn out with numerous Toils; and even in sleep
Sighs seem to heave his Brest, his Eyes to weep.
Nor is that Color of his Face his own,   1425
That sooty Veil, for some Disguise put on,

To keep the Nobler Part from being known;
For 'midst of all—something of Sacred Light
Beams forth, and does inform my wondering sight,
And now—arises to my View more bright.   1430
Ha—can my Eyes deceive me, or am I
At last no true presaging Deity?
Yet if I am, that wretched Rustick Thing,
Oh Heavens, and all your Powers, must be the King.
—Yes 'tis the King! his Image all Divine   1435
Breaks thro' that Cloud of Darkness; and a Shine
Gilds all the sooty Vizar! —but alas,
Who is't approaches him with such a Pace?
Oh—'tis no Traytor, the just Gods I find
Have still a pitying Care of human kind.   1440
This is the Gallant, Loyal *Carles*, thrown
(By the same Wreck by which his King's undone)
Beneath our Shades, he comes in Pious Care
(Oh happy Man! than *Cromwel* happier far
On whom ill Fate this Honor does confer)   1445
He tells the King the Woods are overspread
With Villains arm'd to search that Prize, his Head:
Now poorly set to sale; — the Foe is nigh,
What shall they do? Ah whither shall they fly?
They from the danger hasty Counsel took,   1450
And by some God inspir'd, ascend my Oak,
My Oak, the largest in the faithful Wood;
Whom to receive I my glad Branches bow'd.
And for the King a Throne prepar'd, and spread
My thickest Leaves a Canopy o'er his Head.   1455
The Misseltoe commanded to ascend
Around his sacred Person to attend,
(Oh happy Omen) straight it did obey,
The Sacred Misseltoe attends with Joy.
Here without fear their prostrate Heads they bow,   1460
The King is safe beneath my shelter now,
And you, my Nymphs, with awful silence may
Your Adorations to your Sovereign pay,

And cry, all hail, thou most belov'd of Heaven,
To whom its chiefest Attributes are given;   1465
But above all that God-like Fortitude,
That has the Malice of thy Fate subdu'd.
All hail!
Thou greatest now of Kings indeed, while yet
With all the Miseries of life beset,   1470
Thy mighty mind cou'd Death nor Danger fear,
Nor yet even then of safety cou'd despair.
This is the Virtue of a Monarch's Soul,
Who above Fortunes reach can all her Turns controul;
Thus if Fate rob you of your Empires Sway,   1475
You by this Fortitude take hers away;
O brave Reprisal! which the Gods prefer,
That makes you triumph o'er the Conqueror.
The Gods who one day will this Justice do
Both make you Victor and Triumpher too.   1480
That Day's at hand, O let that Day come on,
Wherein that wonderous Miracle shall be shown:
May its gay Morn be more than usual bright,
And rise upon the World with new created Light;
Or let that Star whose dazling Beams were hurl'd   1485
Upon his Birth-Day, now inform the World,
That brave bold Constellation, which in sight
Of Mid-day's Sun durst lift its Lamp of Light.
Now, happy Star again at Mid-day rise,
And with new Prodigies adorn the Skies;   1490
Great *Charles* again is born, *Monk*'s valiant Hand
At last delivers the long labouring Land.
This is the Month, Great Prince, must bring you forth,
May pays her fragrant Tributes at your Birth;
This is the Month that's due to you by Fate,   1495
O Month most Glorious, Month most Fortunate:
When you between your Royal Brothers rode,
Amidst your shining Train attended like some God,
One would believe that all the World were met
To pay their Homage at your Sacred Feet.   1500

151

The wandering Gazers, numberless as these,
Or as the Leaves on the vast Forest Trees.
He comes! He comes! they cry, while the loud Din
Resounds to heaven: and then, Long live the King:
And sure the shouts of their re-ecchoed Joys   1505
Reach'd to the utmost Bounds of distant Seas,
Born by the flying Winds thro' yielding Air,
And strike the Foreign Shores with awful Fear.
O 'tis a wonderous Pleasure to be mad,
Such frantick Turns our Nation oft has had.   1510
Permit it now ye Stoicks, ne'er till now,
The Frenzy you more justly might allow,
For 'tis a joyful Fit that ends the Fears,
And wretched Fury of so many years.
Nor will the Night her Sable Wings display   1515
T'obscure the Lustre of so bright a day.
At least the much transported Multitude
Permits not the dark Goddess to intrude;
The whole Isle seem'd to burn with joyful Flames,
Whose Rays gilt all the Face of Neighbouring *Thames*.   1520
　　But how shall I express the Vulgars Joys,
Their Songs, their Feasts, their Laughter and their Cries;
How Fountains run with the Vines precious Juice,
And such the flowing Rivers shou'd produce,
Their Streams the richest Nectar should afford: 1525
The Golden Age seems now again restor'd.
See— smiling Peace does her bright Face display, ⎫
Down thro' the Air serene she cuts her way,   ⎬
Expels the Clouds, and rises on the Day.   ⎭
Long exil'd from our Shores, new Joy she brings,   1530
Embracing *Albion* with her Snowy Wings;
Nor comes she unattended, but a Throng
Of Noble *British* Matrons brings along.
Plenty, fair Fame, and charming Modesty,
Religion, long since fled with Loyalty,   1535
And in a decent Garb the lovely Piety:
Justice from Fraud and Perjury forc'd to fly;

Learning, fine Arts, and generous Liberty.
Blest Liberty, thou fairest in the Train,
And most esteem'd in a just Prince's Reign.   1540
   With these, as lov'd, Great *Mary* too return'd,
In her own Country who long Exile mourn'd.
You, Royal Mother! you whose only Crime
Was loving *Charles*, and sharing Woes with him.
Now Heaven repays, tho slow, yet just and true,   1545
For him Revenge, and just Rewards for you.
   Hail, mighty Queen, form'd by the Pow'rs divine,
The Shame of our weak Sex, and Pride of thine,
How well have you in either Fortune shown,
In either, still your Mind was all your own.   1550
The giddy World roll'd round you long in vain,
Who fix'd in Virtues Centre still remain.
   And now, just Prince! thou thy great Mind shall bring
To the true weighty Office of a King.
The gaping Wounds of War thy Hand shall cure,   1560
Thy Royal Hand, gentle alike and sure:
And by insensible Degrees efface
Of foregone Ill the very Scars and Trace.
Force to the injur'd Law thou shalt restore,
And all that Majesty it own'd before.   1565
Thou long corrupted Manners shalt reclaim,
And Faith and Honor of the *English* Name;
Thus long-neglected Gardens entertain
Their banish'd Master, when return'd again.
All over-run with Weeds he finds, but soon   1570
Luxuriant Branches carefully will prune,
The weaken'd Arms of the sick Vine he'll raise,
And with kind Bands sustain the loosen'd Sprays.
Much does he plant, and much extirpate too,
And with his Art and Skill make all things new.   1575
A Work immense, yet sweet, which in future Days, ⎫
When the fair Trees their blooming Glories raise, ⎬
The happy Gard'ners Labor over-pays.   ⎭
Cities and Towns, great Prince, thy Gardens be

With Labor cultivated, worthy Thee.   1580
In decent Order thou dost all dispose:
    Nor are the Woods, nor Rural Groves disdain'd;
He who our Wants, who all our Breaches knows,
    He all our drooping Fortunes has sustain'd.
As young Colonies of Trees thou dost replace   1585
I'th'empty Realms of our Arboreal Race;
Nay, dost our Reign extend to future Days;
And blest Posterity, supinely laid,
Shall feast and revel underneath thy Shade.
Cool Summer Arbors then thy Gift shall be,   1590
And their bright Winter Fires they'll owe to thee.
To thee those Beams their Palaces sustain,
And all their floating Castles on the Main.
Who knows, great Prince, but thou this happy Day
For Towns and Navies mayst Foundation lay   1595
After a thousand years are roll'd away.
Reap thou those mighty Triumphs then which for thee grow,
And mighty Triumphs for succeeding Ages sow.
Thou Glory's craggy Top shalt first essay,
Divide the Clouds, and mark the shining Way;   1600
To Fame's bright Temples shalt thy Subjects guide,
Thy *Britains* bold, almost of Night deny'd.
The foaming Waves thy dread Commands shall stay,
Thy dread Commands the foaming Waves obey.
The watry World no *Neptune* owns but thee,   1605
And thy three Kingdoms shall thy Trident be.
    What madness, O *Batavians!* you possest,
When the Sea's Scepter you'd from *Britain* wrest,
Which Nature gave, whom she with Floods has crown'd,
And fruitful *Amphritite* embraces round;   1610
The rest o'th'World's just kiss'd by *Amphritite*,
Albion sh'embraces, all her dear delight.
You scarce th'insulting Ocean can restrain,
Nor bear the Assaults of the besieging Main,
Your Graafts and Mounds, and Trenches all in vain.   1615
And yet what fond Ambition spurs you on?

You dare attempt to make the Seas your own.
O'er all the vast Ocean, which no Limit knows,
The narrow Laws of Ponds and Fens impose:
But *Charles* his lively Valour this defies,   1620
And this the sturdy *British* Oak denies.
O'er empty Seas the fierce *Batavian* Fleet
Sings Triumphs, while there was no Foe to meet.
But fear not, *Belgian*, he'll not tarry long,
He'll soon be there, and interrupt thy Song,   1625
Too late thou'lt of thy hasty Joys complain,
And to thy Native Shores look back in vain.
Great *James*, as soon as the first Whisper came,
Prodigal of his Life, and greedy but of Fame,
With eager Haste returns, as fast as they   1630
After the dreadful Fight will run away.
   And now the joyful *English* from afar
Approaching saw the floating Belgian War.
Hark what a Shout they give, like those who come
From long *East-Indy* Voyage rich loaden home,   1635
When first they make the happy *British* Land,
The dear White Rocks, and *Albion*'s Chalky Strand.
   The way to all the rest, brave *Rupert* show'd,
And thro' their Fleet cuts out his flaming Road,
Rupert, who now had stubborn Fate inclin'd,   1640
Heaven on his side engaging, and the Wind:
Famous by Land and Sea, whose Valour soon
Blunts both the Horns of the *Batavian* Moon.
   Next comes illustrious *James*, and where he goes,
To Cowards leaves the Crowd of vulgar Foes,   1645
To th'Royal Sovereign's Deck he seems to grow,
Shakes his broad Sword, and seeks an equal Foe.
Nor did bold *Opdam*'s mighty Mind refuse
The dreadful Honor which 'twas Death to chuse.
Both Admirals with haste for Fight prepare,   1650
The rest might stand and gaze themselves a War.
   O whither, whither, *Opdam*, dost thou flie?
Can this rash Valor please the pow'rs on high:

It can't, it won't— or, woud'st thou proudly die
By such a mighty Hand? no *Opdam*, no: 1655
Thy Fate's to perish b'yet a nobler Foe.
Heav'n only, *Opdam*, shall thy Conqu'ror be,
A Labor worth its while, to conquer thee.
Heav'n shall be there, to guard its best lov'd House,
And just Revenge inflict on all your broken Vows.   1660
The mighty Ship a hundred Canons bore,
A hundred Canons which like Thunder roar;
Six times as many Men in Shivers torn,
E'er one Broadside, or single Shot't had born,
Is with a horrid Crack blown up to th'Sky   1665
In Smoak and Flames o'er all the Ocean nigh,
Torn, half-burnt Limbs of Ships and Seamen scatter'd lie.
Whether a real Bolt from Heav'n was thrown
Among the guilty Wretches is not known,
Tho likely 'tis: *Amboina*'s Wickedness,   1670
And broken Peace and Oaths deserv'd no less,
Or whether fatal Gunpowder it were
By some unlucky Spark enkindled there;
Even Chance, by Heaven directed, is the Rod,
The fiery Shaft of an avenging God.   1675
The flaming Wrack the hissing Deep floats o'er,
Far, far away, almost to either shore,
Which even from pious Foes wou'd pity draw,
A trembling pity, mixt with dreadful aw.
But pity yet scarce any room can find,   1680
What Noise, what Horror still remains behind?
On either side does wild confusion reign,
Ship grapples Ship, and sink into the Main.
The *Orange* careless of lost *Opdam*'s Fate
Will next, To attack victorious James prepare,   1685
Worthy to perish at the self same rate,
But *English* Guns sufficient Thunder bear;
By *English* Guns, and human Fire o'erpowr'd,
'Tis quickly in the hissing Waves devour'd.
Three Ships besides are burnt, if Fame says true,   1690

None of whose baser Names the Goddess knew;
As many more the Dolphin did subdue.
Their Decks in Show'rs of kindled Sulphur steep,
And send 'em flaming to th'affrighted deep.
So burns a City, storm'd and fir'd by night,   1695
The Shades are pierc'd with such a dreadful Light;
Such dusky Globes of Flame around 'em broke
Through the dark Shadow of the Guns and Smoke.
   Can Fire in Water then such Licence claim?
Justly the Water hides it self for shame: 1700
The dreadful Wrack outstretching far away
Vast Ruins o'er its trembling Bosom lay;
Here Masts and Rudders from their Vessels torn,
Here Sails and Flags across the Waves are born,
A thousand floating Bodies there appear,   1705
As many half-dead Men lie groaning here.
If any where the Sea it self's reveal'd
With horrid purple Tracks the azure Wave's conceal'd.
All sunk or took, 'twere tedious to relate,
And all the sad variety of Fate   1710
One day produces — with what Art and Skill
Ev'n Chance ingenious seems, to save or kill,
To spare, or to torment who e'er she will,
The vulgar deaths, below the Muse to heed
Not only Faith, but Number too exceed,   1715
Three noble Youths by the same sudden' Death,
A brave Example to the World bequeath;
Fam'd for high Birth, but Merits yet more high,
All at one fatal Moment's Warning die,
Torn by one Shot, almost one Body they,   1720
Three Brothers in one Death confounded lay.
Who wou'd not Fortune harsh and barbarous call,
Yet Fortune was benign and kind withal,
For next to these — I tremble still with fear,
My Joys disturb'd while such a danger near,   1725
Fearless, unhurt, the Royal Adm'ral stood,
Stunn'd with the Blow, and sprinkled with their Blood.

Fiercer he presses on, while they retir'd,
He presses on with Grief, and Anger fir'd.
Nor longer can the *Belgian* Force engage   1730
The *English* Valor, warm'd with double Rage.
Breaks with their Losses, and a Cause so ill
Their shatter'd Fleet all the wide Ocean fill,
Till trembling *Rhine* opens his Harbors wide,
　　Seeing the Wretches from our Thunder fly: 1735
From our hot Chase their shatter'd Fleet he'd hide,
　　And bends his conquer'd Horns as we go by.
In sacred Rage the *Dryad* this reveal'd,
Yet many future wond'rous things conceal'd,
But this to grace some future *Bard* will serve,   1740
For better Poets this the Gods reserve.

A
Congratulatory
POEM
TO HER
Sacred Majesty
QUEEN MARY
UPON HER
ARRIVAL in ENGLAND

While my sad Muse the darkest Covert Sought,
To give a loose to Melancholy Thought;
Opprest, and sighing with the Heavy Weight
Of an Unhappy dear Lov'd *Monarch's* Fate;
A lone retreat, on *Thames's* Brink she found,   5
With murmering Osiers fring'd, and bending Willows crown'd,
Thro' the thick Shade cou'd dart no Chearful Ray,
Nature dwelt here as in disdain of Day:
Content, and Pleas'd with Nobler Solitude,
No *Wood-gods*, *Fawns*, nor *Loves* did here Intrude,   10
Nor Nests for wanton Birds, the Glade allows;
Scarce the soft Winds were heard amongst the Boughs.

   While thus She lay resolv'd to tune no more
Her fruitless Songs on *Brittains* Faithless Shore,
All on a suddain thro' the Woods there Rung,   15
Loud Sounds of Joy that *Jo Peans* Sung.
Maria! Blest *Maria*! was the Theam,
Great Brittains happy Genius, and her Queen.

   The River Nimphs their Crystal Courts forsake,
Curl their Blew Locks, and Shelly Trumpets take: 20
And the surprising News along the Shore,
In raptur'd Songs the wondring Virgins bore;
Whilst mourning Eccho now forgot her Sighs,
And sung the new taught Anthem to the Skyes.

All things in Nature, a New Face put on,   25
Thames with Harmonious Purlings glides along,
And tells her Ravisht Banks, she lately bore
A Prize more great than all her hidden Store,
Or all the Sun it self e're saw before.

The brooding Spring, her Fragrant Bloom sent out,   30
Scattering her early Perfumes round about;
No longer waits the Lasie teeming Hours,
But e're her time produc'd her Oderous Flowers;
Maria's Eyes anticipate the *May*,
And Life inspired beyond the God of Day.   35

The Muses all upon this Theam Divine,
Tun'd their best Lays, the Muses all, but mine,
Sullen with Stubborn Loyalty she lay,
And saw the World its eager Homage pay,
While Heav'n and Earth on the new Scene lookt gay.   40
But Oh! What Human Fortitude can be
Sufficient to Resist a Deity?
Even our Allegiance here, too feebly pleads,
The Change in so Divine a Form perswades;
Maria with the Sun has equal Force,   45
No Opposition stops her Glorious Course,
Her pointed Beams thro' all a passage find,
And fix their Rays Triumphant in the Mind.

And now I wish'd among the Crouds to Adore,
And constant wishing did increase my Power;   50
From every Thought a New-born Reason came
Which fortifyed by bright *Maria's* Fame,
Inspired My Genious with new Life and Flame,
J. R. And thou, Great Lord, of all my Vows, permit
My Muse who never fail'd Obedience yet,   55
To pay her Tribute at *Marias* Feet,
Maria so Divine a part of You,

Let me be Just- but Just with Honour too.

    Resolv'd, She join'd her Chorus with the Throng,
And to the listning Groves *Marias* Vertues Sung;   60
Maria all Inchanting, Gay, and Young.

All Hail Illustrious Daughter of a King,
Shining without, and Glorious all within,
VVhose Eyes beyond your scantier Power give Laws,
Command the VVorld, and justifie the Cause;   65
Nor to secure your Empire needs more Arms
Than your resistless, and all Conquering Charms;
Minerva Thus alone, Old *Troy* Sustain'd,
VVhilst her Blest Image with three Gods remain'd;
But Oh! your Form and Manner to relate,   70
The Envying Fair as soon may Imitate,
'Tis all Engaging Sweet, 'tis all Surprising Great;
A thousand Beauties Triumph in your Air,
Like those of soft Young Loves, your Smiles appear,
And to th'Ungarded Hearts, as dangerous are.   75

    All Natures Charms are open'd in your Face,
You Look, you Talk, with more than Human Grace;
All that is Wit, all that is Eloquence.
The Births of finest Thought and Noblest Sense,
Easie and Natural from your Language break,   80
And'tis Eternal Musick when you speak;
Thro' all no formal Nicety is seen,
But Free and Generous your Majestick Meen,
In every Motion, every Part a Queen;
All that is Great and Lovely in the Sex,   85
Heav'n did in this One Glorious Wonder fix,
Apellis thus to dress the Queen of Love,
Rob'd the whole Race, a Goddess to improve.

    Yet if with Sighs we View that Lovely Face,
And all the Lines of your Great Father's Trace,   90

Your Vertues should forgive, while we adore
That Face that Awes, and Charms our Hearts the more;
But if the *Monarch* in your Looks we find,
Behold him yet more glorious in your Mind;
'Tis there His God-like Attributes we see,   } 95
A Gratious Sweetness, Affability,
A Tender Mercy and True Piety;
And Vertues even sufficient to Attone
For all the ills the Ungrateful VVorld has done,
VVhere several factions, several Intrests sway,   100
And that is still it'h Right who gains the Day;
How e're they differ, this they all must grant,
Your Form and Mind, no One Perfection want,
Without all Angel, and within all Saint.

    The Murmering VVorld till now divided lay,   105
Vainly debating whom they shou'd Obey,
Till You Great Cesar's Off-spring blest our Isle,
The differing Multitudes to Reconcile;
This Stiff-neckt *Israel* in defiance stood,
Till they beheld the Prophet of their God;   110
Who from the Mount with dazling brightness came,
And Eyes all shining with Celestial Flame;
Those Awful Looks, dispel'd each Rebel Thought,
And to a Just Compliance, the wilde Nations brought.

FINIS

POEMS

FROM

THE HISTORY OF ADOLPHUS

A SONG in Dialogue. By Mrs. A. B.

She. Silvio, when will you be kind,
Ah, *Silvio*, when will you be kind.

Sil.. When Constancy in Swains I find,
Ah, when Constancy in Swains I find.

She.. Ah, my *Sylvia*, you're too Fair,
E'er to give me cause to change,
Ah! do not let me then despair,
For my Heart's not given to range.

Sil. Men will Sigh, Protest and Weep
Ah! what a coyle with Love you'll keep,
Till our Blushes you o'er-come:
Ah! till the blessing you have won,
Which, having once obtain'd, you fly:
Or if, by chance, you linger on,
Can see us Sigh, can see us Dye,
And Triumph when we are undone.

She. Oh! may my Flocks forget to feed
And Wolves into my Sheepfold break:
May Heaven forget me in my need,
And thou disdain me when I speak,
If ever I thy Love betray,
Or with false Vows thy faith repay.

Sil. Then take my hand, which ne'er to Swain
    Was render'd, on the score of Love:
  But, oh! I give it you with pain,
    For fear you shou'd Inconstant prove.

Another SONG. By Mrs. A. B.

Morpheus, Morpheus, God of Sleep,
This Hero from all danger keep,
Let soft Dreams around him rove,
Dreams of kind delights in Love.
What-ever toyls pursue the day,
Do thou at Night chase all away.
Make soft Garlands for his Head,
With Roses and with Poppies spread.
Let soft Musick fill his Ears,
Musick from the Tuneful Sphears,
While *Cupids* round his Couch still play,
And wanton in the breaking day.

COMMENTARY

PROLOGUE TO *LIKE FATHER, LIKE SON*

SOURCE: Broadside: *A Prologue By Mrs.* Behn *to her New Play, Called Like Father, Like Son, or The Mistaken Brothers,* Spoken by Mrs. Butler. (Colophon) London, Printed for J. V. 1682. (O'Donnell, 62-63)

'Like Father, like Son' must have been a *rifacimento* of Thomas Randolph's *The Jealous Lovers,* for Mrs Behn herself identified it as such when she reprinted a version of the Epilogue in her 1685 *Miscellany* and called it 'Epilogue to the Jealous Lovers. By Mrs. Behn, in 1682.' Langbaine mentions the revival of Randolph's comedy at the Duke's House in 1682. Summers gives no source for his assertion that the revival 'met with extraordinary success' in March, or for the cast list he supplies, John Nokes, as Asotus the prodigal, and speaker of the Epilogue, Anthony Leigh as Ballio the Pimp, Joseph Williams and John Bowman. As Summers does not mention the Broadside, we may assume that he did not know of its existence. Luttrell's copy now in the Huntington Library, is dated '5. April. 1682'; the cast includes Mrs Butler, John Williams, John Wiltshire, John Bowman, 'Mistris Corall', probably Mrs Currer, Richards, a child actress called Betty, and Jevon, who spoke the Epilogue. It is possible that *The Jealous Lovers* opened in late February or early March with great success, but if this is the case Behn's prologue must have been written for later performances after the court had removed to Newmarket. It laments the fact that the court and all its hangers-on have followed the king to Newmarket, where on March 11, 1682 he was joined by his brother, James, Duke of York, Heir Presumptive to the throne, who had travelled down on the yacht *Henrietta* from Leith to Yarmouth. According to Luttrell (I, 171) the Duke 'was received by His Majesty with all the expressions of kindness imaginable, and since his arrival there hath been waited on by most of the nobility to pay their respects to him.'

The libel on the Whigs, which is the occasion of the printing of the broadside, may have got Behn and Mrs Butler into trouble with the city authorities; in August of the same year Behn and Lady Slingsby were arrested in the charge that 'by acting and writing at his Royall Highnesse theatre' they had 'committed severall Misdemeanors and made abusive reflections upon persons of Quality, and have written and spoken scandalous speeches without any License or Approbation of those that ought to peruse and authorize the same...' The specific occasion has always been thought to be the speaking by Lady Slingsby of Behn's Epilogue to the

anonymous play, *Romulus and Hersilia*, with its reflections upon the Duke of
Monmouth, but the wording refers to repeated offences.

No copy of Behn's revision of Randolph's play can be found; in her 1685
Miscellany she prints a version of the Epilogue only, and that in a curiously
botched version.

Mrs Butler: Charlotte Butler was the daughter of an impoverished knight.
It is thought that she played the part of an African woman in Crowne's
'Masque of Calisto' at court in 1675 and no lesser than the king himself
advised her to try her fortune on the stage. Professor J. H. Wilson states
that she was also a prostitute (Wilson, 80). In an anti-court satire 'on three
late marriages' dated by references to the visit of the Russian Court as of the
same period, Butler is described as having a 'goose skin arse and of the
chestnut brown' as a result of her outdoor sexual activity. In August 1682 she
spoke the prologue to *Romulus and Hersilia* and played Charlot in Behn's
anti-Whig play *The City Heiress* in which Sir Timothy Treat-all is an
obvious caricature of Shaftesbury. It is likely that Butler's identification
with the ultra-Tory court party is the sole ground of the libel which, she
being female, is expressed in exclusively pornographic terms. No scholar
should assume on such evidence that she was ever a common prostitute.
Although references to her dark colouring are frequent, Summers waxes
lyrical about 'that sweet-voiced blonde, winsome Charlotte Butler'
(Summers, I, xlii).

Printed for J. V.: i.e. James Vade, who, according to Plomer, was not active
before 1677 or after 1681, when he was arrested in connection with a charge
brought by Bartholomew Sprint against a group of booksellers, for assault
(C.P.R. Trin. 33 Chas II, 2992, m. 256). Luttrell reports that on 13 October,
1681, 'Vile, Janeway, Baldwin, Vade and others have been before the councill,
for publishing severall scandalous and seditious pamphlets against the
government, and are ordered to be prosecuted thereon.' Vade, a Catholic,
who published no fewer than eighty pamphlets on the Popish Plot, was
included with the Whig publishers arraigned 'to make the list look impartial'
(Kitchin, p. 285). He published nothing else by Behn, and the broadside may
well have been pirated, for Vade's case was not heard until May, 1682 and he
was still under indictment.

2 *Conventicling was put down*: the Act against Conventicles of 1670 outlawed
all non-conformist religious gatherings of more than five persons, and was
prosecuted with the utmost severity (*English Historical Documents, 1660-
1714*, 384-386).

3 *to* Newmarket *gone*: 'their majesties, with the whole court,' left for
Newmarket on March 4 (Luttrell, I, 168) It seems unlikely then that *The*

Jealous Lovers alias *Like Father Like Son* could have been performed in March with great success, as Summers claims.

4-5 Though the reference may be to the decline of the power and influence of the lords of the city party may be general, these lines could more particularly refer to the estrangement between Buckingham and Shaftesbury.

5 *a heartless* Whigg: at this period the name Whig was applied to those who wished to exclude the King's brother, James, Duke of York, from the succession on the grounds that he was a Catholic.

7 *the* Association: at the time of Shaftesbury's arrest in November, 1681, plans to set up a republican association were found among his papers.

9 This line is corrupted; perhaps it ought read 'Whom his perverted Grace betrays and Cozens'. Such an error is usually the result of oral transmission.

11 *Pensive State Puss*: cat imagery was often employed to describe the country party in implied contrast with the lion of the monarchy; 'Satyr A Song' ('Astrea's Booke', p. 31) identifies Shaftesbury as 'that old Catt of State'; 'An Essay upon Satyr' (Bodleian MS Don. b. 8, p. 637) describes Dorset 'purring like a thoughtfull Catt'; the identification with Dorset would fit in with the references to Moll Howard (if such they are) in ll. 24-26. This editor feels nonetheless that this 'State Puss' is more likely to be the Duke of Buckingham, who retired from public life at the beginning of 1682, dissociated himself from the Whig cause, and began to spend most of his time in retirement in the country; 'The Cabal' describes Buckingham as one

...who from a glorious Bully,

Retir'd from Court, to be the City's Cully;

The City's minion; now their scorn and sport;

There more despis'd then once ador'd at Court;... (Phipps, 33)

Another broadside dated by Luttrell, April, 5, 1682 (Yale Broadsides L 3366) refers to Buckingham in similar terms.

Buckingham a statesman would be thought,

And reason geud that he should bear that rev'rend name;

Since he was ene of them that first began the Plot,

How the King might banter and three kingdoms sham;

Majestick: tall, handsome and graceful, Buckingham was the noblest looking of Charles's courtiers; among the charges at Shaftesbury's trial was that he said that Buckingham had 'as much right to be king as any Stuart in England.'

13 *Verses*: Buckingham is thought by some to have paid Shadwell to write *The Medal of John Bayes* in answer to Dryden's *The Medal*. He may have commissioned other poems of state and he also penned his own verses; in an

Epilogue he added later to his version of Fletcher's *Philaster*, Buckingham
sneered at Shaftesbury as one who would abolish popery by becoming
pope. One difficulty with this identification should however be noted;
Behn's play, *The Young King*, published in 1683, is dedicated to 'Philaster',
a name associated with Buckingham as well as meaning 'lover of Astrea'.
However the evidence of the dedication itself indicates that the play was
written and dedicated long before its printing in 1683, when Behn could not
refer to hers by any stretch of the imagination as 'infant-Poetry' inspired by
a 'Virgin-Muse'. One intriguing possibility is that Behn gave Buckingham
her play at an earlier period when he was her patron, and he gave it to the
printers in 1683, in silent reproach.

17 *His Highness comes*: Charles decided after long discussions with James at
Newmarket to bring his brother back to London with him. He arrived on
April 8, (see Dryden's *Prologue to His Royal Highness, Upon his First Appearance at the Duke's Theatre since his return from Scotland*). Behn's Prologue
must have been written after that decision was taken, and may in fact have
been the first public announcement that the Duke's arrival was imminent.
It cannot, therefore, have been the Prologue written for a putative first
performance of the play at the beginning of March.

21-22 The Whigs are profiting by the absence of the court party to plot
further attacks against the prerogatives of the crown.

24 In a poem attributed to Behn in *Familiar Letters* (1718) , 'A Letter to the
Earl of Kildare, dissuades him from marrying Dorset's crony, Mary Howard, on the grounds that

> Whoring has all her lifetime been her Trade,
> And D[orset] says, she is an exc'lent Baud:
> But finding both will not defray Expence,
> She lately is become an *Evidence*;
> Swearing against all that won't her Lust supply,
> And says, they're false as Hell to Monarchy. (Summers, VI, 396)

Kildare's first wife died in 1683; the poem must date from before his second
marriage in 1684. 'Astrea's Booke' contains a ballad called 'Evidence Moll'
addressed to 'You Whigs and you Torys, you Trimmers and all', vilifying
Mary Howard because

> She came and she swore
> With impudence more
> Than *Oats, Prance* or *Bedlow* or any before (p. 42)

In other satires she is called ironically 'silent Moll'.

Conversely, the well-known procuress, Madam Cresswell, was thought
by L'Estrange to be in the pay of the Whigs, (*Observator*, No. 78, 7

December, 1681). Her name was frequently associated with that of Sir Thomas Player, Whig Treasurer of the City of London, who had run up a long score with her and was thought to have embezzled £400,000 of city funds (*POAS*, III, 295, 384-5).

EPILOGUE

Mr Gevan:; Thomas Jevon, son-in-law to Thomas Shadwell, joined the Duke's Company in 1673 when he was twenty-one. He played Don Antonio in *The Rover* (1677), Foppington in *The City Heiress* (1682), Bearjest in *The Lucky Chance* (1687) and Harlequin and Prologue in *The Emperor of the Moon* (1687).

4 *Patriot*: Shaftesbury, see e.g. *Absalom and Achitophel*, l. 179

6 *Scandal worth Eight Hundred Pound*. in March, 1682, 'at the assizes held at Southwark... was tryed an action brought by Mr. Bolsworth against Mr. sheriff Pilkington, for words spoken to this effect: You are a broken fellow, goe home and pay your debts. The plaintiff could not prove he had any damage thereby; and the defendant prov'd the plaintiff first very rudely provok'd him; yet the jury to the astonishment of most, brought in 800*l* damages for the plaintiff.' (Luttrell, I, 174).

10 *Some Body*: though in the *Miscellany* Behn edited in 1685, *somebody* is identified as 'Rebell Ward' i.e. Sir Patience Ward, (1629-1696) elected Lord Mayor of London in 1680, in office until 29 October, 1681, Pilkington must be meant. Ward was tried for perjury in the case of the Duke of York v Pilkington in mid-1683 and fled to Holland, but in March, 1682 he is far from conspicuous whereas, the Lord Mayor, Sir John Moore, having been won over by degrees to the Court party, Pilkington had taken over leadership of the Whig faction. When Behn was preparing the *Miscellany*, both Ward and Pilkington were in prison.

11 *Reflections on damn'd witnesses*: Sir Robert Pilkington was reprimanded by the judges for excessive partiality in returning the Grand Jury in Shaftesbury's trial in November, 1681 (North, *Examen*, 1, 1, 3). In August, the same year, Behn referred to Whig perjurors again in the 'Prologue to Romulus', mocking

> Your *Burlesque Oaths*, when one *Green-Ribbon-Brother*
> In Conscience will be perjur'd for another. (Summers, VI, 398)

13 Salamanchian *Doctorships*: Titus Oates claimed to have a degree from the university of Salamanca, but the university authorities denied it. Though Oates's credibility had been waning for a year, Whig authorities were quick to silence anyone who impugned him openly; in June, Nat Thompson was

convicted, pilloried and fined for publishing refutations of the case against the Papists in the matter of the death of Sir Edmund Berry Godfrey.

20 Joe *and* Jack: identified by the side notes as the players, Joseph Williams and John Wiltshire. Summers identifies them as Joseph Williams and John Bowman, and says that they played Tyndarus and Pamphilius, respectively. In this, the longer version of the Epilogue, Bowman is separately noticed. Joseph Williams played the title role in *Sir Patient Fancy*, (1678), Pietro in *The Feign'd Curtezans* (1679), the title-role in *The False Count*, (1682), Sir Anthony Meriwill in *The City Heiress*, Sir Feeble Fainwou'd in *The Lucky Chance* and Scaramouch in *The Emperor of the Moon*.

22 In the version printed in the 1685 *Miscellany* this line is corrupted to 'He's for Mischief all, and carry's it on' apparently referring to Leigh, and the reference to Bowman is suppressed. John Bowman (1651-1739) played Bredwell in *The Lucky Chance*, Dresswell in *The City Heiress*, and Cavernio in *The Widdow Ranter* (1690).

25 *Sweet Mistris Corall*: Mrs Corror or Currer or Cory who played Ariadne in *The Rover* II (1677), Lady Fancy in *Sir Patient Fancy*, Isabella in *The False Count*, Diana in *The City Heiress*, Prologue and Marcella in *The Feign'd Curtizans*, Mopsophil in *The Emperor of the Moon*. and the title role in *The Widow Ranter*.

29 *Mistris Betty* : a child actress

31 *Mr Richards*: John Richards (1629-1688), a founder member of the Duke's company who played Stephano in *The Rover*, Hunt in *The Rover* II, Zarrack in *Abdelazar* (1677), and Curry in *Sir Patient Fancy*.

34 *Joe* Haines*'s Grace*: the player Joseph Haynes travelled to France in the train of the Duke of Buckingham in 1670, but his name was connected too with the Duke of Albemarle.

POEMS FROM THE 1685 *MISCELLANY*

SOURCE: *Miscellany, Being a Collection of Poems By several Hands, Together with Reflections on Morality, or Seneca Unmasqued*. London, printed for J. Hindmarsh, at the Golden Ball over against the Royal Exchange in Cornhill 1685. (O'Donnell, 217-222)

Judging by the name 'A. Behn' appearing as the signature to the dedicatory epistle 'To Sir William Clifton' Behn was the compiler of this miscellany; her failure to indicate her authorship of 'A Letter to Mr Creech at Oxford, Written in the last Great Frost' and 'Ovid to Julia' can be adequately explained by the political sensitivity of references in both poems. Although he seems to have realised that 'A Letter to Mr.Creech'

was by Behn, (Summers, I, xxxiv) Summers printed only the ten poems
actually attributed to Aphra Behn or, rather, 'Mrs. A. B.' in the text.

A LETTER TO MR. CREECH

'A Letter to Mr Creech' is Behn's only hudibrastic epistle. Tetrameter
couplets with comic feminine rhymes were used to great effect by Samuel
Butler in the the famous burlesque poem *Hudibras* (1662). Behn creates for
herself a *persona* in the Horatian mode, a female *civis in urbe* who drinks
more than is good for her, who is obliged to dun her Augustus, who is in
poor health, and who very easily finds herself absurdly discomfited.
Mr. Creech: Thomas Creech (1659-1700). As his family was less than affluent,
the expenses of his education were defrayed by various benefactors, who
were rewarded by seeing him elected to a fellowship at Oxford in 1683. How
the young Oxford don and the female wit from London can have developed
the kind of relationship indicated in her poem is something of a mystery.
Along with her colleagues Dryden, Tate and Otway, Behn contributed a
commendatory poem to the second edition of *T. Lucretius Caro. The
Epicurean Philosopher, His Six Books De Natura Rerum Done into English Verse,
With Notes* (by Thomas Creech) published at Oxford in 1683. She dated her
poem 'Jan. 25. 1682', i.e. 1683 and addressed Creech in it by his coterie name
of Daphnis, as she does here. Creech or his editor bowdlerised her poem
and removed her injudicious references to 'dull Religion' and 'Faith, the
last Shift of routed Argument'. In an undated letter to Jacob Tonson
(present whereabouts unknown, see Summers, I, xlv-xlvi) asking for £30 for
her *Poems on Several Occasions* (published 1684), she writes, 'As for Mr.
Creech, I would not have you afflict him wth a thing can not now be help'd,
so never let him know my resentment.' When *Poems on Several Occasions
with a Voyage to the Island of Love. By Mrs. A. Behn.* was published by the
Tonsons in 1684, the original irreligious text of the commendatory poem
was included. Summers does not collate the two versions.
the last great Frost: 'About the 15th,' writes Luttrell in December, 1683 'began
a frost, which continued all this month, freezeing very bitter, raiseing the
price of all commodities; and great part of the river of Thames was frozen
over'; in January, 'the 7th the frost began to break, but at night it froze
again; the Thames was quite frozen over, and thousands of people went
upon it, and booths built on it in divers places.' 'The 15th, the frost still
continues at that excessive rate...' 'The 23rd a bull was baited on the ice of
the river Thames'. On February 4, 'the great frost began to thaw at night:

it began to freeze moderately at first, but after a fortnight it froze very hard and so continued, and, for the time, was the sharpest and hardest ever known...' (Luttrell, I, 294-300).

5 *Tonsons*: bookseller Jacob Tonson, who published Behn's *Poems on Several Occasions* had two shops, one 'at Gray's Inn Gate next Gray's Inn Lane' and the other 'at the Judge's head at Chancery Lane End near Fleet Street' which seems to be the one Behn refers to.

8 At their last meeting, Behn promised to leave an invitation for Creech at the bookshop. She hastens to forestall his assumption that because they were drinking on that occasion, she has simply forgotten. Talk of drinking in company and of wit being thereby enhanced is a part of the convention of the familiar epistle.

8 *Billet Deux*: a *billet doux*, or short note, such as might be exchanged by lovers

12 *Shie Wine*: 'sherrie wine', presumably. There seems to be a slight corruption here; Behn's abbreviation has been kept, while a supernumerary syllable *that* has crept in.

19 —- *who has no wit*: the scansion of the line is difficult; the likeliest name for insertion would be one of the Whig poets, Shadwell or Settle, possibly.

21 *that's my Tryal*: Behn claims that her only criterion is whether or not a writer is true Tory; cf. *Postscript*, l. 7.

26-30 Behn explains how the invitation was lost and could not be left at Tonson's. It must be remembered that writing materials were more expensive and cumbersome than they are now; Behn could not simply have called for paper, ink, a shaker and a sharpened pen at the bookshop and written another note. She claims that she has been to Whitehall to dun the king, called here with more than a pinch of irony 'His Sacred Majesty', for payment for writing anti-Whig propaganda to order. Her route from the palace of Whitehall would have taken her along King Street to Charing Cross and up the Strand to the Temple and Chancery Lane.

31 *the Alpian Hills*: the Alps

36 *Temple*: the walled enclosure containing the Middle and Inner Temple, and the Temple church, owned and administered by the Benchers of the two Inns of Court

38 *cured of Simple*: disciplined for foolish behaviour. There may have been stocks or a pillory on this corner. Certainly gibbets were erected at Temple Gate on occasion; Captain Ayloffe was executed there in 1685.

39 *Sign of Whore called Scarlet*: the Pope's Head Tavern in Chancery Lane
40 *My Coachman*: the possessive adjective could indicate that Behn was using her own coach; it seems more likely however that she was travelling

in a hackney; *laid Pilgarlick*: the meaning seems to be similar to that in 'There got he a knock and down goes pilgarlic' (*OED*) i.e. that as the coach took the corner into Chancery Lane too fast in the ice and slush, the coachman was thrown off the box on his head.

41-42 Behn was evidently hurt in the accident, unless the reference indicates that she was already afflicted with the joint inflammation that was to cause her so much suffering.

45 *Honest H—le*: John Hoyle, Behn's Amintas, the Gray's Inn Lawyer who 'unto her was friend in Buzzum'. This line reveals that Behn did not meet Creech through Hoyle as might have been supposed.

50 *when Plot broke out*: Behn is probably referring to the Rye House Plot (June, 1682) which was supposed to have failed when Charles and the Duke of York left Newmarket earlier than expected and avoided assassination, but the attempts of the Whigs to regroup and to revive anti-papist feeling involved them in countless conspiratorial meetings, many of which were observed by Charles's agents.

52-53 In 1681 Charles decided that parliament should meet at Oxford, away from the mobs that supported Shaftesbury and the Exclusionists; the parliament was opened in March 21 and summarily dissolved on March 28.

52 *Rowley*: an affectionate nickname for Charles, so called after one of his own stallions

54 *Perkin*: James Scott, Duke of Monmouth, so named by Nell Gwyn, because he like Perkin Warbeck wanted to be a kingmaker; *God of Wapping*: Monmouth was a favourite with the seamen of Wapping, who constituted themselves his honorary bodyguard.

56 Monmouth, illegitimate son of Charles II by Lucy Walters was the Whig candidate for the succession; if he had been able to prove his legitimacy he and not the Duke of York would have been James II. Shaftesbury's fall led to his banishment.

57 *native Scounderell*: when Charles met her at the Hague, Monmouth's mother was the mistress of Robert Sidney, a younger son of the Earl of Leicester. After the birth of her children by the king, she continued to live an irregular life and eventually died in Paris, of syphilis, according to some reports.

63 *Brawn in sowsing drink*: boar meat that has been placed in brine or vinegar for pickling. As a result of the accident Behn is dripping wet.

64 *Lazarello*: Lazarillo de Tormes, see, e.g. *Lazarillo or the Excellent History of Lazarillo de Tormes, the witty Spaniard...* (London, 1653), Part II, Chapter iv, Sig. N2 ff. which tells how Lazarillo, who was shipwrecked when drunk, was hauled up from the bottom in a fishermen's net and then exhibited in

a tub of water as a humanoid fish.

Postscript: sic

79 *Twelfth Night*: January 6, Feast of the Epiphany

80 *lamentable Cake*: for the closing festivities of the Christmas season at Twelfth-Night, a special spiced cake was baked and ornamented with sugar frosting (*OED* 'Twelfth-cake'). It seems Behn's version was not entirely successful.

OVID TO JULIA

'Ovid to Julia' is better known in the *rifacimento* entitled 'Bajazet to Gloriana', as printed in *Poems on Affairs of State* 1697. The 1697 text follows 'Ovid to Julia' for the most part closely. Some of the variants in 'Bajazet to Gloriana' are the result of authorial emendation; others are interpolations by a clumsier hand.

There is no historical foundation for the notion that Ovid dared to court Julia, the granddaughter of the emperor Augustus, although the co-incidence of her banishment at the same time as his has given rise to speculation. The cause of the poet's banishment has never been established; Ovid himself said that it was the result of a mistake rather than a crime and compared himself to Acteon.

References to Ovid's apocryphal love affair with Julia are frequent in Restoration poetry; Nat Lee's *Gloriana, or the Court of Augustus Caesar*, acted at the Theatre Royal by the King's Company in 1676, presents a profligate Julia who, though immoderately fond of spending time in cool recesses 'With tall young men that make immortal love', wishes to be united with Ovid, rather than her father's chosen, Marcellus,

> For wit to me is more than Empire's charms,
> Or all the surfeits of a monarch's arms.

Anne Wharton used this as the theme for her unpublished play, 'Love's Martyr, or, Witt above Crowns A Tragedy' (BL Add MS 28,693) in which Julia stabs herself upon hearing of Ovid's banishment and dies on stage. In Lee's play, Gloriana is the daughter of the deposed ruler, Pompey; after the Revolution 'Gloriana' would have been a more appropriate sobriquet for the Princess Anne than 'Julia'. Calling Mulgrave 'Ovid', moreover, was conceding too much to his vanity.

Behn's epistle cannot be read simply as straightforward dramatic monologue in the person of Ovid. Various circumstances have been altered specifically to strike the analogy with current affairs: Ovid was not a military man; the Roman Julia was not in the line of succession; and the vain young

COMMENTARY, p. 18

fool of ll. 60-66 is clearly Monmouth. The situation that corresponds is the
attempt by John Sheffield, Earl of Mulgrave, to woo Princess Anne, second
daughter of James, Duke of York, by his first wife, Anne Hyde, which
became public knowledge towards the end of October, 1682, when
Mulgrave's was stripped of his offices and the Duke of York forbade him to
frequent the court. Mulgrave was a constant butt of court satire, which
harped upon his ugliness, his rough manners, his arrogance, his 'lobcock
tarse', his 'hopper-arse', sneering at him as 'King John'; he was himself a
poet and translator, quite good enough to have appreciated the elegance
and subtlety of Behn's treatment of his fall.

Behn's claim to have written 'Ovid to Julia' rests first on its quality;
there is none among her contemporaries who could have written a dramatic
monologue that is at once so light and graceful and so telling. Brice Harris
(1933) lists two almost contemporary attributions. In the 1707 edition of
Poems on Affairs of State an advertisement denouncing the incompleteness
of the 1705 edition refers to '"Bajazet to Gloriana" by Mrs Behn' as among
the deleted material; the anonymous author of 'The Female Laureat',
(*POAS*, II, pp.138-144) ironically praises Astraea's accomplishment in this
poem:

> Next awful Bajazet's more awful Flame,
> Her Wit has plac'd in the first Rank of Fame.
> Go on then, mighty Poetress go on,
> And finish what's so happily begun;
> In lofty Language and adventurous Verse,
> Your Patron Bajazet's great worth rehearse.

This attack on the author of 'Ovid To Julia'/'Bajazet to Gloriana'
assumes complicity between her and the Earl of Mulgrave. In 'A Voyage to
the Isle of Love' published with her *Poems on Several Occasions* in 1684, Behn
herself returns to the Mulgrave theme; the Princess of Hope has two
suppliants:

> One, so above his Aim had made pretence,
> That even to hope, for him, was Impudence;
> Yet he 'gainst Reasons Arguments makes War,
> And vainly swore, his Love did merit her.
> Boldly Attempted, daringly Addrest,
> And with unblushing Confidence his flame confest.

In response the Princess of Hope

> ...animates the haughty to go on!
> Says — *A Town long besieg'd must needs be won.*
> *Time and Respect remove all obstacles,*

> *And obstinate Love arrives at Miracles,*
> *Were she the Heir to an illustrious crown,*
> *Those charms, that haughty meen, that fam'd renown,*
> *That wondrous skill you do in Verse profess,*
> *That great disdain of common Mistresses;*
> *Can when you please with aid of Billet Deux,*
> *The Royal Virgin to your Arms subdue,*
> *One skill'd in all the Arts to please the fair,*
> *Shou'd be above the Sense of dull despair:*
> *Go on, young noble Warrier, then go on,*
> *Though all the fair are by that Love undone. (Summers, VI, 246-247)*

Here again, the unmistakeable portrait of Mulgrave is coupled with a lament for Monmouth drawn to his ruin by 'a Politick throng.' In 'Upon these and other Excellent Works of the Incomparable Astraea' prefixed to Behn's *Poems on Several Occasions* (1684) the anonymous poet, who is sometimes thought to be Dryden because he specifically refers to Behn's collaboration on *Ovid's Epistles translated by several Hands*, argues that if Behn had lived in Rome Ovid would have written one poem less:

> Then the great *Caesar* to the *Scythian* plain,
> From Rome's gay court had banish'd him in vain,
> Her plenteous Muse had all his wants supplied,
> And he had flourish'd in exalted pride:
> Nor barbarous *Getans* had deprav'd his tongue,
> For he had only listned to her Song,
> Not as an Exile, but proscrib'd by choice,
> Pleas'd with her Form, and ravish'd with her voice.
>   His last and dearest part of Life,
>   Free from noise and glorious strife,
> He there had spent within her softer Armes,
> And soon forgot the Royal *Julia's* charmes. (Summers, VI, 128-129)

Dryden was not shy of acknowledging his work, nor is there any reason why he should have been; the most likely author of these verses is Mulgrave himself, speaking here through the character of Ovid. In 'Satyr on the Poets' ('Astrea's Booke', p. 180) we find an interesting reference to 'A Voyage to the Isle of Love':

> *Astraea*, with her soft gay-sighing Swains,
> And rural Virgins on the floury Plains,
> The lavish Peers Profuseness may reprove,
> Who gave her Guinneys for the *Isle of Love*.

Poems on Several occasions with a Voyage to the Isle of Love is dedicated to the

Earl of Salisbury, a circumstance hardly worthy of remark; the satirist appears to be referring to a situation rather less straightforward.

The use of the description of the career of one arriviste, Mulgrave, to attack another, the Duke of Monmouth, is not only consistent with Behn's fixation on the king's handsome, rabble-rousing bastard, but represents a chance for Mulgrave to turn a disastrous situation to some political effect, by warning the king that tolerating one illegitimate and easily manipulated pretender to the throne can encourage others.

Another reference to Mulgrave as Ovid can be found in 'A Supplement to the Late Heroick Poem', *Roxburghe Ballads*, IV, 561:

> Ah, *Mulgrave*! why art thou a garter'd Knight?
> Thou might'st have kept thy knaveries out of sight,
> Safely have cheated as a private Spark,
> But now thy Star betrays thee through the dark:...
> In game thy cheats, in verse thy thefts abound;
> Thou hast driven many Flocks from *Dryden's* ground,
> Which by their generous stature well are known,
> Too loftie for thy pigmie Brains to own.
> Yet thou wouldst be the Ovid of the age,
> And with a Princess would'st thy heart engage...

1 *Julia*, grand-daughter of the emperor Augustus, conversely Princess Anne, elder daughter of James, Duke of York, by Anne Hyde, third in the line of succession to the throne; *a Youth*: pastoral convention; Mulgrave was thirty-four.

4 Promethius *sin*: Prometheus stole fire from heaven and brought it to earth.

11 Mulgrave's hauteur was proverbial: he was known slightingly as 'Grandio'. Though he was thought to have enjoyed many of the court ladies, he appears to have loved none of them. Behn suggests that because his ambition was involved in the affair with Princess Anne, he really did love her and her alone.

15 *th'Arcadian plains*: this lover's complaint is set in the pastoral convention. Ovid/Mulgrave is depicted as a shepherd rich in 'Flocks and Herds'.

16 Mulgrave enjoyed an extraordinary degree of success with the most beautiful women at court; he was supposed to have been initiated by the widowed Duchess of Richmond, to have seduced Henrietta Wentworth; he was admitted to the order of the Garter at the instance of the Duchess of Cleveland for, it is presumed, amorous services rendered.

31-32 Mulgrave was said to have been the lover of 'stately Cary Frazier', 'as fine as hands or point could make her', who was one of Queen Catherine's maids of honour. She had many suitors of whom Mulgrave was the least constant, and eventually jilted her. In 1679 she became pregnant by Charles, Viscount Mordaunt, who, despite court gossip that the child was not his, eventually acknowledged prior contract and married her, 'Mulgrave's painted whore' according to the satirists. In 'To Captain Warcup' (Wilson, 160, dated June, 1686) appear the following lines:

> Never for women was so bad a time,
> Falseness in man is grown a common crime,
> Which Frazier doth lament in tender rhyme.

Wilson assumes this to be Cary's brother, Charles, despite the clear inference that the poet's subject is man's inconstancy. A more likely explanation is that Cary Frazier herself wrote poetry, and that, being red-haired she has every right to be called 'Ephelia' (the freckled one) and that she is the author of some though not all of the *Female Poems on Several Occasions* published under that name in 1679. It would follow too that she is the Ephelia of 'Ephelia to Bajazet', and the 'poor ragged jilt' of the lampoon, having been publicly discarded first by Mulgrave, and then by Mordaunt who refused to acknowledge her as his wife. These connections are made however with a caveat; court wits were more than ready to write in each other's personae, Sir George Etherege, for example, being supposed to have written 'Ephelia's lamentation', i.e. 'Ephelia to Bajazet'. Ephelia is at least partly a fictionalised character. In the same way that Sylvia in Behn's *Letters from a Nobleman to his Sister* both is and is not Lady Henrietta Berkeley, Ephelia both is and is not Cary Frazier. There is no point however, in Behn calling her readers to 'witness how oft, all careless of their Fame' women languished for Ovid/Bajazet/Mulgrave, if there were not something to witness, i.e. the poetry of 'Ephelia'.

33 *my cold reserve*: Mulgrave had a reputation for disappointing women:

> Oh, Mulgrave 'twas not done like cavalero
> To tantalise her with your lobcock tarse,
> Then leave her, and but only clap her arse. (Wilson, 82, 34-36) The lady

in this case was Henrietta Wentworth, whom Mulgrave is supposed to have initiated into sexual practices before Monmouth fell in love with her.

39 See 'Satire on the Court Ladies' (Wilson, p. 36) Spring 1680, l. 65:

> For Mulgrave triumphs in varieties.

He was said to have consorted with the foullest whores as well as the grandest court ladies.

42 *gust*: keen relish, appreciation or enjoyment (*OED*).

43 *From her first bloom*: Anne was born in 1665; the implication here is that Mulgrave had formed an attachment to her when she was very young; she

was only rarely at court between 1679 and 1682. Mulgrave may have indeed justified his cavalier treatment of other ladies on the grounds of a prior attachment.

63 *the vain young Fool*: Monmouth; *with all his mother's parts*: i.e. with nothing of his royal father; Lucy Walters or Barlow as she later called herself was thought to be both dissolute and dim-witted. These reflections on Monmouth are the reason why Behn did not acknowledge authorship of 'Ovid to Julia'; milder satire on him in the epilogue to *Romulus and Hersilia* had resulted in her arrest.

64 Monmouth's stupidity was a Tory commonplace.

65 *with Crowds and unmatch'd nonsense*: Monmouth was very popular with the protestant populace. His Whig advisers staged public appearances where his good looks and affable manners enchanted the crowds. The mobs who acclaimed him were easily incited to attack his enemies with cudgels and stone-throwing.

A PINDARICK ON THE DEATH OF OUR LATE SOVEREIGN

SOURCE Broadside Pamphlet, *A Pindarick on the Death Of Our Late Sovereign With An Ancient Prophecy on his Present majesty*. Written by A. Behn. London, Printed by J. Playford for Henry Playford, near the Temple-Church, 1685. (O'Donnell, 98-99)

The death of Charles II occasioned seventy-eight elegies, of which the best-known is Dryden's *Threnodia Augustalis* (Alden, *passim*). Behn's is the only one known to be by a woman. Her friends, Thomas Durfey, Thomas Otway, and Nahum Tate, were also among the elegists.

1 The king's seizures began at eight o'clock on the morning of Monday, 2 February, 1684/5.

14 Cf. Dryden, *Threnodia Augustalis*:

At once the general voice declar'd
Our sacred Prince was dead.

21 Cf. Sir Francis Fane, *A Pindarick Ode on the Sacred Memory Of Our Late gracious Sovereign King Charles II. To which is added, Another Essay On the same Occasion by Sir F.F. Knight of the Bath...* London,1685:

But why no *Prodigy* at all?
No *Beacon-Comet* fir'd above?
No *Monstrous* Births, no *storms*, no *Whale*,
Or to *presage* Great *CHARLES* thy *Fall*,
Or to *attend* thy *Funeral*

34 *So much a God!*: Behn's understanding of the divine right of kings is uncommonly literal.

35-39 After being copiously bled the king rallied towards evening; on Tuesday, when he seemed to be continuing to improve, messengers were sent to all parts of England to announce his recovery. By Thursday morning when the *London Gazette* ran a story that 'the physicians conceive his Majesty to be in a condition of safety and that in a few days he will be freed from his distemper' his condition had worsened and he was understood to be dying.

47-60 This conceit, which likens the temporary remission of the king's final illness to the Resurrection, Transfiguration and Ascension of Christ, seems extraordinarily miscalculated and overdone.

75 Charles is here compared with Moses.

77 *the Golden Calf*: the religion of the dissenters

79 *Joshua*: the Duke of York, Charles's brother, heir presumptive to the throne; cf. 'Funeral Tears to the Sacred Memory of our late Sovereign King Charles the Second':

> That god-like Joshua fills thy Royal Seat,
> Who thy unfinish'd wonders shall compleat.
> (Thompson, *A Collection of 86 Loyal Poems...*, 343)

91 The king is supposed to have asked James to look after his natural children, of whom the Dukes of Grafton, Southampton, Northumberland, St Albans and Richmond, were present at his bedside.

TO HIS SACRED MAJESTY, KING JAMES II

SOURCE: As above. This section of Behn's poem appears without attribution in *A Collection of 86 Loyal Poems, All of them written on the late Plots, viz., the horrid Salamanca Plot in 1678, And the Present Fanatical Conspiracy in 1683; To which is added Advice to the Carver, written on the Death of the late Lord Stafford with Several Poems on their Majesties Coronation, Never before Published.* Collected by N[athaniel] T[hompson] Printed by N. T. at the Entrance to the Old-Spring Gardens near Charing Cross, 1685, pp. 349-350. The closeness of Thompson's version to the broadside text and layout suggests that the broadside is in fact his source.

1-2 In May 1682 James's ship was wrecked on the Lemmon Ore, a sandbank in the Yarmouth Road, as he travelled to Scotland to collect his wife, then far advanced in pregnancy, and bring her to court.

4-10 As a volunteer in Turenne's army 1654-5 James distinguished himself for gallantry and was feted in Paris as a hero; his exposure of his person at the Siege of Ardres was considered foolhardy.

11 In 1657 Charles ordered James to leave the French army and join that of Spain, to fight against his erstwhile allies and loyal friends.

17 In an attempt to forestall the attacks of the exclusionists upon the monarchy, the king ordered his Catholic brother to leave England before the meeting of parliament in the spring of 1679; on March 4 the Duke and Duchess embarked for Holland, and eventually took up residence in the house in Brussels that Charles had occupied while awaiting the Restoration. When Charles fell ill at the end of August, 1679, James made a secret visit to Windsor and obtained permission to take up residence in Scotland, rather than Belgium, and he lived there from November, 1679 to February, 1680, and from October 1680 until he was recalled to court in March, 1682.

A POEM HUMBLY DEDICATED TO ...THE QUEEN DOWAGER

SOURCE: Broadside Pamphlet *A Poem Humbly Dedicated to the Great Patern of Piety and Virtue Catherine Queen Dowager. On the death of her Dear Lord and Husband King Charles II.* By Mrs. Behn. London, Printed by J. Playford for Henry Playford, near the Temple-Church: 1685. (O'Donnell, 101)

Luttrell's copy of this broadside, preserved at Harvard, notes that it was offered for sale at the price of two pence, and dates it '4. aprill'.

Catherine: Catherine of Braganza (1638-1705), daughter of King John of Portugal, sister of Alfonso IV, was first proposed as a wife for Charles in 1645. Negotiations were several times renewed; in 1660 an Anglo-Portuguese alliance was proposed, in which Catherine to bring as her dowry Tangier, Bombay and 2,000,000 crusados, in return for protection for Portugal from the Dutch and Spanish, who vigorously opposed the treaty. The king's mother, Henrietta Maria, brought the French to support the marriage which was duly solemnised on May 21, 1661. The queen's upbringing had been extremely secluded; she spoke neither English nor French. To Charles's courtiers she seemed both provincial and arrogant, pious to the point of bigotry and at the same time frivolous. Though she resisted with spirit, she was obliged to accept as her lady-in-waiting the king's mistress, raised to the nobility as Countess of Castlemaine. In later years she treated all the king's mistresses, and his illegitimate children, with kindness and consideration. It was commonly thought that she intrigued for the re-establishment of the Church of Rome and that her chapel was a place of resort for Catholics and conspirators against the very life of the king.

13 *dear lov'd husband*: though Catherine was forced to tolerate her husband's

liaisons, all the evidence shows that she was only too happy to welcome any signs of affection in him. For his part, he refused to put her aside on any pretext, despite pressure to make Monmouth legitimate or to take a British wife who might prove fruitful.

16-17 As soon as she heard the news of Charles's seizure Catherine went to his apartment and watched speechless with shock as his doctors let copious quantities of blood, and applied a cautery to his head, in futile attempts to relieve the congestion that darkened his face and distorted his features. Eventually she collapsed in convulsions and was carried bodily out of the room. Her medical attendants then compounded the effects of shock by repeatedly bleeding her. When the king came to his senses he called for her but she was obliged to ask his pardon for she was not physically able to come to him. Her doctors allowed her to re-enter the king's chamber later, and she seems to have attended his bedside intermittently during the first days of his final illness, but more and more she was to be found lying senseless in her adjoining apartment. When his brother and heir, James, Duke of York, was urging the king to be reconciled to the Catholic Church and receive the last sacraments, Catherine was once more fainting and being bled by her doctors in her apartments.

31 *the Saint* : the sincerity of Catherine's piety was never in doubt.

39 *perjuries so black and foul*: In November, 1678 the murder of Sir Edmund Berry Godfrey was laid to the charge of the Queen's priests and her Catholic servants at Somerset House, where she was living apart from the king while the Duchess of Portsmouth, Louise de Kéroualle, was playing the part of the king's consort at Whitehall. Titus Oates went so far as to accuse the Queen of plotting to murder the king. He deposed on oath, absurdly enough, that he had seen a letter from her catholic physician, Sir George Wakeman, conveying the Queen's consent to a scheme to poison her husband; Bedloe gave evidence that he had overheard a conversation in the Queen's chapel between her secretary, Edward Coleman, Lord Belasise and some Jesuits, in which it was said that the Queen's assent though reluctant had been gained, and moreover that she was willing to administer the poison herself. On November 28, Titus Oates, advancing to the bar of the commons, accused the queen of high treason. As a consequence of the perjured testimony of Miles Prance, a silversmith who ocasionally cleaned the silver in the Queen's chapel, three of her servants were unjustly executed. Catherine attended the trial of Stafford and heard her own name cited again and again by the witnesses against the Catholic lords as a chief mover of the plot against the king's life. Stafford was found guilty 'on testimony that ought not to be taken on the life of a dog' and executed on

29 December, 1680. In 1681 the exclusionist faction found a new tool, a pensioner of the Duchess of Portsmouth called Fitzharris, who revived all the accusations against the queen. This time the king dissolved parliament and had Fitzharris arrested.

48 *your vertue they profan'd*: Catherine's fidelity to the king was in no more doubt than his infidelity to her. In the satiric literature of the time she figures rarely and then usually to be reviled only for her infertility and her low stature; in *The Queen's Ball* (1670) which attacks the partisans of the Portuguese marriage through the medium of a cruel personal lampoon, the queen's infertility is ascribed to the heat of her womb, 'a Hell which always burns', with the insinuation by extension that her passion for dancing and her childlessness are both the effects of inordinate sexual desire, in which she is more rabid than Diana's hunting dogs. In terms of contemporary physiology such an explanation of childlessness in women was quite logical.

> If bold Actaeon in the waves had seen
> In fair Diana's room our puppet queen,
> He would have fled and in his full career,
> For greater haste have wish'd himself a deer,
> Preferr'd the bellies of his dogs to hers,
> And thought 'em the more cleanly sepulchres.
> What stupid madman would not choose to have
> The settled rest and silence of a grave
> Rather than such a hell, which always burns,
> And from whom Nature forbids all returns?

61-62 The king had realised from the beginning that all the accusations against his wife were baseless. He had proved to his own satisfaction that Oates was a liar by questioning him about circumstantial details such as the physical appearance of Don John and the layout of the queen's apartments in Somerset House. When it became clear in that Catherine was in real danger both from the mob and the Shaftesbury faction which was making political capital out of anti-papist agitation, he brought his wife back to Whitehall and under his protection. He replied to suggestions from Shaftesbury that a marriage with Monmouth's mother, Lucy Walters, might be proved, with a proclamation that he had only ever had one wife and Catherine was she. When it was suggested to him that he might put Catherine away and take a fruitful wife he declared that it was against his conscience; according to Burnet, who is generally unsympathetic to Catherine, he said 'that considering his great faultiness towards her, he thought it would be a horrid thing to abandon her.' On his death-bed as she knelt to beg his pardon for any fault she might have committed against him, he replied 'that she had offended in nothing, but that he had been guilty of many offences against her and asked her pardon.'

67 *your pleading eloquence*: when the queen arrived in England she could speak only Portuguese and Spanish, and could not converse with the king even in French. Behn's point is, of couse, that she would not have needed eloquence, not that she possessed it.

72 Behn here implies that the queen's return to Whitehall was in the nature of a renewal of her nuptials, and that the king courted her anew. The Countess of Sunderland in a letter to her brother-in-law at the Hague, described the queen as now the king's mistress, 'his passion for her is so great.' Poor Catherine was no match for the beautiful and sophisticated women who surrounded the king, who was soon as uninterested in her as ever.

104 *So the blest Virgin*: Behn's comparison of Catherine of Braganza mourning her unfaithful husband with Mary fainting at the foot of the Cross is one of the most hyperbolic manifestations of absolutist sentiment in English literature. Protestant feeling against the cult of the Blessed Virgin was so strong that pictures of the Madonna and Child were burnt in public bonfires.

108-110 Behn extends the image of Mary at the Crucifixion to a proso-popoiac vision of the mourning queen as the Pieta, the Virgin with the dead Christ in her arms.

114-115 Behn takes a slight risk here in foreseeing that the queen-dowager, who was forty-seven at the time of her husband's death, would never remarry. In fact she did not, although gossip suspected her of a relationship with her Lord Chamberlain, Louis Duras, Earl of Feversham.

126ff Catherine received those who came to offer their condolences lying on a bed of mourning in a chamber lit only by tapers and hung from ceiling to floor with black draperies that excluded all daylight and muffled all sound.

A PINDARICK POEM ON THE HAPPY CORONATION

SOURCE: Broadside Pamphlet *A Pindarick Poem on the Happy Coronation of His Most Sacred Majesty James II and His Illustrious Consort Queen Mary*. London, Printed by J. Playford for Henry Playford, near the Temple-Church: 1685.

The poem was printed in two versions; the second was partially reset, from Div to the end, incorporating not only corrections but new material, removing stanxa XVII, renumbering the stanzas and inserting a revised version of Stanza XVII as Stanza XXVII. Though the title-pages are identical the second version must be recognised as a separate edition. As the emendations are all authorial the second edition has been taken as my copy-text.

Luttrell's copy of the emended version, at Princeton, is marked '6d' and dated '13. May'; the poem was entered in the Term catalogue for Easter, 1685 (II, 126). The text was followed by an Advertisement of pamphlets available from the bookseller: 'A Pindarick on the Death of our late Sovereign, with an Ancient Prophecy on His Present Majesty. Written by Mrs. *Behn;* A Poem Humbly Dedicated to Her Sacred Majesty *Catherine* Queen Dowager, on the Death of her dear Lord Husband King *Charles* the Second, by Mrs. *Behn;* A Pindarick Ode on the Sacred Memory of our Late Gracious Sovereign King *Charles* the Second: To which is added another Essay on the same occasion, by Sir *F.F.* Knight of the *Bath.*; The Vision: A Pindarick Ode: Occasion'd by the Death of our Late Sovereign King Charles the Second, by *Edm. Arwaker*, M.A. [together with] The second Part of the *Vision*, a Pindarick Poem on the *Coronation*, by *Edm. Arw.;* A Poem on the Sacred Memory of our late Sovereign: with a Congratulation to his Present Majesty. Written by Mr. *Tate.* The Elegies are sold single or in one Volume by *Henry Playford* near the *Temple-Church.*'

The Coronation of James II and his consort, Mary of Modena took place on St George's Day, April 23, 1685, which fell in Easter week .

12 *little Gods that tun'd the spheres*: amoretti

22 *Charming Swain*: David when he sang before Saul

26 *Godlike Patron*: in 1681 Behn dedicated the second part of *The Rover* to James, Duke of York although she dreaded to appear one of those 'Insolent and Saucy Offenders' who would take advantage of his absence in Scotland 'to commit ill-mannered Indecencies.' In her dedication she claims that his Highness was 'pleas'd to give the Rover' encouragement 'at his first appearance' and that he expressed 'concern' 'for his second'. The Duke was the titular patron of the Duke's Company which produced all of Behn's plays until the union of the theatres in 1687.

3 *first Messenger of Heaven*: Michael who defended the gates of Eden against Adam and Eve with a flaming sword

40 *Laura*: the reference is obviously to Maria Beatrice Eleonora D'Este of Modena. Laura was in fact her mother's name.

42 *Guardian-Angels*: according to Catholic doctrine each human soul has a guardian angel to protect it from evil.

72 *Ten thousand Angels*: Behn sets the scene of the coronation amid ranks of angelic entities, as if it were a painted *trionfo* or a staged *opera seria*.

84 *Awake*: By tradition the monarch should sleep at the Tower on the eve

of his coronation and process through the city of London to Westminster. As James and Mary slept at St James's Palace the populace was denied the spectacle.

100 *So bodies when refin'd*: only when the soul is released from the body can it see the glory of God which would blind mortal eyes; only James can behold the celestial beauty of Mary of Modena and live to tell the tale. The realities of the royal marriage-bed in no way resembled Behn's glowing vision of monogamous sexual bliss.

142-164 James is here described in the kind of imagery more usually to be associated with Louis XIV of France, the Sun King,

165 *Dunkirk's bloody field*: in June 1658 James, who was commanding two thousand exiled Britons in the service of the King of Spain, took on Cromwellian troops fighting on the French side in the Battle of the Dunes outside Dunkirk. They fought until James was forced to withdraw through the French lines with the twenty men remaining to him to the village of Zudcote (see Haswell, 115-119). In the Dedication of the second part of *The Rover* to James in 1681, Behn referred to Dunkirk, where James's courage and virtue taught even his 'Enemies so intire an Obedience, that asham'd of their Rebel Gallantry they have resigned their guilty Commissions and vow'd never to Draw Sword more but in the Royal Cause'; a side note explains 'Some of Oliver's Commanders at Dunkirk.'

169 *Thus spoke*: what follows is Behn's invention.

181 *defus'd*: diffused, i.e. poured out

192 *His early courage*: As a volunteer in Turenne's army 1654-5 James distinguished himself for gallantry and was feted in Paris as a hero; his exposure of his person at the Siege of Ardres was considered foolhardy.

Stanza X The Queen was not dressed by 'loves and graces' but by the Countess of Peterborough, Groom of the Stole, her ladies of the bedchamber, Lady Sophia Bulkeley and Frances, Countess of Bantry, and her tiringwomen, Mrs Elizabeth Bromley and Mrs Margaret Dawson, who attended her throughout.

265-266 Once more Behn employs the conceit of superhuman attractions destroying lesser mortals, this time rather cunningly invoking Jupiter's adultery with mortal females. Semele was destroyed because she demanded that Jupiter show himself to her not in disguise as a mortal, but in his glory.

271-2 Mary of Modena had much need of prayer. Her husband was obsessed by other women, she had no living child, and the life she was forced to lead was in many instances repugnant to her.

296-301 The extreme vagueness and generality of Behn's hyperbolic eulogy bears out her own statement of her distance from the court and her obscurity.

314 *the gilded Barges*: Only the king went by barge from the Privy Stairs at Whitehall to the Parliament Stairs at Westminster. The queen went by her chair to Whitehall, and then by the Privy Gardens into Channel Row and across New Palace Yard to Westminster Hall.

328-348 James was appointed Lord High Admiral of the British Fleet in March, 1665, and commanded at the Battle of Solebay.

338 *that Senat*: the parliament which repeatedly endeavoured to exclude James from the succession on the grounds of his Catholicism

350-1 After the victory at Solebay the Dutch fleet was allowed to escape while the Duke was resting, owing to the misjudgment of Brouncker.

Stanzas XIV-XVI: These stanzas are by way of hymns, XIV to Jove, XV and XVI to Juno.

377 *all the shining tropies of the East*: the Queen's regalia was new made for this coronation, for the regalia used by Anne of Denmark in 1603 had been plundered during the Interregnum; its value was assessed at the fabulous sum of £111,900.

405 *Ten Thousand Garlands*: Mrs Mary Dowie, hereditary herb-woman to the king, directed three pairs of damsels in strewing fresh aromatic herbs along the path trod by the king and queen from Westminster-hall to the west door of Westminster Abbey. It is doubtful however that Behn's evocation of generic floral tributes refers to this specific circumstance.

447 In the first edition Stanza XVIII ran as follows:

> Behold the *Royal Hero* on the shore!
>
> Voices and Canons now with louder Accents roar;
>
> Wild with their joy, even rudly they express
>
> Its vast concern, its vast excess!
>
> All stretch themselves beyond their native height,
>
> At more advantage to Survey the sight;
>
> That Glorious sight which though each day we view...

and so on as in Stanza XXVII. Stanza XVIII is the original XIX, and so on until after Stanza XXVII when the original numbering is restored.

453-463 Behn seems here to be referring to her hopes of royal favour, which was never forthcoming.

464 *and now the Royal Robes are on*: the Queen had been vested in her robes of purple velvet trimmed with ermine and looped with ropes and tassels of pearls, and her cap of purple velvet, held on with a circlet of large diamonds, before leaving St James's Palace; Behn's sequence of events has the royal couple travelling down the Thames to an investiture and then, after resting, appearing robed before the crowds.

490 *She comes!*: Behn now describes the order of the procession from Westminster Hall, through New Palace Yard, into King Street and across the Great Sanctuary to the West Door of Westminster Abbey exactly as it was given in *An Account of the Ceremoniall at the Coronation Of their Most Excellent Majesties King James II and Queen Mary, published by order of the Duke of Norfolk, Earl Marshall of England.* (London, 1685).

491 *The Ivory Scepter*: usually called the ivory rod, surmounted by a dove,

499 *DORSET*: Charles Sackville Lord Buckhurst, fourth Earl of Middlesex and sixth Earl of Dorset (1638-1706) minor poet, member of the Kit Kat Club, friend of Rochester, Etherege, Sedley, Buckingham and Jacob Tonson, patron of Dryden, Prior and numerous other writers, and loyal Whig, was at first in favour with James, but was deprived of his offices in 1688. He served William and Mary as Lord Chamberlain and member of the Privy Council.

504 *all he e're spoke or writ*: Dorset was severe upon the Duke of York, whom he called Charles's 'hair-brain'd brother' in 'On the Young Statesmen' (c. January 1680), ironically praising his wit in 'My Opinion' (1681-2). Behn may have had in mind too his squib 'on the Countess of Dorchester'. Dorset's most withering attacks on James II are all of later date than Behn's Coronation poem, the best known and most devastating being 'A Faithful Catalogue of our most Eminent Ninnies' (1688). These lines from 'Julian's farewell to the Muses' (1685)

> My great Maecenas, awful Dorset, came,
> And as a mark of his censorious wit
> Paid double fees for what himself had writ, (*POAS*)

imply that Dorset was the principal financier of Julian's activities as distributor of MS lampoons and satires, including some written by Dorset himself, and it may be to these propagandist activities that Behn is referring.

505 *The golden Scepter*: the Queen's sceptre with the cross; *RUTLAND*: John Manners, Earl of Rutland

512 *BEAUFORD*: Duke of Beaufort; *the sacred Circle*: the crown with which the Queen was actually crowned, as distinct from the circlet of diamonds she wore on her way into Westminster Hall, and the small crown she wore during the coronation banquet.

547-552 See Revelations, 12, 1-2

554 *NORFOLK*: Mary, Duchess of Norfolk, daughter and heiress of Henry Mordaunt, second Earl of Peterborough, who became the subject of one of the most clamorous court scandals of 1685 when she was caught by her husband in the act of adultery with John Jermain, and sent to a monastery

in France.

559 *YOUNG DIANA'S*: in bearing the queen's train the Duchess was assisted by Lady Jane Noel, daughter of the Earl of Gainsborough, Lady Anne Herbert, daughter of the Earl of Powis, Lady Anne Spencer, daughter of the Earl of Cumberland, and Lady Essex Roberts, daughter of the Earl of Radnor, all of whom were unmarried.

569 *AYLESBURY*: Robert Bruce, Earl of Aylesbury; *GRAY*: Henry Yelverton, Lord Gray of Ruthyn

570 *the Marshall Staff*: usually known as St Edward's Staff; *the Spur*: the golden Spurs

615-618 These lines refer to the power Edward the Confessor had of curing the King's Evil, or scrofula, by the laying on of hands, a power believed to have been inherited by all in the line of direct succession.

577 *PETERBOROW*: Henry Mordaunt, second Earl of Peterborough, ambassador extraordinary and proxy in James's marriage to Mary of Modena, Groom of the Stole, First Gentleman of the Bedchamber, and a catholic

582 *the Treasure that he bore*: the Sceptre with the Cross, also known as St Edward's Sceptre

583 *PEMBROKE*: Thomas Herbert, eighth Earl of Pembroke (1656-1703) who raised the militia against Monmouth in the summer of 1685, but was dismissed from office in 1687

589 *the Sword*: the sword of justice to the spirituality, or the third sword

591 *DARBY*: William Richard George Stanley, Earl of Derby; *SHREWSBURY*: Charles Talbot, twelfth Earl of Shrewsbury (1660-1718) who turned against James in the year of his accession and was one of the signatories to the invitation to William of Orange in 1688

596 *the pointed... Sword*: the sword of justice to the temporality, which has a longer point than the third sword; *more honour'd Broken Sword*: the Sword of Mercy, known as Curtana, has its point broken off.

597 *OXFORD*: Aubrey de Vere, twentieth Earl of Oxford, (1626-1703) first earl of the realm, who refused to support the repeal of the test act and was stripped of his offices in February, 1688, carried the Sword of State in its Scabbard.

604 *GRAFTON*: Henry Fitzroy, first Duke of Grafton, second natural son of Charles II by Barbara Villiers, Countess of Castlemaine; both he and his brother defected to William in the last weeks of 1688.

605 *England's High Constable*: Grafton, dressed in his robes of state and wearing the coronet of a duke, and the collar of the order of the Garter, also carried the staff and mace of the Lord High Constable.

616 *NORFOLK*: Henry Howard, seventh Duke of Norfolk, who refused to

carry the sword of state before James into his (Catholic) chapel and resigned his regiment of foot in June, 1686; *the greatest Subject*: Norfolk was premier duke.

623 *MÆCÆNA of my Muse, my Patron Lord*: in 1682, Behn dedicated the book of *The City Heiress* to 'Henry, Earl of Arundel and Lord Mowbray' as he was known before succeeding to the dukedom in 1684; possibly, in his capacity as Earl Marshall, Norfolk had commissioned the coronation ode from Behn; ceratinly her account of the ceremonial is based entirely upon the official order published by the Earl Marshall's office, which she may have been shown before it was available to the general public.

624 *ORMOND*: James Butler, Duke of Ormonde, who went over to William in 1688

636 *the Sacred Diadem*: Ormond carried St Edward's Crown, which is the one used for the actual crowning, in his capacity as Lord High Steward of the Realm.

638 *that grac'd his hand before*: Ormond performed the same office at the crowning of Charles II.

640 *SOMERSET*: Charles Seymour, sixth Duke of Somerset (1662-1748) who refused to introduce the Papal Nuncio to James's court and was immediately dismissed from all his offices

643 *Worlds Emblim*: the Orb with the Cross.

646 *ALBEMARLE*: Christopher Monck, second Duke of Albemarle, whom see below.

651 *the Peaceful Scepter*: the King's Scepter with the Dove

678 *the kind* Confirmers: those who ratified James's right to the Succession

691 *land-pirates*: looters of ship-wrecked vessels

697-698 Using the biblical analogue that Dryden made irresistible in *Absalom and Achitophel* Behn refers to the struggles of the Country party to exclude James from the succession.

700 *NORTHUMBERLAND*: George Fitzroy, Duke of Northumberland, second son of Charles II by the Countess of Castlemaine, walked behind the king, bare-headed and unrobed, because he was under age, in the dress uniform of Captain of the Troop of his Majesty's Horse Guards in waiting.

722 Incense: incense

750 *Ely's* Sermon: the coronation sermon was preached by James II's old Chaplain, Francis Turner, Bishop of Ely.

758 Ariosto was not himself of the d'Este family; his first patron was Cardinal Ippolito d'Este, whose service he left in 1517 to enter that of his brother Alfonso, Duke of Modena, Maria Beatrice's ancestor.

ÆSOP'S FABLES

SOURCE: *Æsop's Fables with his life in English, French and Latin newly translated. Illustrated with One hundred and twelve Sculptures. To this Edition are likewise added, Thirty one New Figures representing his Life.* By Francis Barlow, and are to be sold by Chr. Wilkinson at the Black-boy against St. Dunstan's Church in Fleet Street, Tho. Fox in Westminster Hall, and Henry Faithorne at the Rose in St. Paul's Church-yard. M.DC.LXXXVII.

Francis Barlow (1625/6-1704) is considered the first English sporting artist; his native birds and animals are meticulously observed and rendered with a spontaneity and authenticity rare in animal depiction at any time. His first edition of the Fables, *Æsop's Fables with his Life in English, French & Latin.* The English by Tho. Philipott Esq., The French and Latine by Rob. Codrington M.A. Illustrated with One hundred and Twelve Sculptures by Francis Barlow, London, Printed by William Godbid for Francis Barlow, and are to be sold by Ann Seile at the Black-Boy against St. Dunstan's Church in Fleetstreet, and Edward Powell at the Swan in Little Britain. M.DCLXVI. sometimes appears dated 1656, giving rise to a ghost in Wing. A second engraved title-page advertised that Barlow also sold copies from his shop at the Golden Eagle in New-street near Shoe Lane. It has been supposed that this edition is relatively rare because Barlow's stock was destroyed when New Street was engulfed in the Great Fire (September, 1666). In the late seventies Barlow began to prepare a second edition using his original plates, and preparing thirty-one full page illustrations for the life of Æsop, most of which were engraved by Thomas Dudley. For this edition Barlow used a new French version of the life, and the new French translation of the fables by Baudoin. In the 1666 edition the English verse paraphrases of Philipott had been engraved directly on the copper plates bearing the illustrations; for the new edition his verses were erased, and Behn's new versions engraved in a different, italic script, almost certainly by Barlow himself, in their stead.

Barlow engraved very little besides his Æsop, and apologised for the quality of his engravings. Indeed, as engravings, his plates for *Æsop's Fables* are not in the first rank; as illustrations they have almost never been equalled. Though Barlow provided illustrations for the enlarged edition of Ogilby's *Æsop Paraphras'd* (1668) he did not engrave the plates himself. He was primarily an inspired animal portraitist, and was very probably in demand for records of sporting events, which he would have enjoyed a great deal more than labouring with metal and acid. Vertue tells us that he was 'a sociable and pleasant gentleman much loved by the gentry', unlike the generality of engravers who are not gentlemen but artisans. In 1653 Barlow was paid the considerable sum of £8 for a picture of a fish; he could not expect to make this kind of money engraving. The first depiction of an English sporting event is Barlow's drawing of the last race meeting attended by Charles II, at Dorset ferry near Windsor in August 1684, which he eventually engraved.

The most likely explanation for the preparation of a second edition of Barlow's Æsop in 1687 is that someone among Barlow's friends and patrons urged him to it. The edition is dedicated to William, Lord Cavendish, who inherited as 4th Earl of Devonshire in November, 1684. Rake, sportsman, and the builder of Chatsworth, he had more than sufficient means, taste and generosity to have persuaded Barlow to undertake a new edition. He was a lover 'of ladies and plays' (Wilson, p. 234) and might also have suggested Behn as the best person to supply the new English version of the Fables.

The ascription to Aphra Behn of all the captions for Barlow's engravings in the 1687 edition is justified by Barlow's statement in the address to the readers: 'The Ingenious Mrs. A. Behn has been so obliging as to perform the English Poetry, which in short comprehends the sense of the Fable and Moral: whereof to say much were needless, since it may sufficiently recommend it self to all Persons of Vnderstanding.' The new edition was a long time preparing; some of the new plates are dated 1678 and 1679. We do not know when Mrs Behn was approached to provide new verses, but there can be no denying the evidence of hasty composition, as well as hasty transferring of the text from her manuscript to the plates. Mrs Behn clearly had the 1666 edition by her as she struggled to produce a hundred and ten potted fables. The new verses appearing as captions to the full-page illustrations of Æsop's life are very probably hers too, and therefore I have included them, until evidence should appear that they are by another hand.

The appearance of the second edition of Barlow's Æesop coincides with the development of a veritable mania for fables among English littérateurs. It is a great pity that Behn could not indulge her own creativity in the writing of original fables or even allow herself the luxury of developing her own version of Æsop beyond the constraints imposed by the engraved plates, which allowed her only a gnomic four lines, and a concluding couplet. Even so, Behn's personality emerges with startling vividness from this very uneven work; her obsessions, with Monmouth, with the marriage of young women to old men, with foppery of all kinds, keep resurfacing only to sink again under a weight like that of the repulsively anti-feminist and far-fetched 'morall' of Fable LXXIII.
XII Cf. Philipott,

> While the quick fouler, sought wth busy skill
> A Stock Dove on a neighbouring tree to kill,
> An Adder lurking in the ye grass beneath
> His death did with a fatall bite bequeath
> Who now from an assaulted heart did feele,
> Whilst he ey'd her, the viper ey'd his heele.

the young usurper: Monmouth landed in the west of England on June 11, 1685.

a victim: the Duke of Monmouth was found guilty of high treason and his beautiful head clumsily struck off on July 17, 1685.

XIV Cf. Philipott:

> A Horse whom gaudy trappings did array
> Commands a loaded Ass to yeild the way...

XXI Cf. Philipott:

> Good Counsell's eas'ly given, but the effect
> Oft renders it, uneasy to transact.

XXII The moral is Behn's own injunction and clearly political; Philipott's moral is closer to the spirit of Æsop:

> Thus Povertie its right hath oft foregone
> When by injurious greatnes trod upon.

XXIII Once more Behn introduces a political reference, which may indicate that she was working on Cowley's *Sylva* at the same time, and his references to the Boscobel oak were running in her mind; Philipott would have been aware of the same commonplace but his version reads simply:

> Do not ye humble wth neglect dispise,
> A Mouse a Lion rescu'd from Surprize.

XXIV *late pitty'd president;* i.e. recent pitiable precedent, Monmouth. Once again the Tory propagandist intervenes to point our understanding of Æsop's moral. (Unfortunately for Behn both Barlow and the Earl of Devonshire were Whigs.) Philipott has:

> Thos yt from schooles & warme disputes doe come
> Are unawares by beautys charmes struck dumbe.

XXV Behn's version is inferior to Philipott's original:

> So bold Impietie doth often boast,
> In those loose actions men dishonour most.

XXVI This time Behn slips into the idiom of the literary lampoonist; Philipott makes the more general point:

> Nature in one does not her guifts entwine
> Therefore let none at his first state repine.

XXVII Behn keeps close to Philipott:

> When first the Fox the Shaggy Lion saw

Congeald wth feare & child with reverend awe...

XXIX Again Behn's moral is idiosyncratic; Philipott has:

Som with keen Envie would themselves anoy
So those they Emulate they might destroy.

XXXV Again Behn's preoccupations lead her to the theme of Monmouth: Philipott makes the more general point rather more verbosely:

Thus factious men wth their intestine Jarrs
Fix on their Contreys such destructive scarrs
That being wasted wyth their mutuall wounds
A foreign force thyr interest confounds.

XXXVI Cf. Philipott:

The Froggs implore a king, but Iove detests...

XXXVII Again Behn's moral is her own; Philipott's frame of reference is very different:

When you'l decline a thing disgustful see
You not contract a worse calamitie.
So hapless seamen oft to save themselves
Do shun the Rocks to split upon the shelves.

XXXVIII Behn keeps close to Philipott:

Thus oft from Realmes by mutuall conflict torne
Away by a third power, the Scepters borne.

XL Behn makes rather a mess of Philipott's moral:

By subtilty ye tenure first was gain'd
And now by force ye title is mainteyn'd.
Empire by fraud is oftentimes made good
By ye more rough designs of warr & blood.

XLV Again Behn keeps close to Philipott, but perhaps not close enough:

The gay plum'd Peacok wth a nice disdaine
Slights ye cheap clothing of ye long-beakt Crane...
Scorne not the indigent. their minds may be
Richer then all thy gaudy pedigree.

LIV Behn's is an exact transcription of Philipott's moral.

LVI Cf. Philipott:

A Clowne an Ambush strew'd for cranes & Geese
Whose ravage wasted his sowne fields; wth these
A storke surprisd did for his life request...

LVII Though the expression of Philipott's moral is more than usually infelicitous, Behn retains it:

So a Luxuriant power oft makes its will
The only cause of Rough oppression still.

LXII Behn has Philipott's moral in mind:
> He says, Lo how by concord things obtaine
> New vigour, which discord dissolves again.

LXIII Again Behn's moral is a version of Philipott's:
> Cowards by nature with no magic can
> Be heightned to the valor of a man

LXV 3-4 Cf. Philipott:
> Wee'l curb your pride, henceforth yor head shall weare
> No hornes alone, but what is worse no eare.

LXVI Cf. Philipott:
> Winnow all Councell, for you'le find most tend
> To private ends, when they your good pretend.

LXX Cf. Philipott:
> Mean parts by Industry those things doe Act
> Which greater wou'd, foyld by their dull neglect.

LXXIII Cf. Philipott:
> Thus our too swelling hopes abortive are,
> And fall like towers whose basis is the air.

LXVII Cf. Philipott:
> Envy not others vertues, providence
> Guifts fitted to each genius does dispence.

LXXIX Cf. Philipott:
> In Civill broyles ye Indigent are free'd
> While still ye rich doe in their purses bleed

LXXX Cf. Philipott:
> Since for the shaddow he the substance lost.

LXXXV Cf. Philipott:
> The Fox the Crane did solemnly invite...
> But a glass viall did her Cates conteyne...

LXXXVI Cf. Philipott:
> Oft pettier Princes b'ing too much persu'd
> Have Mightyer Monarchs wth joint strength subdu'd.

Behn ignores the sense of the French, 'que les grands doivent apprehender la colère des Petits'.

LXXXVIII Cf. Philipott:
> But thou design'd (said he) far greater ill,
> Who men each other does excite to kill.

LXXXIX Cf. Philipott:
> No wonder says she that they me annoy
> When they themselves with their own hate destroy

XCII Cf. Philipott:
>...the Fox replyes,
>The Asses fate had taught him to be wise.

XCIV Cf. Philipott:
>But from this petty gayne his loss began
>For he ere since hath servant been to man.

XCV Cf. Philipott:
>But his imagin'd mine and vaine desire
>Did with his Goose together both expire.

XCVII Cf. Philipott:
>...my Master, said the Dog
>T'appease my fierceness there annext a clog.

CI Cf. Philipott:
>Though wrackt wth various tortur life doth please
>Still more then death, though death all pressures ease.

CIII Cf. Philipott:
>Oft injur'd innocence is eas'd to see
>Ill men as Scourges to Ill men to be.

CIV Cf. Philipott:
>A Prince elected should be still indu'd
>Not with gay forme but inward fortitude.

CV Cf. Philipott:
>Wild Hectors this discribes who boast t'have don
>Acts, which they never durst adventure on.

CVII Cf. Philipott:
>Our ruin oft does from those Arts commence
>Our feares at first contriv'd for our defence.

CIX Cf. Philipott:
>Love so Captves us wth its powerfull charmes
>It both our prudence & our strength disarmes.

CX Cf. Philipott:
>Promise not Princes what you cant make good
>Only to raise your selves. theyr Royall Blood
>Doe not inflame. 'tis dangerous them to mock
>It oft procures a Halter or the Block.

TO CHRISTOPHER, DUKE OF ALBEMARLE

SOURCE: Broadside Pamphlet *To the Most Illustrious Prince Christopher*

Duke of Albemarle, on his Voyage to his Government of Jamaica. A Pindarick. By Mrs. A. Behn, London, Printed for John Newton over against the Inner Temple Gate in Fleet Street. 1687. (O'Donnell, 123)

Christopher Monck (1653-1689), son of George Monck, first Duke of Albemarle, succeeded to the title on his father's death in January, 1670 when he was only seventeen. At first he was a crony of Monmouth; when the beadle, Peter Vernell, who surprised Monmouth and Viscount Dunbar at a disorderly house in January 1671/2 was killed, Albemarle was with them (Ward, 50 and *passim*). In 1673 Albemarle was made colonel of a regiment of foot, in 1675 privy councillor, lord lieutenant of Devonshire and joint lord-lieutenant of Essex; in 1678 he was made colonel of the Queen's Regiment of horse. Though an unshakeable protestant, he was equally unshakeable in his loyalty to Charles II, if remiss in his duties as Gentleman of the Bedchamber. When Monmouth returned unbidden from exile in the Netherlands, struck out the bar-sinister on his coat of arms and set off on a progress in the West, the king gave Albemarle Monmouth's Captaincy of the King's Life Guards of Horse, and the First Troop of Horse; in 1682 he was appointed Chancellor of Cambridge University, displacing Mon-mouth once again. After playing his part in the coronation of James II and Mary of Modena he withdrew to Newhall, his estate in Essex, and ignored all summons to come to court. When Monmouth invaded, he was obliged to lead the Devonshire militia against the rebels, but his troops were disaf-fected, and the organisation of the county militias deficient. At Axminster in June 1685, he ordered a retreat, despite his numerical superiority. On July 6 a letter from the Earl of Sunderland informed him that the Frenchman, Louis Duras, Earl of Faversham, had been appointed commander in chief; on July 31, the day after a long interview with the king had left tears standing in Albemarle's eyes, he laid down all his commissions and announced his retirement from the chancellorship of Cambridge University, thus becom-ing the first of the protestant lords to withdraw from the service of James II.

Proponents of the view that Aphra Behn was both a catholic and a jacobite will have to account for her writing this poem to this man at this time (as well as her fulfillment of commissions from Mulgrave and Dorset). It is possible that Albemarle had come to Behn's assistance in August 1682 when she and Lady Slingsby were taken into custody for reflections upon Monmouth in the prologue to *Romulus and Hersilia*, and he may have aided her in her exposure of Monmouth's co-conspirator and leading Whig, Ford, Lord Grey of Warke, anti-hero of *Letters from a Nobleman to his Sister*, who had been Albemarle's sworn enemy ever since February 1679 when their candidates had opposed each other at the poll of Essex. (Price, 41-44).

Within a few days of the death on April 11, 1686 while on a visit to
England, of Sir Philip Howard, Governor of Jamaica, Albemarle had gone
to see the king at Windsor, kissed his hand and asked for the governorship
of the colony, which was granted on May 31. There was a popular outcry,
from Albemarle's supporters in Devon, and from the loyal protestants who
saw their influence at court much weakened by his exile, brought about
more by his own haughty impatience than the Machiavellian malice of the
king. The vociferous Whigs chose to misrepresent the situation. A satire of
June, 1686 (Wilson, 167) lists Albemarle among the clients of the fortune-
teller, Madam Le Croix:

> In comes a duke, from mighty place
> And merit fallen into disgrace.
> She views his hand and bids him joy,
> Calls him Excellence Viceroy!

'On the Camp' (Bodleian MS Firth c. 15, p. 192) is m ore explicit:

> Next, is an Officer of late disgusted,
> Whose Court Quarrel newly is adjusted:
> Heav'n ne'r design'd him for the politick Trade,
> All his best part of Flesh and Bones are made,
> Perhaps He always means well; but his best
> Was Stumbling on some Service in the West:...
> But now is business found will fit him to a Hair;
> To teach wild *Indians* (not Stratagems of War,
> But) to drink Punch, Wrestle and throw the Bar.

The Monck family had long had connections with the Americas;
George Monck, the first Duke, had held grants in the Carolinas, and
pursued interests in Barbados; since 1882 his son had served on the Committee of the Lords of Trades and Plantations. Albemarle's secretary, Arthur
Fairwell, was from a Massachusetts Bay family. Sir Thomas Modyford,
governor of Jamaica to 1680 was a second cousin. When he was arrested at
the suit of Spain after the Sack of Panama, it was Albemarle who success-
fully petitioned for his release. It is not impossible that Aphra Behn yearned
to revisit the scenes of her girlhood, if only in search of relief from her joint
pain; after all, her friend and colleague Edmund Arwaker was travelling
with the Duke as his chaplain. The duke did not leave England to take up
the governorship of Jamaica until 12 September, 1687.

2 *the Heroe*: in 1673 Christopher Monck, then Lord Torrington, had been
one of the eight lords commissioned by Charles to raise new regiments for
the Dutch war; he accompanied his regiment to Holland in July and
evidently served in the Lowlands for some months; thereafter his military

duties were limited to exercising his militias in Devon and Essex. He went ostensibly to join the army in Holland in 1677, but stayed less than two months. He went to Holland again in 1678 only to find that hostilities had ceased for the moment, returned and raised a regiment of horse for the king's service. His deportment during Monmouth's attempted invasion was not considered heroic even by his supporters. Dubbing Albemarle hero after such an unimpressive career involves more than poetic licence. Behn must also have known of Albemarle's surrender of his sword to Lord Grey of Warke, who needled him into issuing a challenge in May, 1682 (Price, 72-73). Conversely she may also have known of Albemarle's bravery when a fire that broke out at Wapping on the night of November 19, 1682, destroyed more than a thousand houses.

18 *youth*: Albermarle was thirty-four.

30-35 Sir Hans Sloane, who accompanied Albemarle to Jamaica as his physician described him as 'of a sanguine complexion, his face reddish and his eyes yellow, as also his skin, and accustomed by being at court to sitting up late and often being merry.' The Duke seems to have been fairly addicted to sherry, and to have exhibited signs of liver disorder from late 1685, if not before.

44 *that memorable day*: when James and Charles returned to England

53 *Hereditary loyalty*: Christopher Monck was the son of George, who despite his royalist sympathies had been commissioned by Parliament to command its forces in the Irish war, and in Scotland. After Cromwell's death, Charles's advisers saw Monck as the most likely instrument of the king's restoration, as he and his soldiers were the only effective power in the country. It was by Monck's advice that Charles withdrew to Breda and announced the general pardons that made possible his return.

62 *a prince whom no ignoble interest sways*: a conventional compliment, but hardly fitting. In June, 1687, Albemarle began fitting out a third treasure-hunting expedition to Haiti; there was furious interest in treasure trove at the time; most of the proceeds of salvage operations were being illegally disposed of in Jamaica. Albemarle did not leave England until he had secured patents gaving him and the crown rights in all recovered treasure, and over all mineral wealth in Jamaica. He was also a commissioner of the Royal African Company which had a monopoly of the British slave trade.

62-65 In 1686 Albemarle and the committee of Gentlemen Adventurers, with Sir James Hayes, Sir John Narborough, Lord Falkland, Francis Nicolson and Isaac Foxcraft, invested in a scheme to recover sunken treasure from a Spanish wreck on a reef on the north-east coast of Haiti, which a year later netted him the fabulous sum of £90,000.

72 *with him his Princess*: The Duchess did indeed accompany her husband to Jamaica.

75 Newcastle'*s name*: Elizabeth Cavendish (1654-1734), who was married to sixteen-year-old Christopher Monck at the bedside of his dying father on December 30, 1669, was the eldest daughter of Lord Ogle, heir to the Duke of Newcastle.

78 *Poet*: William Cavendish, first Duke of Newcastle, wrote poetry.

81 *like that Bright Vertue*: in the summer of 1682 when the Duchess became mentally disturbed, her father claimed that it was because she had received a love-letter and her husband had come to know of it, 'which had made her dissemble herself distracted.' (*Verney*, 301). In fact she suffered from a progressive mental disorder.

85 *such as has never blest*: the Duchess was by far the highest-born female to have visited the American colonies.

91 *high in his favour*: Albemarle carried the scepter with the dove at the coronation of James and Mary, but already he was in difficulties at court, having come drunk into the presence of the queen.

96 *the Muses best lov'd theme*: poems about the duke are in truth few. Nahum Tate, collaborator and friend of Behn, eulogised Albemarle in the continuation of *Absalom to Achitophel* (1682) thus:

> Brave Abdael with the first (i.e. his father) a place must claim.
>
> Proceed illustrious, happy chief, proceed!
>
> Foreseize the garlands for thy brow decreed;
>
> While th'inspir'd tribe attend with noblest strain,
>
> To register the glories thou shalt gain;
>
> For sure the dew shall Gilboah's hill forsake (etc)
>
> Before the Muses leave their patron's praise.

Albemarle's patronage of poets seems to have been of the same order as his military achievement, expected but never realised though Wharton in a note recalled him as 'liberal' as well as loyal. He preferred hunting, horseracing and gaming to more literary amusements; he is mentioned as patron of 'Mr Haynes, an actor in the King's House' (1676), and Tom D'Urfey was one of his boon companions.

97 *To whom their noblest Verse they Recommend*: at his installation as Chancellor of Cambridge University, 11 May, 1682, Albemarle inspired twomediocre panegyrics which were later printed without attribution, one by Nat Thompson in London, the other by John Hayes in Cambridge.

99 *you*: Jamaica. Behn here addresses the colony; it is possible that copies of the poem were taken to Jamaica as part of the propaganda exercise of establishing Albemarle as an effective governor. The colony was actually

run by freebooters and privateers, who were generally unimpressed by Albemarle's letters patent.

128 Albemarle was in poor health when he left England; he died in Jamaica on October 6, 1688. The Duchess brought his body back for burial in the family vault in Westminster Abbey in June the following year. She outlived him forty-eight years, for most of them completely mad. Ralph Montagu, Earl of Halifax, learning that she would consider remarriage only with a monarch, disguised himself as the Emperor of China in order to marry her and get control of her fortune. To the last her attendants pretended that she was indeed Empress of China.

...ON THE UNIVERAL HOPES FOR A PRINCE OF WALES

SOURCE: *A Congratulatory Poem to her most sacred majesty on the universal hopes of all Loyal Persons for a Prince of Wales.* By Mrs A. Behn. London, Printed for Will. Canning at his Shop in the Temple-Cloysters, 1688 (O'Donnell, 129-132)

Her most sacred Majesty: Mary of Modena (1658-1718). For five years after the consummation of the marriage by proxy of the fifteen-year-old queen to the forty-year-old duke, she was continually pregnant; she miscarried in May, 1674, and bore her first child, the Princess Catherine, on 10 January, 1675, only to see her die of convulsions on 3 October the same year, when she miscarried again. Her second daughter, Isabella, was born 18 August, 1676, and survived until 4 March 1681. On 7 November, 1677, Mary bore a son, Charles, Duke of Cambridge, who was carried off by the small-pox on 12 December. On 15 August, 1682 another little girl, Charlotte Maria, was born, only to die of convulsions eight weeks later. In October 1683 and again in April 1684 Mary miscarried. At the time of James's accession to the throne in 1685, she had no living child. She was in poor health and deeply depressed. Her husband was involved in an affair with one of her ladies in waiting, Katharine Sedley, whom he created Countess of Dorchester in 1686. After taking the waters at Bath in September, 1687, the queen found herself once again pregnant.

universal hopes: the hopes of male issue to continue the Stuart dynasty were far from universal. The king was known to be a papist; Mary was the symbol of ultramontane interference in English affairs. In November, Luttrell noted that 'her majestie been 2 months gone with child, hath been lett blood to prevent miscarrying' (I, 422). On 23 December a royal proclamation ordered public prayer and thanksgiving throughout the kingdom for the Queen's pregnancy; three of the Bishops were commanded to draw up a form of service which was celebrated in London on January 15. Behn's poem was licensed by Sir Roger L'Estrange on February 17, 1688. We may infer from the fact that the sheets were later bound in with the second edition of *A Congratulatory Poem to the King's Most Sacred Majesty on the Happy Birth of the Prince of Wales* and re-issued with a cancellans title page as *Two Congratulatory Poems to their Most Sacred Majesties* that there were not many persons willing to display their loyalty by buying it.

Prince of Wales: The first reports of Mary's pregnancy were greeted by coarse lampoons and common jokes, such as that she had been sent Our Lady's smock and Christ's baby clothes by the Pope, and that the Virgin had appeared to her and told her that she would bear a son. Common prejudice, alarmed by James's concerted attacks on the judiciary and the protestant clergy, was only to ready to believe that the pregnancy was another popish plot. It was certainly not in the best interests of the Stuart monarchy that loyal persons should display certainty before the event that the outcome would be a living male child. Superstitious Catholics may have believed that the Queen's pregnancy was a miracle and actually felt that confident predictions of the birth of a son were no more than the expression of pious faith and hope; prejudiced protestants were implacably convinced that the whole repulsive display of a pious and refined woman breeding by a diseased profligate was a gross fraud.

1 *Blessing*: pregnancy. Behn's congratulations on the achievement of the Queen's ninth pregnancy would seem tasteless even if Mary Beatrice had not been known to be delicate, and widely believed to have been infected by her husband with syphilis, which would make childbirth specially risky for both her and the infant.

3 *Long did the Almighty pause and long debate*: Behn refers to the five years that had elapsed between the birth of the Queen's last child and the announcement of this pregnancy. The all-knowing God cannot be uncertain about this or any other matter but Dryden makes a similar blunder, in attributing the Prince's conception to a conspiracy of the Trinity (*Britannia Rediviva*, 25-26).

4 *For MONARCHS are not fashion'd at a Heat*: the making of kings takes time and deliberation: a ridiculous hyperbole.

7 *the coming God*: Behn risks the imputation of blasphemy in comparing the coming of the Prince of Wales with the birth of the Messiah, her caveat in l. 9 notwithstanding.

28 *Arrests the* Wheel: the iconography of Fortune shows her turning a wheel signifying the rise and fall of human hopes.

33 *second* Bless'd: i.e. after the Virgin Mary, mother of God

44 Behn asks why other poets have not celebrated the pregnancy. In fact response to the order for general rejoicing was embarrassingly lukewarm. *A Poem Humbly dedicated to the Queen, on the occasion of her Majesty's happy conception*, by Edmund Arwaker struck a number of false notes:

> At last the rich, the royal Field
> That once did fertile Plenty yield,
> But long has unsuccessfully been till'd,
> Does happy signs of a new Product wear...

but even Arwaker does not assume the foetus to be male.

47 Lutes... *on the Willows hung*: the kingdom's poets are still in mourning for the death of Charles

49 MARS the god of war. Since Monmouth's invasion in the summer of 1685, Britain had been preoccupied by war and the threat of war.

64 *A young* APOLLO; Behn hopes that unlike his father and grandfather the new prince will be a munificent patron of poets.

A CONGRATULATORY POEM ... ON THE HAPPY BIRTH

SOURCE: Broadside pamphlet: *A Congratulatory Poem to the King's Most Sacred majesty, on the Happy Birth of a Prince of Wales*. By Mrs. A. Behn. London. Printed for Will. Canning, at his Shop in the Temple-Cloysters. 1688. (O'Donnell, 136-138)

The text is followed by an advertisement: '*On* Wednesday *next will be Published the most Ingeniousand long Expected History of* Oroonoko: or, the Royal Slave. By Mrs. Behn'. Luttrell's copy in the Weidener Collection at Harvard is marked 'id' in the left-hand corner, and dated '13. June. 1688'. The broadside was first issued separately, and then a second edition was bound in with a re-issue of *A Congratulatory Poem to her Most sacred Majesty on the Universal Hopes of all Loyal Persons for a Prince of Wales* with a conjugate cancellans title-page, as *Two Congratulatory Poems to their Most Sacred Majesties. The First, Occasion'd by the Universal Hopes of all Loyal Persons for a Prince of Wales. The Second, On the Happy Birth of the Prince. By Mrs. A. Behn.*

James Francis Edward, Prince of Wales, was born at St James's Palace at 10 a.m. on Sunday, June 10, 1688. Nothing abashed by the foolhardiness of her poetic prophecy, or the widely voiced scepticism about the genuineness of the queen's confinement, Behn here boasts of her prescience and goes on to spell out other auguries, all of which proved false. The child's birth was the precipitating factor in the bloodless Revolution of 1688, which deposed the crowned king and sent the heir to the throne into life-long exile.

15 *No MONARCH's Birth*: in fact the new-born prince shared his birthday with Edward, the Black Prince, as Dryden noticed in his celebration of the birth, *Britannia Rediviva*.
39-40 The summer solstice falls on June 22/23.

TO POET BAVIUS

SOURCE: Broadside Pamphlet *To Poet Bavius occasion'd by his Satyr He Writ in his verses to the king, upon the queens being Deliver'd of a son.* Permissu Superiorum. London, Printed for the Author. MDCLXXXVIII.

    To Poet Bavius has survived in ten copies in three states, for three lines were accidentally dropped at the beginning of A3ᵛ and subsequently restored in a stop-press correction, with an intermediate state in which the old catchword was inadvertently retained. The Huntington copy belonged to Narcissus Luttrell, who has written upon it 'By Mrs Behn' and dated it '23. June'. He also noted that Behn was 'severe on Poet Baber', which seems to indicate that Baber had more claim to be considered a poet than would be adduced from the works printed with his name. Behn herself appears to have known him and to have known of other literary attempts by him.
Bavius: John Baber, son of Sir John Baber (1625-1704), physician in ordinary to both Charles and James, who was instrumental in negotiations between the Presbyterians and the crown. He was knighted by Charles II for services to the crown in 1666, and created Gentleman of the Privy Chamber in 1679. Mentions of his son as a member of court circles date from 1680. John Baber junior seems to have had ambitions to set up as a Court wit and to have written ballads, elegies, panegyrics and satires, none of which have been identified. 'Astrea's Booke' has an unusual number of anti-Baber references, beginning with 'A Song' (p. 7) which complains that

> Baiber, that fine Aeiry Sparke
> Is growne an Arrant Clowne.

A Ballad usually dated 1683 but dated on internal evidence by J. H. Wilson as about August, 1682 (Wilson, 92-93) discusses whether any of the satirical attacks on the court ladies was to be attributed to Baber:

> Some say 'tis the labor
> Of sly Mr. Baber.
> Who's a plaguy sharp writer of satire;
> But for one to say true,
> Give the devil his due,
> He's a Tory and can't be a traitor.

His best friend to jeer,
He can hardly forbear,
And that way employed his pen is.
Once I did hear whisper
A brisk holy sister,
'He's better at that than at tennis.'

On July 6, 1683 a search was made for the daughter of Sir Thomas Draper, a city knight (*CSPD*, 1683, 59) who had been 'taken by force' from her father's house; on July 14 it appeared that she had run away with Baber (*Hatton*, II, 30). In 'Astrea's Booke' 'Satyr B:' (pp. 20-21) asks

How offt has *Baber*s follys bin the Theam
How offt the excrement of every Pen
Till to compleat his Wondrouse farce of Life,
He ended with that Luckey Jest, a Wife...

In 'The Present State of Matrimony' (pp. 90-91) Baber is described at length:

But here we must leave Reviling for a While,
And change our Sharp for an Obleging stile
For when so aire we Babers praise begin
Envys dumm and Satyrs Cease to grin
His Gracefull meen, Resistless Charmes Impart
And Glids Unfelt into a femall heart
While on his Lips such smooth discourse is hung
His Persons less Attractive then his Tounge
In Julians Book his Choycest Vertues shine
And Dart fresh Lusture Out att every Line
Nor is the Hero less Admird in Myne
Tho had he scap'd the Matrimoniall snare
And still drest on like Andrew in the faire
Bin Buble, Cully, Whimsicall or dull,
Or in Translating Buttler Cracked his scull
He might have scaped the Notion of a foole,
Wich now is fixt as lasting as his Life
For Deaths the Surest Refuge from a Wife.

In April, 1685 Baber published *Poem on the Coronation*. At the beginning of 1686 he was mentioned as amongst the dullest of the members of James's dull court:

Poets are next the scandal of our age,
And D'Urfey is the dullest of the stage.
Parsons and Baber, in the same degree,

> Excel in melting elegy.

A few months later the satirist tells us:

> Baber hath left the panegyric strain,
> And now to ballad-making turns his brain... (Harl MS 7319, 393)

He is named too in 'The Lovers' Session' of June, 1687 as a fop. (Wilson, 177) *To the King upon the Queen's being Deliver'd of a Son*, published by Mary Thompson in 1688, is his only other printed work. Behn's answer, which was published at her own expense, is not a defense of the crown but a defense of herself, for the opening section of Baber's poem is a scathing condemnation of her pindaric *On the Universal Hopes*.

Maria Beatrice of Modena gave birth to the Old Pretender, James Edward Stuart, on June 10, 1688 in St James's Palace. If Mrs Behn's answer was published as Luttrell suggests on 23 June, Baber's poem must have been published very shortly after the prince's birth; however, divergences between Behn's quotations from Baber's poem and the published version suggest that she may have seen the poem in manuscript.

2-4 Most of Behn's direct references are to the opening section of Baber's poem:

> Nine Months a Loyal Zeal had fir'd my Breast;
> Which for Nine Muses could not be at Rest:
> Who long have struggling and in Labour been
> To give the *KING* a *SON* before the *QUEEN*:
> But Duty has Controul'd the Muses Pow'r,
> And check'd my Rage to wait Her Happy Hour.
> Some could not bridle their Officious Rhyme,
> But must bestow an *Heir* before the Time:
> Where each Well-wisher Honestly intends,
> Good Will for Paultry Lines, must make Amends:
> Who can more easily Fore tell and Guess,
> Than when It is arriv'd good News express:
> Better had they in Church or Closet stay'd,
> Devoutly for the future Blessings Pray'd;
> Then with too Early Rhymes a Son bespeak,
> And thus the *Queen* and *Heav'n* their Debtors make:
> Then with Abortive Joyes the Nation fill
> And make the *CONSORT* bear the burden still;
> For till the long'd for Heir was Born, and *She*
> Was safe, my Muse could never Pregnant be...

One of the crasser aspects of Behn's poem on the queen's pregnancy is that she betrays no awareness of the risk that the pregnancy offered to the

Queen's health, or of any of the other possible disasters that were only too likely to result from a genuine confinement.

11 This line does not appear in the published version of Baber's poem.

27 Baber appears to have been an acquaintance of Mrs Behn.

28-33 Sir John Baber lived in Covent Garden; his son evidently haunted the playhouses; In 'Utile Dulce' January, 1681 (Harl MS 6913, p. 151) he is numbered among the sparks who 'strut i'th'pit'.

32 *famous in Julians Song* Robert Julian was a collector and distributor of unprintable lampoons and libels from about 1673. In May 1684 he was arrested for a libel on the king; unable to pay the 100 marks fine he stayed in prison until June 1685. (Brice Harris, 'Captain Robert Julian, Secretary to the Muses', *ELH*, X, 4, December, 1943, 294-309; Judith Slater, 'The Early career of Captain Robert Julian Secretary to the Muses', *N&Q*, N.S., XIII, 7 (July,1966), 260-262 etc.) 'Astrea's Booke' contains an unusual number of items connected with Julian, e. g., 'A Letter to Julian' ('Julian how comes it of late we soe' 1681-2, p. 10), 'To the Secretary of the Muses. A New Year's Gift' (p. 16), 'Julian's Farewell to the Muses' (p. 52), 'A Consolatory Epistle to Mr Julian in his Confinement (p. 53), 'To Julian' ('Dear friend, I fain would try once more', p. 97), 'Julians Farewell to the famely of the Coquets' ('Give o're Yee poore Players depend not on Witt' , p. 161), 'A New Letter to Julian' ('Tell me thou Treasury of Spight', p. 189).

40-4 Baber appears in lampoons on the court party from as early as 1680; A Satire from the Spring of 1680 (Wilson, 44) lumps Baber with Robert Leke, Henry Savile, Sir Thomas Isham, Behn's dedicatee, Sir William Clifton and other court half-wits. Goodwin Wharton in the same poem is called 'as much impertinent as Baber was' and accused of taking 'more pains to make himself an ass.' The latest mention I have found is in a satire of 1692/3 beginning 'Declining Venus has no Force o're Love' (Bodleian MS Eng. Poet. c. 18, p. 244) which describes Lady Mary Ratcliffe as 'Painted and Patch'd, with Baber for her Spark'.

49-50 Maces and Furs, the accoutrements of the Lord Mayor

52 Baber's line actually reads:

> Bleak looks a *Trading City*, and despis'd,

and goes on to list the classes of public officials that the King has estranged in the course of his repeated attempts to force their allegiance to the Catholic Church:

> A Body without a Soul, the *Charter* seiz'd;
> *Maces* and *Furrs* , their Princes favour gone,
> Neglected look, like *Roses* after *June*.
> My Lord, the *Judge*, divested of his *Chain*,

> Takes fees, and pleads below the *Bar* again;
>
> The stubborn *Prelate*, whom his Prince Rebukes,
>
> With Heav'n it self then out of Favour looks.
>
> The Flock their Pastor both suspects and fears,
>
> When in sheep's Clothing He a Wolf appears.

In April 1686 the King had dismissed four of the senior judges who would not support him in his proposed repeal of the Test Act, which required that candidates for public office be members of the Church of England. When Baber's poem appeared, the seven bishops who refused to ratify the Declaration of Indulgence were in prison in the Tower awaiting trial.

49-50 Behn's questions purport to be Baber's exact words cited as if to show that his serious point about the revoking of the charter is not simply overstated but outright nonsense.

79 *Primitive Roman Church*: evidently the Catholic Church

82 *establish'd Faith profest*: here Behn refers to Baber's earlier *Poem upon the Coronation*,

> Safely on Him may *England's* Church depend,
>
> Pious he is, and will the Faith defend.
>
> The faith I mean of our Progenitors,
>
> We by our Practice scarce can call it Ours.

83 *Bewrayst*: foulst

84 *the amphibious Batt*: the image is to be found in Aesop's fables, but also in 'Epistle to Julian,' (c. 1677) l. 68, where Sir Carr Scroope is described as neither wit nor fool but something of both like 'Aesop's bat, half bird half beast' also 'An Exclamation against Julian' etc. *POAS* 1705, p. 421;

88 *Almanzor*: the bombastic hero of Dryden's *Conquest of Granada*.

90-91 Baber's lines actually read:

> *White-staff* discarded, Lame and Helpless seems
>
> Though he walk Lusty, with substantial Limbs.

The white staff was a sign of high office, carried by the Lord High Treasurer the Lord Chamberlain and the Steward of the King's Household among others; there was at this time some question that the White-staves would be dismissed for adhering to their religion. Laurence Hyde, Earl of Rochester and Lord Treasurer, was dismissed in January 1687.

94-99 refer to Baber ll. 334-37:

> A Colonel in Commission Insolent,
>
> Cashier'd his haughty Carriage does repent,
>
> As on a Death-bed Contrition does begin
>
> With them who did run on long Scores in Sin:

101 Again Behn's quote is inaccurate: Baber's line reads:

No Coats Galloon'd to's *Levee* do repair,

102-103 Baber's point is actually the opposite:

Honours are, without Royal Favour, Dreams,
And all are cold not warm'd with Royal Beams;
No Badge of Greatness, wonted Lustre bears,
But like a Garment out of fashion wears.

104-107 Cf. Baber:

The Garter him that wears it may delight,
'Tis the Kings Favour that brings up the Knight;
But stript of that, he's for an *Idol* spoil'd.
His *Star* looks Tarnish'd and his *Ruban* soil'd.

108 *Beau Bavius Belt*: another reference to Baber's odd style of dress, like a Merry-andrew, see above.

110 Permissu Superiorum: by permission of the authorities

125 Hudebras: Butler's Poem, *Hudibras.* See 'The Present State of Matrimony' quoted above. No French version by Baber is known.

TO SIR ROGER L'ESTRANGE

SOURCE: Broadside Pamphlet: *A Poem to Sir Roger L'Estrange, on his Third part of the History of the Times; Relating to the Death of Sir Edmund Bury-Godfrey* by Mrs. A. Behn. London, Printed for Randal Taylor, near Stationers-Hall. 1688. (facing the title-page) Licensed, *April* 22. 1688. *Rob. Midgley.* (*O'Donnell, 136*)

Sir Roger L'Estrange: royalist journalist and Tory pamphleteer (1616-1704). Sentenced to death by the House of Commons in 1644, he was released from Newgate in 1648, fled to Holland, returned in 1653 and after the dissolution of the Long Parliament in 1659 began propagandising in favour of the restoration. In 1662 he was granted a warrant to seize seditious publications, and exercised great rigour in doing so. In 1663 he was made 'Surveyor of the Imprimerie' and set about publishing his own newspaper, *The Intelligencer.* He was also one of the licensers of the press. From its inception he denounced the fabrications of the Popish plot as unworthy of credence. At the beginning of 1680 he was obliged to flee to Holland, so strong was public feeling against him; though the London crowds burned him in effigy in November, he returned to London in February to answer the libels against him and to found the satirical weekly, *Heraclitus Ridens.* When Oates was arrested in June, 1684, and convicted of perjury, it was largely as a result of L'Estrange's tireless campaign against him. L'Estrange was knighted by James II on April 30, 1685, but his decisive rejection of the

Declaration of Indulgence led to his muzzling in March, 1687. At the revolution he was deprived of his office of licenser of the press and in December, 1688 he was imprisoned.

The Third Part of his History of the Times: the first series of *The Observator* ended in January 1684, with No. 470, for the periodical now appeared three or four times a week; the second ran to 270 numbers; the third and last series began in February, 1685 and ran until March 1687. Each series was issued in bound form; the volume of the third series also contained 'A brief History of the Times' with L'Estrange's final confutation of Oates's case that the Catholics had murdered Sir Edmund Berry Godfrey.

Sir Edmund Bury-Godfrey: Sir Edmund Berry Godfrey (16??-1678) was a Protestant Justice of the Peace who was remarkable for the degree of religious tolerance he showed to both Catholics and Non-conformists. In September 1678 Titus Oates made his first depositions alleging the existence of a Popish Plot to murder the King to Sir Edmund, who was loth to foment the panic and persecution of the Catholics that would follow and sought to keep the matter bottled up for as long as possible. Oates threatened him, saying that he would cause a parliamentary inquiry to be made into his laxity in digging out the conspirators. Godfrey's friends begged him never to go about unaccompanied, but Godfrey did not follow their advice. He left home at nine o'clock on Saturday morning, 12 October; on the evening of the following Thursday his body was found in a ditch on the south side of Primrose Hill, lying face downward, transfixed by his own sword. Money and jewellery were still in his pockets; only his pocketbook and his lace cravat were missing. The surgeons who examined him were of the opinion that he had been strangled and stabbed after death. Before his state burial on 31 October, two proclamations were issued offering a reward of £500 for the identification of the murderers. Popular opinion held that Godfrey had been murdered by the Papists, although no motive could be adduced.

32 Wapping-Councils: the men of the Wapping docklands, who formed Monmouth's honorary body-guard, said by Shaftesbury to number ten thousand

38-39 Cf. L'Estrange, *Observator*, No. 89 [15 August, 1682] 'Have we not seen a worthy knight... deliver up the picture of Christ in the arms of his mother... in triumph to the flames; and the multitude hoiting about it and throwing stones at it?' and 'An Elegy upon Sir William Waller, ll. 8-71:

> Then in New Palace Yard of Westminster,
> I most courageously did make a fire,
> And true-dissenter-like, in zealous scorn,

At noonday did my saviour's picture burn...(*POAS*, III, 469)
40 Stafford: William Howard, Viscount Stafford, catholic peer, impeached
30 November, 1678, executed 26 December
45 Golgatha: Golgotha, where Christ was crucified, or Tyburn, public
place of execution for London and Middlesex, where most of the people denounced by Oates, Bedlowe, Prance and company were executed.
47 Among the catholics hung, drawn and quartered at Tyburn was at least
one priest, Father Whitebread (June 13, 1679); Thomas Pickering, executed
17 December, 1678, was a Benedictine lay-brother.
59 Perseus: in Greek mythology, the hero who saved Andromeda from the
sea-monster
61 Curtius: in Roman mythology, a youth who leapt into a chasm to save
Rome from being engulfed
69-81 L'Estrange argued that Godfrey, who suffered from constitutional
melancholy inherited from his father, killed himself.

'OF TREES'

SOURCE: *The Second and Third Parts of the Works of Mr Abraham Cowley, The
Second containing What was Written and Published by himself in his younger
Years: Now Reprinted together. The Sixth Edition. The Third containing His Six
Books of Plants, Never before published in English. Viz. The First and Second of
Herbs. The Third and Fourth of Flowers. The Fifth and Sixth of Trees. : Now
made English by several Hands. With necessary Tables to both parts, and divers
Poems in Praise of the Author.* Licensed and entered. London: Printed for
Charles Harper, at the Flower-de-Luce over against S. Dunstan's Church
in Fleet-Street. 1689. Book IV *SYLVA.* (O'Donnell, 267-268) The side-
notes in the original have here been printed as footnotes.

The Preface 'To the Reader' of the Third Part, signed by Nahum Tate,
remarks that the translation of the Sixth Book 'oe'ertops all the others' and
that the translatress had inserted ideas of her own. The publication of the
work can be dated around July, 1689 when an advertisement was inserted in
the *London Gazette*, but the evidence points to an earlier, possibly much
earlier, date of composition. The book of Cowley's Latin poems 'newly
made English by several hands' was entered in the Term Catalogues for
April 5, 1688; Tate's preface makes no mention of Behn's death on April 16
the following year, although as Sprat had arranged for her burial in the
cloisters of Westminster Abbey, he must have been aware of it, so we may
assume that the book was already in press when she died.

Internal evidence suggests that the composition of Behn's contribution
should be dated more than ten years earlier. The Translatress in her own

person says to Apollo, 'I by a double right thy Bounties claim' (l. 597); in 'A Session of Poets' we read that

> The poetesse Afra next shew'd her sweete face,
> And sure by her Poetry & her black Ace,
> The Laurel by a double right was her owne
> For the Playes she had writt, & the Conquests she had wonne.
> Apollo acknowledg'd 'twas hard to deny her;
> But to deal frankly and ingeniously by her,
> He told, were Conquests & Charmes her pretence
> She ought, to have pleaded a dozen yeares synce.
>
> (Bodleian MS Don. b. 8, p. 588)

Vieth's dating of the composition of 'A Session of the Poets' in November, 1676 is incontrovertible (*ARP*, p. 309). Behn must have known the poem which was widely circulated and widely quoted, and would not herself have drawn attention to so unsympathetic a joke against her by echoing its exact words. We probably ought to assume that the anonymous poet echoes her, in which case, we must also assume that 'Of Trees' had come to his attention before November, 1676. (In any case, attempts to explain the poet's 'black Ace' as a reference to Oronooko are clearly misguided.) Behn's friend, Thomas Sprat, who was Cowley's literary executor, produced a new edition of Cowley's *Poemata Latina* in 1678; he may already have been seeking English translations for a de luxe edition.

We know from Dryden's Preface to *Ovid's Epistles Translated by Several Hands* (1680) that the author of 'Oenone to Paris' being 'of the Fair Sex understood not Latine.' Behn herself in the commendatory poem written for the second edition of Creech's Lucretius animadverts on the deficiencies of her education:

> Till now, I curst my Birth, my Education,
> And more the scanted Customes of the Nation:
> Permitting not the Female Sex to tread,
> The mighty Paths of learned Heroes dead.
> The God-like *Virgil*, and great *Homers* Verse,
>
> Like Divine Mysteries are conceal'd from us.
> We are forbid all grateful Theams,
> No ravishing Thoughts approach our Ear,
> The fulsome Gingle of the times
> Is all we are allow'd to understand or hear. (Summers, VI, 167)

Rather than actually translating Cowley's poem then, Behn must have versified an existing translation. Both Tate and Sprat would have been capable of furnishing her with a literal prose translation of Cowley's 1244 lines of Latin, to which her version, although unavoidably longer, the compression of Latin being both impossible and undesirable in English, remains remarkably faithful. 'Astrea's Booke' contains a version of Prior's satire 'On the Modern Translators' (mis-titled 'Odi – Imitatores Servium Lecus') with its bitter jeers against 'blind translatress Behn' and her contribution to *Ovid's Epistles translated by Several Hands* (p.64). If 'Of Trees' was written in 1676 it may have been held over because Tate, who with Settle, the likeliest author of 'A Session of the Poets', collaborated on *Ovid's Epistles*, was unwilling to expose himself and Behn to further vilification.

There was, as is only to be expected, a political purpose behind the issuing of a vernacular version of Cowley's poem within months of James's flight and William's and Mary's usurpation. Cowley's poem celebrates the miraculous preservation of Charles II when he took refuge in the Boscobel oak, invokes the old legend of Aeneas's great-grandson as the founder of Britain, thus emphasising the continuity of succession, and climaxes in the description of James's victory in the Battle of Lowestoft. While Cowley was in England in 1657, according to Sprat, he undertook to disguise his real activities (as a spy for the royalists) by studying medicine; the sixth book of *De Plantarum* enacts the deception, by disguising a poem on the Civil War as a botanical poem in imitation of Statius, but most if not all of the sixth book was written after the Restoration. By way of issuing a translation of a prestigious work, Tate, Sprat, Behn and the defeated Court party succeeded in publishing a Jacobite poem in the teeth of the triumphing Whigs.

An English version of the sixth book of Cowley's *De Plantarum* was already in existence. In 1680, Samuel Walsall, at the Golden-Frying Pan in Leadenhall Street, published *A Translation Of the Sixth Book of Mr. Cowley's Plantarum, being A Poem on the late Rebellion, the Happy Restoration of His Sacred Majesty, and the Dutch War Ensuing.* Taking as his starting point l. 40 of Cowley, and eliminating all the machinery of the conference of wood-nymphs, and Dryas's 'harangue', the anonymous translator produces 138 quatrains of bald historical summary interspersed with panegyric.

5 *Phoebus*: the sun, and the god of poetry

6 *my Huntress*: the poet's muse

15 *gins*: snares

27 *To thee*: the poet now addresses Charles II in death apotheosed.

40 *Wood-Nymphs, Hamadryades*: hamadryads are wood-nymphs.

41 *Satyrs and Fauns*: again pleonastic

48 *Harangues*: speeches addressed to an assembly

55 Daphne: Ovid, *Metamorphoses*, I. 452ff.

65-74 Cowley's Latin hardly justifies Behn's interpretation:

> Foelix ante alios reges, dum fata sinebant,
> Dúmq; gubernantis tempestas improba rerum
> Non renuebat opem, nunc foelicissimus ultra
> Invidiam, & Divûm lato transgressus honores.
> Nam miseram Vento *Europam* bellante per omnem,
> Et strage informi sylvas lacerante vetustas;

75 *Peace*: here symbolised as a dove

83 *fruitful Goddess*: the goddess of peace, who safeguards prosperity. Cf. *A Translation* (1680) iv: 'Nor did the fruitful Goddess sit in vain...'

85 Cornucopia: the horn of plenty, an attribute of the goddess Pax

87 When Saturn was expelled from heaven by Jupiter, he ruled with Janus in Latium, civilised the Italians, and taught them agriculture, and the useful and liberal arts.

91-100 Once more Behn's imagination elaborates Cowley's latin:

> Et levitas hominum pulchram temeraria mutat
> Pellice deformi Uxorem; *mutatio pulchra est.*

114 *in my tenth year*: i.e. in 1628.

135 Monk: George Monck, first Duke of Albemarle, 1608-1670. As commander of the Parliamentary forces, he managed the restoration of Charles II in the interests of public order, and served the crown faithfully thereafter both as a military and naval commander in the Dutch war, and as keeper of public order during the great plague and the Fire of London.

166 *Monsters of the* Caledonian *Woods*: creatures of the Loch Ness variety

167 *Schismatic Crowds*: the sectarians who proliferated during the Interregnum

168 Cromwel: Oliver Cromwell (1599-1658) Lord Protector of England under the Commonwealth

180 Dryads: wood nymphs indwelling in the trees and dying when they die, akin to the Roman *genii* , spirits of place

186 Cowley's footnote: 'Ex animalculis intra gallas quercuum enatis, recepta est apud rusticos venturi anni divinatio, si vermis in iis generetur, caritatem fingum(?), si aranea, pestilentiam, Musca, bellum instare praedicunt.'

205 *Spinturnix* and Sidenote: The 'Aruspices' or Haruspeces were specialists in the art of reading the entrails of blood sacrifices; Cowley's note quotes Pliny, *Naturalis Historia*, Lib.X, 13 and Dalecamp.

214-217 The ash was considered fatal to serpents. The successful nesting of the serpent in the ash is taken as an ominous portent.

232-239 See William Camden, *Britain, or a chorographicall description of the most flourishing Kingdomes...* Translated... by Philemon Holland, London, 1637, p. 358.

249 Behn's parenthesis

260 Dryas: daughter of Faunus, who never appeared in public

262-263 The British navy, with ships constructed of British oak, is now acknowledged ruler of the seas.

281 Alcides: one of the names of Hercules, so-called for his grandfather, Alcaeus. Cowley cites Virgil.

281-285 Hercules was crowned with poplar during his descent into Hades, or, in some versions, he wove himself a crown of poplar after he had killed the giant Cacus. The surfaces of the leaves that that touched his brow turned white; so the legend explains the darkness of the upper side of the leaves of *Populus niger*, contrasting with the pale undersides. (Cowley miscalls the English poplar, *Populus alba*.)

286 Phaetonian Alder: the Heliades, sisters of Phaeton, weeping for his disgrace, were changed by Jupiter into poplars, some say alders, some aspens, and their tears to precious gum. Cowley identifies the genus as *Alnus* (alder).

290 Willows: symbols of mourning especially for lost love

291 Olesicarpians: Cowley's note supplies Homer, Odyssey 10 and Pliny Lib.XVI,xxvi, as the sources. The willows' connection with chastity and the separation of lovers probably derives from the fact that most members of the genus are dioecious, i.e. male and female catkins are borne on separate plants.

296 Salamanders: mythical lizards that live in fire

300 Elders: *Sambucus niger*

313 Birch: the genus *Betula*

325 Maples: the genus *Acer*

331 Behn has skipped 8 lines relating to the cedar and the hornbeam. Cowley uses the Greek name, and supplies the Latin, *Ulmus*, in a footnote.

335 Oxias: from the Greek name for the genus *Fagus*

376 Ash: the genus *Fraxinus*. For its properties see Pliny Lib.XVI,xiii.

378 Achilles *Spear*: *Iliad* 16

384 Phylira: Greek name for the linden, the genus *Tilia*

400 Orcimelis *and* Achras: Cowley's footnote explains '*Achras...* & *Orci-melis*' as 'Pyri & Mali sylvestris'; the sidenote 'Wood-pear and Crab-apple' has them in the wrong order.

406 Ouas: Greek name for the genus *Sorbus*

408 Oxyacantha: from the sidenote 'Bar-berry' the genus *Berberis* must be

meant, however John Ray's *Trilingue* gives Oxyacantha as both the botanic name and the Greek name of Hawthorn or Whitethorn.

403 Castanis: the genus *Castanea*, chestnut

417 Hawthorn: the genus *Crataegus*, glossed by Cowley as 'Spina alba. (*Heythorn.*)'

421 Behn appears to have skipped a line:
Utilior latrante *Cane* armatoque *Priapo.*

433 Cowley supplies Pliny, Lib. XVI, xviii as his source.

442 Bramble: Cowley supplies *Rubus.*

452 Pyxias: from the Greek name for the genus *Buxus*

487-489 Cowley translates the Greek *Agrias* as 'Aquifolium. (Holly.); more correctly *Ilex aquifolium*. A foot-note to the Latin explains that bird-lime comes not from holly but *ex illa viscum*, from the mistletoe that grows on holly.

499 Camaris: actually *Comaris* from the Greek, for *Arbutus unedo.*

500 Craneia: members of the genus *Cornus*, also known as cornels or dogwoods

501 Carya: from *Caryon*, the Greek name for the walnut, the genus *Juglans*

502 Corylus: the genus *Corylus*, or hazelnut family

502-504 During the Golden Age people fed upon acorns and the fruits of the arbutus.

505 Cowley's Phillyrea is explained in his note from Dioscurides as '*Alaternus ex eus genere*'; it is probably *Ligustrum italicum*. Cowley's 'Prickly Coral-Tree' is possibly *Pyracantha coccinea* introduced into England in 1629.

517-524 Cowley is quite wrong about the yew; *Taxus baccata* is poisonous in both leaves and fruit.

525 Arceuthis: the Greek name for *Juniperus communis*

533 Sabina: *Juniperus sabina*, a shrub, whose leaves have marked emmenagogic properties and have been used since antiquity to procure abortion

545 Cyparissus was changed into a cypress by Apollo, when he pined with grief after accidentally killing a stag of which Apollo was very fond (Virgil, *Aeneid*, 3, 680; Ovid, *Metamorphoses*, 10, 121).

549 *his lov'd Dear*: Behn seems not to have realised that the 'dear' was also a 'deer', unless the pleonasm represents a compositorial error.

566 *the Fair Nymph*: Daphne changed by Apollo into a laurel, i.e. *Laurus nobilis*, the bay-tree

595-596 The well-known satire 'A Session of the Poets for the Bays' seems to refer directly to these lines (see above). The idea that women poets have a double right to the bays is a commonplace, see e.g. 'Philo-Philippa', 'To the Excellent *Orinda*' ll. 1-8 (*KTR*, 204). and 'To Mrs. B. Wright on her

Incomparable Poetry':

> *Daphne* to Laurel turn'd, a *Female Brow*
> Has the best title to a *Female Bough*.

from Poems and Translations Written upon Several Occasions. By a Late Scholar of Eaton, London, 1689.

597 Sappho *and* Orinda: Behn refers to the Sappho of antiquity, rather than any modern poet so-called; Orinda is Katherine Philips (1632-1664) the most respected woman writer of the century.

600 Elate *next, and* Peuce: Cowley's note gives '*Abies. Pinus*.' and translates the former as 'Firre'; the latter is of course the pine.

601 *Sister-Nymphs*: both genera, *Abies* and *Pinus*, are members of the family of the Pinaceae.

610 Ossa...Pelion: the highest two mountains in Thessaly

613 Behn appears to have missed a number of lines relating to the holm oak and transferred some of its attributes to the conifers.

725 *both the valu'd* Indies: the East Indies and the West; cf. Dryden, *To His Sacred Majesty, A Panegyrick on His Coronation*, 123-124.

730 *Plantan*: plantain

755 Tripos: three-legged stool

757 Dodonian: from Dodona, the most ancient shrine of Zeus, where the oracle spoke through the rustling of the wind in the leaves

760 *Bacchanals*: the devotees of Bacchus, who roved the wilds in tranced states

780 Chaonian: from a district of Epirus in Greece, where oaks abounded

799 *Brutus*: great-grandson of Aeneas, who killed his father, Sylvius, and was banished from Troy; the inverted commas should not appear at the head of these lines until l. 820.

83 Epirus: a region bordering the Ionian Sea

805 Brutus is supposed to have fathered the race of Britons.

820 Sylvia'*s Blood*: the descendants of Sylvia, mother of Romulus and Remus

826 *th'Western* Cales: the western Isles?

838 Charles's Wain: the constellation *Ursa major*

839 *Grandsire* Jove: the nymph Callisto was translated to the constellation after she was raped by Jupiter in the form of a bear.

841 *The Bear too*: Charles's Wain is the Bear; Behn has omitted Cowley's references to Bootes.

843-844 Cowley reads:

> ...Tua dextra Tyrannos
> Bis senos *Gomeritarum* sub tartara mittet
> Praetereuntis opus;...

Gomerstish therefore would seem to be an error for *Gomeritish*, meaning barbarian.

896-907 Cowley has simply:

Fontemq; recludens
Purpureum, in medio furiis operata Senatu est.
Magnorum invidia Vir magnus, Plebis ineptae
Integer injustis odiis...

The unknown author of *A Translation* also understands this to refer to Strafford (St. 26) but he stops short of Behn's sneer at 'the privilege of the *House*'.

914 Kintonian: Sidenote: 'Keinton-Field Edge-Hill.' i.e. Kineton in Warwickshire, where the battle of Edgehill was fought on October 23, 1642.

918 Rupert: third son of Charles II's aunt, Elizabeth Stuart, and Frederick V, the Elector Palatine, commander of the horse at the battle of Edgehill

919 Charles: Charles I

927 Orcades: Orkneys

931 Eumenides: a euphemistic name for the Furies

934 Newberry: Newbury where three battles of the Civil War were fought

935 Philippi's *Fields*: where Brutus and Cassius were routed by Octavius and Mark Antony in B. C. 40

943 Naseby: the New Model Army inflicted a decisive defeat on the royalist troops at Naseby on 14 June, 1645.

980 The Scottish Army escorted Charles who had surrendered to them at Newark under guard to Newcastle and kept him there, from 13 May, 1646 until they delivered him into the hands of the Parliament on 30 January, 1647, for which service they were paid.

995 *the* Isle of Wight: Charles escaped from Hampton Court and made his way to Carisbrooke Castle on the Isle of Wight, hoping to take refuge there, but the governor was loyal to the Parliament and he found himself a prisoner.

1005 Ribla: the Ribble, in reference to the battle of Preston

1009 Colchester: where in 1648 Sir Charles Lucas with 4,000 royalist soldiers resisted despite a long siege

1026-1033 Charles I was executed on 30 January, 1649 on a specially erected scaffold before the palace gate of Whitehall.

1177 Charles II with an inadequate escort landed in Scotland 16 June, 1650.

1209 Charles was crowned at Scone, 1 January 1651.

1211 *the left hand of the kingdom*: out of deference to the Presbyterians the crown was put on Charles's head not by a clergyman but by Archibald Campbell, seventh Earl of Argyll, who persuaded Charles to sign the

Covenant.

1239 Charles invaded England 13 July, 1651.

1265-1279 Charles had expected to be joined by volunteers as he marched south, but the expected rally to his standard did not eventuate.

1275 Torpedo's *Touch*: contact with the electric ray

1282 Sabrina's *Stream*: the river Severn

1283 Red Hill: a sector of the battlefield at Naseby

1284 Worster: Charles's forces were all but annihilated at Worcester on 3 September, 1651.

1297 Darby: James Stanley, seventh Earl of Derby, 1607-1651, who was executed for his part in the royalist insurrection on 15 October; Willmot: Henry Wilmot, first Earl of Rochester (1612-1658) who accompanied the king throughout his wanderings and arranged his escape to France

1298 Buckingham: George Villiers, second Duke of Buckingham (1628-1687)

1300 Achates: the beloved companion of Aeneas

1342 Salop: Shrewsbury

1352 White Lady: or White Ladies, a residence of the Giffard family, about half a mile from Boscobel House

1361 *all his mourning Friends*: the king was accompanied by Buckingham, Darby, Lauderdale, and Wilmot

1366 *Blew Garter*: the insignia of the Order of the Garter, of which king was the head; *Saint* George: the garter star which has the figure of St George in the centre

1385 The king wandered on to Moseley, Bentley, disguised as Jane Lane's maid to Leigh, near Bristol, to Trent, near Sherbourne, and thence to Brighton, where he took ship for France.

1441 Carles: William Carlos, Carles or Careless, royalist officer, was hiding in the oak in Boscobel wood, when, at about 5 a.m. on the morning of 6 September, he invited Charles, whom he did not recognise, to share his hiding place, while the Parliamentary soldiers searched the wood for them.

1447 *that Prize, his Head*: a price of £1,000 had been placed on Charles's head.

1481 *that Day*: Charles was born on 29 May, 1630, and restored to his throne on 29 May 1660.

1485 *that Star*: on the day Charles was born a star was seen at midday, some thought it a new star, and others that it was the Evening Star, i.e. Venus, visible at noonday.

1491 Monk's *valiant Hand*: despite his royalist sympathies Monck had been commissioned by Parliament to command its forces in the Irish war, and later led their forces in Scotland. After Cromwell's death, Charles's advisers saw Monck as the most likely instrument of the king's restoration, as he and his soldiers were the only effective power in the country, Cromwell having instituted himself a virtual dictator. It was by Monck's advice that Charles withdrew to Breda and announced the general pardons that made possible his return.

1497 *your Royal Brothers*: James, Duke of York, and Henry, Duke of Gloucester (1640-1660) who died of the small-pox a few months after accompanying the king back to England

1501 *wandering Gazers*: Charles's progress from Dover to Whitehall was accompanied by huge crowds.

1541 *Great* Mary: Henrietta Maria, who returned to England in October, 1660

1602 Britains: Britons

1607 Batavians: the Dutch

1610 Amphritite: grand-daughter of Oceanus, wife to Poseidon, queen of the moaning sea, whose name means 'wearer away of the shore'

1615 *Graafts*: the dykes of Holland

1620 War was declared by England and Holland in January and February, 1665.

1633 After an English blockade of Dutch ports had been forced to return on account of bad weather, the Dutch mounted a massive naval attack which met the English fleet at Solebay, near Lowestoft on June 3.

1638 Rupert: Prince Rupert was admiral of the white fleet, and led the attack.

1646 *the Royal Sovereign's deck*: James's flagship was the Naseby, renamed on May 23, 1660 the *Royal Charles*.

1648 Opdam: commander of the Dutch fleet

1670 Amboina*'s Wickedness*: the massacre at Amboyna in 1619

1684 Orange: the only ship left behind when the Dutch fleet fled

1692 *the Dolphin*:

1716 *Three noble Youths*: Charles Berkely, Earl of Falmouth, Lord Muskerry and Richard Boyle

TO QUEEN MARY UPON HER ARRIVAL IN ENGLAND

SOURCE: Broadside Pamphlet: *A Congratulatory Poem to her Sacred Majesty Queen Mary upon her arrival in England.* By Mrs. A. Behn. London Printed by R.E. for R. Bentley in Russell-Street in Covent Garden and W. Canning at his Shop in the Temple Cloysters. 1689 Narcissus Luttrell's copy of this poem (Harvard, Widener Collection) is priced at twopence and dated

'1689./8. 26. Febr.', i.e. February 26, 1689. (O'Donnell 149-50)

Behn may have been encouraged to write this rather perfunctory tribute by the suggestion of Bishop Burnet. Burnet, in voluntary exile during the reign of James II, had been invited by William and Mary to take up residence at the Hague, where he enjoyed great favour as a trusted counsellor and architect of the Bloodless Revolution. Evidently he asked Behn to write a tribute to the house of Nassau and Behn replied with *A Pindaric Poem to the Reverend Doctor Burnet, on the Honour he did me of Enquiring after me and my Muse*, (Summers, VI, 407-410) which flatters Burnet's genius, and in particular his powers of persuasion, thanks him for the 'welcome wounds' that he had dealt her before, presumably by his censure, but curiously claims that her Muse, 'never durst like *Cowley* tune her strings, To sing of Heroes and of Kings'. Burnet may have seen her translation of Cowley and have taken the opportunity to recommend that she use her talent rather to commend herself to the House of Nassau than to earn their enmity by rehearsing the heroic exploits of the supplanted Stuarts and their supporters. Behn, who would have known Burnet to have been the author of some of the most libellous pasquinades against James II and Mary of Modena, had no option but to reply with exaggerated obsequiousness. If Burnet expected Behn to celebrate the invasion, on which he accompanied William, he was mistaken. Her refusal was as curt as the courtesy demanded from a needy and dependent social inferior could make it:

> What must I suffer when I cannot pay
> Your Goodness, your own generous way?
> And make my stubborn Muse your Just Commands obey?
> My Muse that would endeavour fain to glide
> With the fair prosperous Gale, and the full driving Tide,
> But Loyalty commands with pious Force,
> That stops me in the thriving Course,
> The Brieze that wafts the crowding Nations o're,
> Leaves me unpity'd far behind
> On the Forsaken Barren Shore,
> To sigh with Echo, and the Murmuring Wind;...

The poem goes on to praise Burnet, and his 'Seraphick Quill' for the 'Mighty Change' in England's political life, comparing him to Ulysses whose cunning accomplished what valour could not do for the Greeks. Behn's intention under the guise of flattery is clearly to accuse Burnet as the arch-traitor to the cause of legitimacy and divine right, and, as nicely as possible, to tell him if he wants praise for William of Orange to write it himself.

The ode to Burnet is usually dated March, 1689, a matter of days after the congratulatory poem to Queen Mary; the *terminus ad quem* relates only to the latest possible date, for after 31 March, when Burnet was consecrated Bishop of Salisbury, it would have been improper to refer to him as Dr Burnet. The ode may have been written before the poem to Queen Mary; Behn might have swallowed her scruples to the extent of writing the poem to the queen as a result of renewed persuasion by the Bishop whose condescension to the poor, sick woman was indeed remarkable. Elsewhere Burnet had referred to Behn as a bad woman, dissuading Ann Wharton in 1680, for example, from having any communication with her (*KTR*, 286-293). He may have been eager to repeat the public relations coup of Rochester's death-bed conversion, and to announce that another notorious Tory had been rescued for whiggery and true religion. 'Astrea's Booke' contains a version of 'Mrs Nelly's Complaint' which ends

> Even Now in Terror on my Bed I lie
> Send Doctor Burnet to me or I dye. (p. 15)

The last lines of the Ode to Burnet are closely related to the beginning of the *Congratulatory Poem to ... Queen Mary*.

> Tho' I the Wond'rous Change deplore,
> That makes me Useless and Forlorn,
> Yet I the great Design adore,
> Tho' Ruin'd in the Universal Turn.
> Nor can my Indigence and Lost Repose,
> Those meagre Furies that surround me close,
>> Convert my Sense and Reason more
> To this Unpresidented Enterprise
>> Than that a Man so Great, so Learn'd, so Wise,
> The Brave Atchievement Owns and nobly Justifies.

Queen Mary: Mary Stuart, Princess of Orange, daughter of James II and his first wife, Ann Hyde, was born at St James's Palace on April 30, 1662. She was married to William Henry Nassau, Prince of Orange, son of the stadtholder, William II, and Mary, eldest daughter of Charles I, on November 4, 1677 and thereafter lived at the Hague. When, in October 1688, her husband led the invasion that drove James II out of England and re-established the protestant monarchy, Mary remained at the Hague attending public prayer four times a day 'with a very composed countenance'. She did not come to England until the wrangles about the precise terms of her joint rule with her husband had been decided. On February 10, 1689, she embarked from Brill, while the crowds lit bonfires along the estuary of the Thames, in which they burned the six-months old Prince of

Wales in effigy. She arrived on the morning of February 12.

4 *unhappy dear Lov'd Monarch*: James II, abandoned by all his supporters, left Whitehall secretly between two and three in the morning of 11 December, 1688 and travelled to Sheerness where he was to take ship, but instead was arrested and forced to return eventually to London. He finally made his way to France, arriving on Christmas Day, 1688.

27 On the day she arrived Mary went by barge from Greenwich to Whitehall-stairs to take possession of her father's palace.

37-39 Behn's panegyric appeared less than two weeks after Mary's triumphant arrival; Mary was not crowned until April 11, five days before Behn's death, hastened according to Gildon by want of care in her physician.

37 *The Muses all but mine*: an astonishing flurry of mediocre poetic activity greeted William and Mary but Behn's silencewas not unique. Dryden wrote nothing in support of William and Mary and was replaced as poet laureate by Shadwell.

61 Mary was twenty-seven.

84 *every Part a Queen*: most of Behn's flatteries are mere convention. Mary was handsome, although she could hardly be as celestially beautiful as Behn is obliged to pretend. Her manners were indeed so informal as to occasion unfavourable comment, on account in particular of her housewifely foraging around the royal apartments, her undisguised jubilation at the elevation in her status, and her lack of feeling for her exiled father, whose personal belongings she did not trouble to return to him although he had asked for them.

POEMS FROM *THE HISTORY OF ADOLPHUS*

SOURCE: *The History of Adolphus, Prince of Russia; And the Princess of Happiness By a Person of Quality With a Collection of Songs and Love-Verses. By several hands. To which is added, Two Letters in Verse from Sir G. E. to the E. of M. with Mr. D. Answer to them.* London, Printed and are to be sold by R. T. near Sationers'-Hall, 1691 (O'Donnell, 269-270).

The hitherto unpublished poems by Behn appear as part of a grouphere printed together (pp. 59-69) of which eight had been published by Behn, *viz.*: from *La Montre, or, The Lover's Watch* (published in August, 1686): '*Advice for a Lover*' ('Cleon, if you wou'd have me true' a version of 'The Example', ('Damon, if you would have me true' Summers, VI, 36); '*On the Modesty of* Aminta' ('Aminta, fear not to confess', Summers, VI, 38); '*On a Lover beginning to Love*' (As free as wanton winds I liv'd', Summers, VI, 56); *On Jealousy. By Mrs. A. Behn.* ('Oh Jealousy! thouPassion most ingrate',

Summers, vi, 70); together with, from *The Lucky Chance, or, The Alderman's Bargain* (1687), *A Song. By Mrs.* Behn. (Rise *Cloris*, charming Maid, arise', Summers, 1915, III, 191; from *Lycidus, or, The Lover in Fashion*, '*Verses. By Mr. H. W.*' ('A Constancy in Love I'll prize' Summers, 1915, VI, 304) and *Advice Against Constancy in Love* ('Let Love no more your Heart inspire' Summers, VI, 314); from *The Emperor of the Moon*, (1687), *A Song.* ('When Maidens are young, and in their Spring', Summers, 1915, III, 429). Most of the other poems appended to *The History of Adolphus* are by George Granville (dubbed Baron Lansdowne in 1701) to whom, only weeks before her death, Behn dedicated her novel, *The Lucky Mistake*. Lansdowne, a vociferous supporter of the cause of James II, was at what Behn called 'this Critical Juncture' living in retirement. His verse panegyric 'To Mrs. B—' is printed in *The History of Adolphus* for the first and only time; the texts of the Behn poems in the volume may have come from copies sent to Granville by her. Behn concluded her dedication,

I must own, Sir, the obligations I have to you, deserves a greater testimony of my respect, than this little piece, too trivial to bear the honour of your Name, but my increasing indisposition makes me fear I shall not have many Opportunities of this kind, and shou'd be loath to leave this ungrateful World, without acknowledging my Gratitude more signally than barely by word of Mouth, ...

1 She: Shepherd
2 Silvio: mistake for *Sylvia*